Travelaid

GUIDE TO GREECE

by Michael von Haag
and Neville Lewis

*To our friends on the
mountain and on the island.*

Throughout this Guide the authors have combined their
often overlapping knowledge and experience.

Photo credits: Acropolis approach (cover), Anafiotika, the
Acropolis from Ardettos, the butcher, the Monastery of
St John on Patmos and Mistra — Michael von Haag. Fishing
boat — Clare Ferguson. Temple of Aphaia — Ian Ferguson.
The Meteora — Neville Lewis.

Illustrations by Clare Ferguson.
Maps, plans, cover design and layout by Colin Elgie.
Typesetting by Dahling Dahling Ltd., 10A Poland Street,
London W1.
Printed in Great Britain by litho at The Anchor Press Ltd.
and bound by Wm Brendon & Son Ltd., both of Tiptree,
Essex.
Published by Travel Aid Services Ltd., 7A Belsize Park,
London NW3.
ISBN 0 902743 12 0

Distribution: The Two Continents Publishing Group Ltd.,
30 East 42nd Street, New York, NY (USA); Dominie
Press Ltd., 55 Nugget Avenue, Unit J, Agincourt, Ontario
M1S 3L1 (Canada); Lonely Planet Publishing, PO Box 88,
South Yarra, Victoria 3141 (Australia); APA Productions
(Pte) Ltd., Room 1021, 10th floor, International Plaza,
10 Anson Road, Singapore (Far East); Nilsson & Lamm bv,
Pampuslaan 212, 1380 AD Weesp (Holland).

CONTENTS

BACKGROUND

Greece reaches down into the Mediterranean like a sweeping hand that has sown a thousand islands upon the sea. The sea is everywhere, not on three sides only, but at every turn, penetrating the broken phalanxes of the coastline. You cannot travel very far across country without meeting the sea and you cannot sail for long upon the sea without an island rising off your bows. Greece is a tough cloth woven from the contrasting textures and colours of rugged mountain land and blue water.

There is a dignity to this land and in the people who live upon it. It is not that Greece was ever simply great in her monuments, in her intellect or in her power, but that her people expressed through these things their hard discovery of the proportions of their existence. Camus wrote that "he who dedicates himself to the duration of his life, to the house he builds, to the dignity of mankind, dedicates himself to the earth and reaps from it the harvest that sows its seed and sustains the world again and again".

The Greek lives his life in this way. Amidst a landscape of stark brilliance where the mountains stand in razor-sharp clarity against the sea and sky, with the hot sun at his neck and the stony soil resisting at his feet, the Greek forces the elements to meet and give him life. The clear, slightly resinated wine is the synthesis of his labours. He drinks life in all its contradictions and knows joy.

The Greek lives out so many contradictions that one suspects he deliberately creates them, partly to nourish his inborn scepticism, partly to make the world more complicated. He will place his lips upon an ikon and then emerge into the sunlight with a sly smile which says that in there we believe, out here we know better. He is a superb businessman and has a great respect for money, but he will also give you the shirt off his back and refuse any repayment. So often he does not give in order to earn, but earns in order to give. He will open a taverna, stand outside, and you will sit down and wait an hour before he bothers to serve you. Then he will insult you into the bargain and finally, having decided that he likes you, will give you a bottle of wine on the house.

He is as passionate about women as any Italian but does his best not to show it. He will say to foreigners, why do you talk with women? Why do you dance with women? Women are for making love to and nothing else. At the same time, you will find no more proud, assured or independent woman in all the Mediterranean than a Greek woman. That Greece was the 'cradle of democracy' is a cliche. It is no less true that the country has been a nursery for tyranny and anarchy. Sometimes the government abuses the people; other times the people abuse the government; and when both the government and the people are abusing each other simultaneously, that is democracy. The cradle is rocked vigorously and the Greek comes through it all with anything but complacency: he is tough and resilient, sharply intelligent and inquisitive; he is his own man, independent of spirit and free.

When Perithoos, king of the Lapiths, invited the neighbouring Centaurs on the slopes of Mt Pelion to his wedding feast, these creatures, half man, half horse, attracted by the unfamiliar fragrance of wine, pushed their bowls of sour milk aside and drank the wine-skins dry. Drunk and lecherous, they dragged the bride off by her hair and raped the nearest women and boys. Theseus, legendary founder of Athens and friend of Perithoos, joined the Lapiths in their day-long fight to drive the savage guests away.

One more outrageous tale of Greek mythology it seems, but an exceptionally popular one in Classical times. With events like the defeat of the Persians to celebrate, the Athenians chose instead to depict the battle between Lapiths and Centaurs on the metope reliefs of the Parthenon, and the same theme appears on the interior frieze of the Temple of Apollo Epikouros at Vassae, high up in the wild mountains of the Peloponnese, and again on the west pediment of the Temple of Zeus at Olympia.

For all the exhilaration the Greeks felt after their victories over Darius and later Xerxes at Marathon, Salamis and Plataea, they understood that these momentous episodes were also only momentary episodes in their struggle for civilisation, a struggle that would have to be waged for endless centuries to come. The battle between Lapiths and Centaurs, between men on the one hand and on the other men who are yet half beasts, expresses a larger, timeless struggle. Sophocles' "moderation in all things" is not the motto of a moderate people — for whom it would be superfluous. It is a warning against the beast in man, a warning that destruction arises from within as well as from without. The Greeks of Pericles' time could be an immoderate people. It was their awareness of this and the prizes they won in their struggle with themselves that was their glory.

This is a guide to the land and its people, and inevitably a guide through time. Even if one shunned the Parthenon and could somehow avoid not stumbling upon a broken

column, a Mycenaean wall, a Byzantine chapel, the land itself has that awesome dawn-of-creation clarity and the people that naked response to it that cannot have changed since Homer's day. Greece today is the same Greece as when man first surveyed the savage landscape about him and within him and dared pit reason and justice against what he found. Time weaves back upon itself. Mycenaean, Classical, Byzantine, modern are not eras within a chronology but each designs upon an ever-present tapestry that portrays the continuing struggle.

Tourist Information. The National Tourist Organisation of Greece is extremely helpful both inside and outside the country supplying maps, brochures (in English, German, French and Greek) and travel information sheets. Their

offices are found in principal cities abroad, including:
Britain: 195-7 Regent Street, London W1 (Tel: 734.5997).
USA: 645 Fifth Avenue, New York, NY 10022 (Tel:
421.5777); 627 West Sixth Street, Los Angeles, California
90017 (Tel: 626.6696); 168 North Michigan Avenue,
Chicago, Illinois, 60601 (Tel: 641.6600).
Canada: 2 Place Ville Marie, Suite 67, Esso Plaza, Montreal,
Quebec H3B 2C9 (Tel: 871.1535).
Australia: 51-57 Pitt Street, Sydney, NSW 2000 (Tel:
241.1663).
Netherlands: Leidsestraat 13, Amsterdam (Tel: 25.42.12).
Belgium: Blvd de l'Imperatrice 62-66, 1000 Brussels
(Tel: 513.02.06).
France: 3 Avenue de l'Opera, Paris 75001 (Tel: 260.65.34).
Germany: Neue Mainzer Strasse 22, 6 Frankfurt/Main
(Tel: 23.65.61); Pacellistrasse 2, Munich (Tel: 22.20.35).
Italy: Via L. Bissolati 78-80, 00187 Rome (Tel: 487.249);
Piazza Diaz 1, Milan (Tel: 66.47.49).
Austria: Kartner Ring 5, 1010 Vienna (Tel: 52.53.17).
Sweden: Grev Turegatan 2, Box 5298, 10246 Stockholm 5
(Tel: 21.11.13).
Switzerland: Gottfried Keller Strasse 7, 8001 Zurich (Tel:
32.84.87).
South Africa: 116 Marshall Street, Johannesburg (Tel:
836.46.31).
Japan: 11 Mori Building, Shiba Nishikubo, Akefunecho
Minato-Ku, Tokyo (Tel: 5035001).

The NTOG's head office in Greece is at 2 Amerikis
Street, Athens (Tel: 3223.111), and there are information
desks inside the National Bank of Greece at 2 Karageorgi
Servias Street, Syntagma Square, Athens and at the East
Main Airport. Regional offices are located in the major
towns and at the border, while the Tourist Police all over
the country can be relied upon for their courtesy and
efficiency in supplying information and finding rooms.

No visas are required of Western European, American,
Australian and New Zealand nationals, amongst others.
A valid passport is sufficient to gain entry for 3 months
(US citizens, 2 months). If you wish to extend your stay,
contact the Aliens Bureau, 9 Halkokondyli Street, Athens
(Tel: 3628.301). Personal belongings such as clothing and
camping gear may be brought through customs duty-free,
as well as one each of the following: cameras, cine cameras,
projectors, binoculars, musical instruments, record players
(with up to 20 records), radios, typewriters, tape recorders,
bicycles and sports gear such as skis and shotguns. It is
forbidden to export any work of art dating from before

1830 without permission. 'Works of art' can include old coins and potsherds. Penalties are severe. Cars and motorcycles brought into the country are entered on your passport to ensure that they are taken out again at the end of 4 months, though this period can be extended to 8 or even 12 months. Trailers will require the completion of a special customs document. The importation of foreign currency is free and unlimited, but sums in excess of the equivalent of US $500 should be declared to ensure free exportation. No more than 750 drachmas in Greek currency may be brought into or taken out of the country. Cholera and yellow fever certificates are required if coming from an infected area.

Climate   Hot summers and mild winters are the rule for all of Greece except in the north, and at higher elevations in the mountain regions, where winters are cold. The highest summer temperatures are usually found in the Peloponnese, Rhodes and the Dodecanese and Crete. July and August are the hottest months. Athens is then stifling, but the islands of the Aegean are cooled by the meltemi which indeed can make them positively windy at times. Crete and Rhodes are the warmest parts of Greece during the winter though certainly do not count on being able to swim, especially in January and February. The very best time to come to Greece is in April and May when it's not too hot, the land has not yet been parched, and all is green and brilliant with wildflowers. Second best is October; most of the vegetation has dried up but the sun has released a herbal scent amongst the hills, and for some plants there is a second flowering.

Travel Notes. Athens is served by major international airlines and charter operators from all over the world, and from within Europe it is also possible to fly directly to Thessaloniki, Corfu, Kos, Rhodes and Heraklion.

Getting there by air

By sea   Piraeus is the port of Athens and the major port of Greece, but you are only likely to arrive there if coming from major European ports like Venice, Trieste, Genoa or Marseille. The more usual sea approach to Greece is from the Italian port of Brindisi, calling at Corfu, Igoumenitsa on the mainland, and Patras in the Peloponnese. Either before sailing or on board ship you can buy a coach ticket from Patras to Athens. If you buy a ticket for Patras but want to spend some time on Corfu enroute, insist that this be noted on your ticket. The run from Brindisi, like the less frequent runs from Bari and Ancona, ferries cars as well.

By land   Coming to Greece by train means passing through Yugoslavia, a hot, crowded, unpleasant journey. It's better to go by train to an Italian port and continue on by boat. The cheapest way of getting to Greece is by bus, but this is recommended only to those with a considerable sense of humour.

Student discounts Students may fly cheaply to Greece on charter flights operated under the aegis of the Student Air Travel Association. They are also eligible for discounts ranging from 10% to 30% on trans-Adriatic shipping lines, and can obtain still more substantial discounts on rail fares. They should contact their local student travel office for details.

Travel within Greece by air Olympic Airways is the exclusive operator within Greece and has a network of routes connecting Athens with Thessaloniki and a few other mainland cities, but is most valuable for getting out to some of the major islands in a hurry: Chios, Corfu, Crete, Kos, Lesvos, Rhodes, Samos, Skiathos, Thera, Zakynthos and a few others. Some of these routes may be dropped during the winter months. Olympic's head office is at 96 Syngrou Avenue, Athens (Tel: 92.921) and there is a booking office in the Athens Hilton (Tel: 9292.445). One flight over the Aegean is worth it for a god's eye view of that ancient blue sea speckled with scores of islands — you can almost see the square sails of Odysseus, Theseus or the Argonauts down below. Air fares compare favourably with first class boat fares.

By sea Voyaging by sea is what Greece is all about and always has been. A mountainous country making overland communications difficult, hundreds of boats still bob along the coastline or from island to island at very low fares. Piraeus is the hub of Aegean routings. For weekly information sheets on sailing times, routes and fares, go to the NTOG office in Syntagma Square. Also you can scan the shipping page of the English-language 'Athens News'. Car ferries operate over many routes. Passengers may travel first or second (tourist) class — that is, with cabins on the longer runs — or deck class.

The joys of a sea voyage Deck class is the cheapest way to travel and for the young or adventurous the most enjoyable. For daytime voyages, like the early morning sailings from Piraeus through the Cyclades, deck class means nothing more than that you may freely wander above and below deck but not into the first-class restaurant and bar.

But for overnight voyages, like the one to Crete, the question of where to sleep arises. Down below, on every available bunk, chair or sheet of newspaper, the Greek passengers have staked out their claims, but first they sit around talking, smoking, drinking, sharing out food from vast parcels (better and cheaper than the food you buy on board). Gipsy women despatch their children to maraud the ship, and themselves sit on beautifully woven cloths selling dresses, blouses, trinkets. Hawkers stand by doorways with trays of nuts, chocolates and honey-cakes. There's a man with a lamb slung over his shoulder who presses through the pandemonium selling raffle tickets.

The soldiers are drunk, the old men are laughing and slapping their knee boots when not playing vicious games of cards, mothers are breast feeding their babies, and then by 2 am, amidst a clutter of paper, bread crusts, bottles and cans, everyone is sprawled out fast asleep in their reserved positions. The air is choked with smoke, damp with sweat, hot with sufficient snoring bodies to sink a ship twice the size of the one you're on, the engine thuds against the floor, the wind chops against the half-open port holes.

Why the Greeks won't sleep on deck, I don't know, but every foreigner with a sleeping-bag is up there (even in mid-summer, sun and wind compete for the sea and by the time the first star appears in the sky, the sea breeze has taken cold possession of the night). Cigarettes glow in windless corners, thick borrowed novels are read beneath the deck lights, life-boats sway with the sea and the copulating travellers who have made their beds inside them. Dark islands slip by in the black Aegean night.

Some Greeks do appear on deck before passing out below. One time, when I was sailing to Heraklion, several were attracted by the noise of a ukelele and the voices of a dozen Germans singing *Gaudeamus Igitur* as though on the deck of a sinking U-boat. One Greek had a flute, another a violin, a third expropriated the ukelele and the rest began dancing with the Germans to wild Cretan music. Several bottles of wine later, the frenzy declined, the moment had come for an older Greek to come forward and dance in that proud measure of a toreador before the horns and soft eyes of a breathless bull.

This old mountain man with stubble on his chin, high boots, threadbare jacket flicked by the wind, danced with a power that held all eyes, and gesturing towards a young and muscular soldier who could have knocked half of us off deck with one sweep of his arm, these two then danced, shoulder to shoulder, the old man's every step a mastery of grace, the soldier following, prettily, deferentially, like a young girl dancing with her father on her wedding night.

There is a sexuality in this dance, perhaps a homosexuality, though I suspect it is a dance of another passion, a challenge to disorder, destruction and death (the Spanish bullfight is a bastardised bull dance, common in the Aegean

3,500 years ago), the older men showing the younger the way. Anyway, they dance on these ships, they sing, they sell and trade and drink and argue, and you fall asleep on the deck, and if you haven't rolled off during the night you wake with the sun in your face, and the old Venetian walls of Heraklion loom close leaving only enough time for a quick coffee.

Bus and train

Both buses and trains are cheap. Buses are faster, more comfortable and a bit less expensive than trains, and reach nearly every nook and cranny of the country. (But students should note that with an ISIC they get a 50% reduction on rail journeys between Athens, Piraeus or any border station to any other station on the line.)

By car

Greece is probably the most expensive country in Europe for car rentals. The great advantage to having a car, your own or rented, is being able to get to inaccessible spots, indeed being able to discover places miles from nowhere which you probably wouldn't have chanced seeking out had it meant waiting hours for a bus or hiking for miles in the mid-day sun. On the other hand, there is the danger of shutting yourself off from the country, in particular missing the lively society of the Greek bus.

Further details

For further notes on internal travel, tours, cruises, taxis, etc., see under place headings in the last section of this guide.

Living Notes. The first thing you should do is learn the Greek alphabet. Greek is not nearly as strange as it looks on first sight: once you know that an upside down L is really a G, that a P is an R and that a B is a V, you're on your way to seeing through the camouflage of peculiar letters which reveals words not all that more difficult than the ones you easily make sense of in French, Italian or Spanish. After all, a fair part of the English language has grown up from Greek as well as from Latin roots.

The alphabet

The more assiduous alphabet-learners among you may want to grapple with the lower-case letters as well, but they make less initial sense than the upper-case ones, and fortunately street names, names of hotels and so on are usually written entirely in upper-case letters.

Two excellent phrase books and dictionaries combined are *Travellers' Greek*, published by Jonathan Cape, and the Penguin *Greek Phrase Book*. Both are available in Greece as well as abroad.

The French, Spanish and Italians are all used to foreigners knowing a few words of their languages, but the Greeks seem not to expect it and are therefore all the more gratified if you can utter the simplest greeting. So it's very much worth your while to get a phrase book, or even just to learn the following words: parakal*o* = please, efcharist*o* = thank you, kalim*e*ra = good morning, kalisp*e*ra = good afternoon or good evening, kalin*i*kta = good night. Kala alone means good, and you can use it when you pat children on the head, comment on a meal or in any situation where you want to convey approval. One of the most common words you'll hear is and*a*xi: it means okay. And as a general greeting or farewell, as when you encounter a goatherd on a hillside, there's yia-soo (that is the familiar singular; the formal and the plural is yia-sas). Yes is ne; no is *o*hi. Here you might run into some trouble. When a Greek says no he also tilts his head back. Sometimes he says nothing at all but just accompanies this gesture with a clicking of the tongue. And sometimes he doesn't even click his tongue. The result is that you ask at a kiosk for a certain newspaper and the Greek cocks his head back. At first you think this means "I beg your pardon?", so you say it again, and again the head flicks back. After you've asked for your newspaper seven times, each time raising your voice, simultaneously trying to enunciate more clearly and to gesticulate fiercely in the appropriate manner, you realise that he has been saying "no" all along and you feel like a numbskull. So along with learning the alphabet and a few words and phrases, you should also learn some gestures. There is a very funny book (all the more funny for being so true to life) by Papas called *Instant Greek* which illustrates this aspect of communication. It is published in Greece and readily available throughout the country.

There are a few other words worth being able to recognise when you're walking around: od*os* = street, plate*i*a = square, leof*o*ros = avenue, st*a*sis = bus stop, xenodoch*i*o = hotel.

This is a good place to apologise for any inconsistencies in our transliteration of Greek words and place-names into English. There is no standard formula. We write odos as odos because it seems simpler to do so, though its pronunciation in Greek is more like 'odhos' (the 'd' in Greek being pronounced like the 'th' in 'that'). We do not overly-mimic the phonetic subtleties of Greek. On the other hand, we have often written place-names as they are pronounced in Greek (indicating also in the index to this guide how they are stressed), partly for flavour, partly so that you can be more immediately understood. Epidauros, for instance, is Ep*i*davros to a Greek and that is the way we have written it. Eleusis is pronounced Elefs*i*s. (A 'u' after 'a' or 'e' is pronounced either 'v' or 'f' depending on what follows.) It may seem incredible that Greeks should speak

A few words

And gestures

A few more words

And an apology

of Zeus as 'Zefs', but after all, he was their god and it is their language. But then we have not always gone so far. Thebes we commonly write as Thebes, noting the Greek 'Th*i*vai' only in brackets. Names of people have usually been written in their Greek form, but occasionally, in recognition of popular usage, Sophocles, for example, might appear instead of Sophokles. Writing leoforos with an 'f' but Phaleron with a 'ph' when both could be either the one or the other can only be explained as an aesthetic idiosyncrasy and our small contribution to furthering the spirit of contradiction which the Greeks themselves, in other matters, are so good at promoting.

Accommodation Depending on your preferences and on what you are prepared to spend, there is a choice of hotels from luxury to fifth class (denoted in this guide as L and A, B, C, D and E), also 'inns' (often dormitory-style accommodation), service flats, rooms in private homes and organised camping grounds. Prices are set by the government and are strictly adhered to. There's no chance of being overcharged, though you can always look at the rate card behind the door to check for yourself. Bargaining can be worthwhile at any time, especially outside of the high season when prices are authorised to go down.

Prices applying to all categories of accommodation throughout Greece, as well as a place by place listing of hotels, etc., will be found in the third section of this guide.

Roof-tops, monasteries and freelance camping It is also possible at many tavernas around the country to get free or very cheap roof space. Monasteries and convents may offer beds (usually to males and females respectively), especially in out-of-the-way places where there is no alternative accommodation, and though these are free, and though an offer of some payment will usually be refused, something should be left in the chapel upon leaving. Freelance camping is no longer allowed; but the law was introduced to stop people from sleeping out in the middle of Athens or along resort beaches (there was considerable abuse, litter and lack of hygiene), so that if you are out of the way and not making a nuisance of yourself it is less likely that this restriction will be enforced. The air is warm, the nights are brilliant with stars, and all of Greece could be yours for the price of a sleeping-bag.

Eating places If there's much distinction to be made between a restaurant (estiatoria) and a taverna, it's that the latter is less formal, at least partly outdoors and its fare uncompromisingly Greek. A taverna meal can be inexpensive and delicious, though the menu will be limited in variety. Greece is not renowned for its cuisine, and though some eating places will serve better food than others, it's probably as much if not more worthwhile basing your choice of where to eat on atmosphere. Greeks themselves frequently dine out as the large numbers of tavernas attests; lunchtime is from 1 to 3, dinner from 9 to 1am (though earlier outside Athens) and at least half the point of going to a taverna for dinner at all is the convivial evening spent talking and drinking.

Like hotels, restaurants and tavernas are officially graded and their prices fixed accordingly. Menus will show the basic price against each item, and then the price with service added. When served by the owner of a small taverna, it's not necessary to tip as the service charge covers this. But in larger places something should be left on the change dish for the employee-waiter, and if a boy has been helping out with the water and retsina, a coin can be left for him under your eating plate. In Athens and major towns and resorts the menu is likely to be in English or French as well as in Greek, though wherever you are it's quite acceptable to go into the kitchen and see for yourself what's there.

Food
A meal might start with soup, pasta or an hor d'oeuvre such as the pink fish roe paste called taramosalata or stuffed vine leaves (dolmades). Fish, common on the islands or by the coast, rare inland, is usually served as a main course. Red mullet (barbounia) and whitebait (marides) are fairly standard; also octopus (ktapodi) and squid (kalamari) which largely depend for their taste on the wine sauce in which they are prepared. Foreigners might prefer the more tender baby squids (kalamarakia), crisply fried. Meat (kreas) is most usually veal (moskari) or lamb (arnaki); also shish kebab, skewered chunks of grilled meat as often called souflaki. Each person might order his own main fish or meat course, but the usual practice is to share vegetables and salads from common plates. The selection will be determined by the season. In spring you should try horta, or greens — in fact dandelion and other leaves plucked from the slopes of the Acropolis, by the roadside, or in someone's back garden — which are served cold in plenty of lemon and oil. Salad (salata) can be all tomato (domata salata), all lettuce (marouli) or mixed, popularly known as Greek or country salad (choriatiki), served with goat's milk cheese (feta). Old standbys include moussaka, a layered pot-pourri of peppers, tomatoes, minced meat, cheese, potatoes, etc. — its flavour and quality varying from day to day, place to place — and macaroni casserole (makaronia). If there's any chance of oil (ladi) being added to anything it will be. So if you don't want oil you had better be fast with "ohi ladi". But anyone spending any time in the sun should

welcome all the olive oil they can get: it finds its way to the skin, lubricates you against the heat and works with the sun to give you a beautiful colour.

Wine Wine (kras*i*) comes either resinated or not. The mouth-puckering retsina, flavoured with resin from pine trees, may seem strange at first taste, but in combination with Greek food it's perfect. Retsina is usually served from the cask in cans and so there are local variations in quality and taste; less often and less interestingly it comes standardised in bottles. Unresinated wine almost always comes bottled, Hymettos and Demestica being two of the most widely available labels. White wine is *a*spro, red is m*a*vro (literally 'black') and rose is k*o*kkino (literally 'red').

Sweets are not usually served at tavernas, nor coffee.
Cafes For coffee you go to a cafe or kafene*i*on, where you might find sweets too though you might have to go to a patisserie (zakaroplaste*i*on). The coffee is usually Greek-style, thick and black in small cups and comes without sugar (sk*e*tto), with sugar (m*e*trio) or with loads of sugar (variglik*o*). If you want Western-style coffee, ask for Nescafe. The favourite kafeneion aperitif is ouzo, colourless and flavoured with aniseed, and usually served with me*ze*, little snacks of cheese, nuts, olives or fish. The most popular sweets are baklav*a*, layered pastry filled with honey and nuts, and kata*i*fi, shredded wheat filled with sweetened nuts.

Shopping Athens offers as broad a range of goods as any European city, though imports are likely to be expensive. The department stores are found mostly around Omonia Square. The yellow kiosks (per*i*ptero) throughout Athens and in other cities and towns of Greece are open for as much as 18 hours a day and are extremely handy for obtaining a myriad of small items. Not only can you purchase newspapers (Greek and foreign), cigarettes, post-cards, chocolate and other items on display, but somehow tucked away within are toothpaste, shampoo, lightbulbs, combs, aspirins, film, razor blades, glue, watchstraps, needles, worry beads, men's contraceptives and still more. Also the periptero will have a public telephone or two for local calls.

Crafts Craft items are found at markets, villages and monasteries as well as in many shops. In Athens, to avoid wasting time searching from one nasty souvenir place to another, go directly to the National Organisation of Hellenic Handicraft, 9 Mitropoleos St, where craft goods are displayed but none sold: when you've found what you want you are given the address of the shop or artisan where purchase may be made. Different towns, islands and regions around Greece have their specialities. Some of the most famous are:

Arta and **Trikala**: kilimi, hand-woven rugs, shoulder bags.
Chania (Crete): leather work.
Corfu: jewellery, embroidery, woodwork.
Heraklion (Crete): onyx and alabaster work.
Ioannina (Epirus): jewellery, metalwork, silver.
Kastoria: furs.
Metsovo: weaving, woodwork.
Mykonos: woven fabrics, clothes.
Pelion: pottery.
Rhodes: jewellery, pottery.
Sifnos: pottery.
Skyros: pottery, embroidery, woodcarving.
Vitina (Peloponnese): woodwork.

Shopping hours

Shopping hours for general trade stores and pharmacies are from 8am to 3pm, Monday, Wednesday and Saturday; from 8am to 1.30pm and again from 4.30pm to 8pm on Tuesday, Thursday and Friday. There may be variations for foodstores, hairdressers and gift shops. There is a move to abolish siesta and keep stores open all day. This may yet succeed, at least in winter. Tavernas, kafeneions, etc., are usually open 7 days a week.

Health

Freelance campers and those hiking about the countryside should consider inoculation against tetanus. Dog bites need immediate treatment. A list of doctors and dentists may be obtained from your embassy (see embassy addresses under Athens at the back of this guide). Urgent cases are dealt with by the roster of hospitals which stay open day and night (phone the Tourist Police — dial 171 — for the hospital on duty), and by the Hospital Control Centre (Rythmistikon Kentron) of the State Hospital on Leoforos Mesoghion, Athens (Tel: 7701.211) and the KAT Hospital outside Athens in Kifissia (Tel: 8014.411). Gastric disorders can be countered by plain unsweetened lemon juice, or a standard preparation can be obtained from any pharmacist. Their advice in all matters is generally knowledgeable. And of course it's a good idea to be medically insured.

Banks and changing money

Banks are open Monday through Saturday (though Saturday openings may soon be abolished) from 8am to 1pm, and some in Athens, the National Bank of Greece in Syntagma Square amongst them, are open as late as 9pm for changing money. Money may also be changed at port of entry and at hotels. Elsewhere around the country post offices and telecommunications centres might also be able to help.

Greek currency

The drachma is the unit of currency in Greece. It is allowed to float and therefore its value is changeable. In recent years its value has varied between 30 and 37 to the US dollar; it would be hazardous to give it even a rough value against the erratic pound. Notes come in denominations of 50, 100, 500 and 1000 drachmas; coins in 1, 2, 5, 10 and 20. And there is a half-drachma coin. Over the last decade or so, Greeks and foreigners alike have been regarding their small change with increasing bewilderment. New coinage has been minted while old coinage has remained in circulation. The monarchy had one coinage, the junta three, and now the democratic government has added a fifth. Don't be afraid to carefully examine your change; even the Greeks have to.

Post office

Post Offices (ELTA) are open from 7.30am to 8pm, Mondays through Saturdays, though certain sections, like parcels, close at 1.30pm. Correspondence marked 'Poste Restante' (to be called for) may be addressed to any post office and is handed to the addressee on proof of identity. A small fee is sometimes charged. Surnames should be written entirely in capitals. Parcels are not delivered, but upon receipt of a notice advising arrival must be collected from the post office.

Telephone and telegrams

OTE is the Greek telephone and telegraph service with offices in all large towns. Though local calls may be made from a periptero, long distance and international calls should be made at an OTE office.

Electricity

Electricity is 220 volts AC except in the most outlying places where it is still 110 DC.

Weights and measures

The metric system of weights and measures was adopted by Greece in 1958, along with its familiar terms: metro for metre, kiliometro for kilometre, etc. However, some liquids, including wines, are measured by weight, not volume, thus a kilo of retsina rather than a litre. The standard unit of land measurement is the stremma, about ¼ of an acre.

In this guide we have stated distances in kilometres as that is how you will encounter them on maps, signs, in conversation, etc. However, altitudes and measurements have been expressed in feet, this being more meaningful to most readers, though the Greeks themselves will use metres. (One kilometre = .62 miles; one metre = 3.28 feet. Or putting it the other way round: one mile = 1.6 kilometres; one foot = .304 metres.)

Time, calendar and holidays	Greek time is 2 hours ahead of GMT: noon in London is 2pm in Greece. All movable festivals are governed by the fixing of Easter according to the Orthodox calendar. The Greek and Western Easters occur on the same day only once every four years. Public holidays are 1 January; Epiphany on 6 January; Shrove Monday; Independence Day on 25 March; Good Friday, Easter and Easter Monday; Assumption on 15 August; 'Ohi' day (when the Greeks said no to the Italian ultimatum in 1940) on 28 October; Christmas Day on 25 December and St Stephen's Day on the 26th.
Tourist police	The Tourist Police operate a 24-hour phone service for any kind of problem affecting tourists. If you've lost your wallet or can't find a hotel, need urgent medical attention or just want information, give them a ring. Their office in Athens is at 7 Leoforos Syngrou (Tel: 171).
Artistic events	**Cultural Notes.** The NTOG sponsors a number of artistic events throughout Greece. The following are presented annually:
Athens Festival	From July through September ancient drama, opera, music and ballet are included in the programme of the Athens Festival at the Odeon of Herodos Atticus against the southern base of the Acropolis. Both Greek and foreign companies of international repute are invited to perform.
Epidavros Festival	Through July to mid-August ancient Greek drama is performed in the famous theatre of Epidavros whose perfect acoustics permit attendance by 14,000 people at a time.
	Similar festivals, usually in August, take place in the ancient theatres of Dodoni, Thassos and Philippi.
Sound and Light	Sound and light shows in several languages bring the history of the Acropolis to life from your vantage point at the Pnyx, and similar shows take place at Rhodes and Corfu. They are presented from early April to the end of October. Information and tickets for all of the above can be obtained at the NTOG Festival Office, 2 Spyrou Miliou Arcade (between Stadiou and Panepistemiou streets, near Syntagma Square), Athens (Tel: 3221.459 or 3223.111).
Song and film festivals	During the first week of the Thessaloniki Trade Fair (September) a Festival of Greek Light Song is held in the Palais des Sports within the fairgrounds; and immediately after the Fair there is a festival of Greek and foreign films.
Demetria Festival	A series of theatrical, musical, ballet and operatic performances follow the Thessaloniki Trade Fair in October, reviving the tradition of Byzantine festive events.
Folk dancing	The Dora Stratou ballet and song troupe present a

programme of Greek folk dancing at the open-air theatre on Philopappou Hill, Athens, from May to September.

Similarly, on Rhodes the Nelly Dimoglou troupe presents Greek folk dancing in the theatre of the old city from June to October.

And from November to March, folk dance performances move indoors to the Aliki winter theatre, 2 Amerikis Street, Athens, home of the Greek Lyceum company.

Museums and archaeological sites

Museums and most archaeological sites throughout Greece require tickets of admission costing from 25 to 50 drachmas per person. Student admission is from 2.50 to 5 drachmas upon presentation of an ISIC. Admission to all state museums is free on Thursdays and Sunday. Additional fees

Fees

are charged for filming or photographing inside museums, or filming at archaelogical sites. Still photography at sites (provided no tripod is used) is free.

Archaeological sites and museums in the Athens area and at Thessaloniki, Olympia, Corinth, Mystra, Delphi, Mycenae, Corfu, Rhodes, Lindos, Heraklion and Knossos are open as follows:

Hours of admission

Weekdays: 9am to 3.30pm from 16 October to 31 March and 7.30am to 7.30pm from 1 April to 15 October.

Sunday and holidays: 10am to 4.30pm in winter and 10am to 6pm in summer.

But note that special hours apply to Sounion and Epidavros:

Weekdays: 11am to 5.30pm in winter and 7.30am to 7.30pm in summer. Sundays and holidays as above.

All other museums and archaeological sites in the country are open as follows:

Weekdays: 10am to 4.30pm in winter and 9am to 1pm and again from 4pm to 6pm in summer.

Sundays and holidays: 10.30am to 2.30pm in winter and summer.

Most museums are closed on Tuesdays (some on Mondays), and all are closed on 1 January, 25 March, Good Friday and Easter Sunday (Orthodox), and 25 December.

Architecture

In the 8th and 7th C. BC the Doric temple developed the features that were to achieve their greatest refinement in Periclean times. The entire structure stood upon a stylobate. The cella housed the image of the god and was at first

The Doric temple

built of mud brick and timber. To protect the cella from the rain a verandah was added on all sides with a peristyle. The pronaos led to the cella and for symmetry's sake the opisthodomos was added at the opposite end.

During the 6th C. BC mud brick and wood were replaced

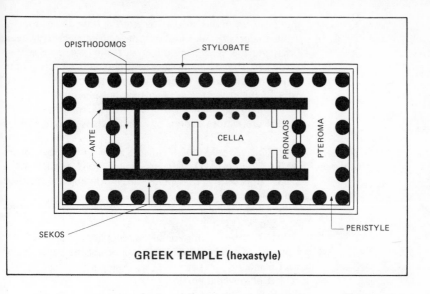

GREEK TEMPLE (hexastyle)

OPISTHODOMOS · STYLOBATE · ANTE · CELLA · PRONAOS · PTEROMA · SEKOS · PERISTYLE

by limestone, the thatched roof by tiles. Stucco covered the limestone to improve its appearance, though towards the end of the century the Athenians improved upon both the strength and beauty of their temples by building them of marble quarried from Pentelikon. The Parthenon, completed in 438 BC, with its fine proportions enhanced by subtle optical effects, marked the perfection of the Doric temple.

The Ionic order   Stagnation following upon perfection was avoided by the introduction to mainland Greece of the Ionic order from across the Aegean. Within a few years of the Parthenon's completion, Athenian architects were complementing Doric maturity with the slenderness and the restrained elaboration of the Erechtheion and the Temple of Athena Nike, both of the Ionic order; while already the Parthenon itself and, soon after, the Propylaia successfully combined elements of both orders.

Church architecture   Christian architecture at first borrowed Classical forms, the earliest churches employing the basilical plan of the pagan temples, when not actually taking over the temples themselves.

The dome   But it was the dome that became the most distinctive feature of later Byzantine churches. Its considerable outward thrust required buttressing: buttresses external to the basilical plan of Western churches supported high Romanesque and Gothic vaults; the Eastern church solved

Cross-in-Square the problem more neatly by setting the dome upon a vaulted superstructure in the form of an equal-armed Greek Cross and then enclosing the cross at the lower level within a square. The structure was entirely self-supporting, the thrust of the dome extending down through the vaulted arms of the cross, the arms in turn bolstered by the square that contained them. The churches at Daphni and Osios Loukas are mature expressions of this cross-in-square style.

Glossary of terms AMPHORA: tall, two-handled jar with narrow neck.

ANTA (plural ANTAE): projecting front portion of a cella's side wall in a temple, often forming an enclosed porch.

APSE: semi-circular domed recess, most frequently at the east end of a church.

ARCHITRAVE: horizontal supporting beam across columns of temple, stoa, etc., supporting the pediment or roof-front.

ATRIUM: covered portico.

BASILICA: church in the form of a long colonnaded hall, usually with one or more apses at the east end, and a narthex at the west end.

CAVEA: concave auditorium of seats in a theatre.

CELLA: enclosed inner 'house of the god', central room of a temple.

CHTHONIC: dwelling in or under the ground, of the earth.

CRYSOBUL: document containing decree of Byzantine emperor.

ENTASIS: slight swelling in a column to counteract the optical illusion of a straight column appearing pinched.

EXEDRA: semi-circular, recessed structure.

EXO-NARTHEX: outer vestibule of a church.

FRIEZE: horizontal band of sculpture comprising either metopes and triglyphs (Doric order) or continuous figures in relief (Ionic order), usually placed above the architrave on the exterior (sometimes also on an interior wall) of a temple.

HEXASTYLE: having six columns along the end of a temple, etc.; octostyle, eight columns; etc.

IKONOSTASIS: screen carrying ikons between the main part of a church and the sanctuary or choir.

KORE: archaic statue of standing clothed young woman.

KOUROS: archaic statue of standing nude young man.

LOGGIA: open gallery.

MEGARON: central main room of Minoan or Mycenaean palace, sometimes also applied to an old temple.

METOPE: square space between triglyphs in a Doric frieze, used for relief sculpture.

NAOS: cella, though sometimes referring to the entire temple.

NARTHEX: entrance vestibule at west end of a church.

NAVE: main body or central aisle of a church.

ODEON: concert hall, roofed over.

ORCHESTRA: flat circular area in front of theatre stage where chorus moved and sang.

PEDIMENT: triangular area below gabled roof of a temple, usually filled with sculpture.

PERISTYLE: row of columns round the outside of a temple.

PITHOS (plural PITHOI): large storage jar.

POLYGONAL: form of masonry in which large blocks of stone, cut in irregular shapes, have been fitted together like a jigsaw.

POROS: a soft, coarse, conchiferous limestone (same as tufa).

PRONAOS: a columned porch, leading to the cella.

PROPYLON (plural PROPYLAIA): entrance gate to a temenos.

RHYTON: drinking vessel terminating in the shape of an animal's head.

ROTUNDA: circular building, sometimes domes.

SKENE: back scene structure behind theatre stage.

SKETE: a community of monks, smaller or of less importance than a monastery.

SQUINCHES: small arches across the corners of a square, enabling support of a circular dome.

STELE: upright stone slab or pillar with an inscription or design, used as a monument or grave marker.

STOA: portico, usually in the market-place of an ancient Greek city, used for shops, discussion, etc.

STYLOBATE: top step or platform on which temple or stoa columns rest, loosely applied to all three levels beneath the columns.

TEMENOS: sacred enclosure, for temples, etc.

THOLOS: round building with conical roof, either a Mycenaean 'beehive' tomb or a special civic structure with surrounding colonnade.

TRANSEPT: northern or southern arm of a cruciform church.

TRIGLYPH: decorative element of Doric frieze above architrave of temple or stoa, imitating primitive wooden beam-ends, with two vertical grooves between three raised vertical panels.

TUFA: same as poros.

ANCIENT GREECE

NEOLITHIC Period			6000 BC	Early settlement at Nea Nikomedia, northern Greece. Later settlements in Thessaly at Sesklo and Dimini and on Crete.
	Mainland	Crete	2800	Invaders from Anatolia, with pre-Greek language, settled near Corinth and in Argolid, eg Lerna. Flourishing settlements in eastern Crete. Worship of Earth Goddess prevalent.
B R O N Z E	Early Helladic	Pre-Palatial		
	Middle Helladic	Proto-Palatial: first palaces at Knossos, Phaestos and Mallia.	2000	First Greeks invade mainland (? 'Achaeans'). Significant settlements at Mycenae, Tiryns and Argos.
A G E	Late Helladic ('Mycenaean') Palaces at Mycenae, Tiryns, Athens, Gla, etc.	Neo-Palatial: palaces rebuilt, palace at Zakros.	1700 / c1600 / c1550	Shaft graves at Mycenae. Acme of Minoan civilisation: 'colonies' in Aegean, eg Thera. Linear 'A' script on Crete.
			c1450	Eruption of Thera. Devastation of Cretan palaces except Knossos. Linear 'B' (Greek) script on Crete.
			c1400	Final destruction of Knossos.
		Post-Palatial	1400 / c1350	Palace at Mycenae enlarged, Cyclopean walls built. Mycenae predominant in Greece: beehive tombs (1500-1300).
			c1300-1200	Tiryns rebuilt. Linear 'B' tablets at Pylos. Trojan expedition (c1250).
			c1200-1100	Mycenae and other palaces destroyed
IRON AGE commences			1100	Dorian invaders occupy most of mainland. Male gods now dominant.
Geometric period (from style of pottery, notably at Athens)			c850	Invention of Greek alphabet.
			c800	Birth of Greek city-state. Athens leader of unified Attica.
			776	First Olympic Games

Rise of HELLENIC CIVILISATION	750	
Archaic Period (Early representational art)		Period of increasing commerce and colonisation throughout Mediterranean, and development of city-states through tyrannies towards democracy.
	c600	Invention of money spurs economic activity.
	600-500	Statues of Kouroi and Korai. Attic 'Black Figure' style on vases. Homer becomes known.
	561-510	Peisistratid tyranny at Athens; Festival of Great Dionysia instituted.
	c540	Doric Temple of Apollo at Corinth.
Classical Period	500	Democracy at Athens (instituted 507)
	490-479	Persian Wars. Marathon (490), Salamis (480), Plataea (479).
	c475	Delphi Charioteer. Acme of 'Red Figure' vases.
	c454	Delian Confederacy becomes Athenian Empire.
		Age of Pericles (died 429). Parthenon completed (438). Sophocles' *Oedipus Tyrannus*.
	431-404	Peloponnesian War between Sparta and Athens ends in Athenian defeat.
	399	Death of Socrates.
	371	Thebans defeat Sparta at Leuktra.
	c370	Fortifications at Messene.
	c360	Hermes of Praxiteles.
	c350	Temple of Apollo at Delphi rebuilt. Aristotle, pupil of Plato at Athens.
	338	Macedonian victory over Greek states at Chaeronea.
	c330	Alexander the Great's conquest of Persia.
	323	Death of Alexander. Lamian War (323-322): Athens' revolt against Macedonia fails.

Hellenistic Period	323 4th C.	Death of Demosthenes (322). Wars of Alexander's successors result in rule of Antigonids in Macedonia. Formation of Greek states into leagues against Macedonian interference.
	280-278	Invasion of Gauls repulsed by Aetolian League.
	c220	Boy Jockey from Artemision.
	220-217	War between Achaean and Aetolian Leagues.
	197	Romans defeat Macedonians at Kynoskephalae, Flaminius proclaims Rome 'protector of Greek freedom'.
	168	Romans end Macedonian Empire after Pydna.
	c150	Stoa of Attalos.
	148	Macedonia becomes Roman province.
	146	Greece becomes part of Roman Empire; Corinth destroyed.
ROMAN GREECE	146	'Pax Romana'.
	88-86	Mithridatic War. Sulla sacks Athens.
	48-31	Battles of Pharsalus (48), Philippi (42) and Actium (31).
	31 BC-AD 14	Reign of Augustus. Greece separated from Macedonia into province of Achaea, capital at Corinth.
	AD 54	St Paul visits Athens and Corinth.
	c130	Temple of Olympian Zeus dedicated by Hadrian.
	c160	Odeon of Herodos Atticus.
	c170	Pausanias writes Description of Greece.
	267	Goths pillage Athens.
	c325-330	Under Emperor Constantine, Christianity becomes official religion of Roman Empire, its capital at Constantinople.
	393	Last Olympic Games.
	395	After further Goth invasion, on Emperor Theodosios' death (395) Roman Empire is divided; eastern half, including Greece, ruled from Constantinople.

BYZANTINE TO MODERN GREECE

BYZANTINE GREECE

Date	Event (right column)	Event (left column / timeline)
AD 395	On division of Roman Empire, eastern half including Greece is ruled from Constantinople (Byzantium).	
5th C.	Church of Agios Dimitrios, Thessaloniki.	
529	Emperor Justinian abolishes pagan University of Athens.	
Early 6th-mid 8th C.	Ikonoclast movement (726-843)	Period of Slav invasions of Greece. Athens sacked c580
783		Slav settlers subjected to Byzantine Empire. Saracens possess Crete.
826-961	Renaissance under Macedonian dynasty (867-1059)	Saracens sack Thessaloniki. Bulgars expand into northern Greece.
904		
10th C.		
963	Foundation of Great Lavra on Athos.	Northern Greece recovered by Empire.
1018		
c1020	Church of Osios Loukas	
1054	Final schism between Eastern Church and Rome.	
c1080	Church of Daphni.	Normans occupy Corfu, penetrate Thessaly.
1081-1084		Roger of Sicily loots Thebes.
1146		Normans loot Thessaloniki
1185		Increasing influence of Venetians.
12th C.		

27

FRANKISH AND VENETIAN GREECE

EPIRUS	MACEDONIA	THESSALY	ATTICA/C. GREECE	PELOPONNESE (except Venetian Ports)	ISLANDS		
Despotate of Greek Angeli	Frankish Kingdom of Salonika 1223		Frankish Duchy of Athens	Frankish Principality of Achaia	1. Frankish County of Cephalonia (Ionian Is.) 1194-1479	1204	Sack of Constantinople by Fourth Crusade.
	Despotate of Epirus —1246—				2. Frankish/Venetian Duchy of Archipelago (Aegean Is.) 1207-1566	1204-1261	Latin Empire of Romania
	Byzantine Empire (1186-1258 Bulgars in northern part)	Duchy of Neo Patras or Great Wallachia		—1262— Monemvasia, Mistra, Mani	3. Venetians held i. Crete 1204-1669 ii. Euboea 1209-1470 iii. Aegina 1451-1537, 1654-1718 iv. Most Ionian islands from 1483-1797 v. Tinos to 1715	1261	Constantinople recaptured by Byzantine Empire of Nicaea.
—1318 Orsinis of Cephalonia —1336— Byz. Empire —1349 Serbians/ Albanians	—1349	—1318 Byz./ Neo Emp. Patras in north —1349 Serbians —1375	—1311 Catalan Duchy of Athens (Sicilian rulers) —1388 Florentine Duchy of Athens	—1318 Angevins —1383 Navarrese Company	4. Genoese held (periodically) Eastern Sporades 14th & 15th C. (Chios to 1566)	c1312	Church of Holy Apostles, Thessaloniki.
	Serbians (except Thessaloniki) —1375 Turks (except Thessaloniki, taken in 1430)	—1393 Turks		—1432 Byz. Empire	5. Knights of Rhodes 1309-1522 (Kos 1315-1522)	14th C.	Renaissance under Palaeologan dynasty. Macedonian School of Painting
—1418 Toccos of Cephalonia —1449 Turks	Ionania 1430		—1456-60 Turks	—1461 Turks	1453-1797 Turks acquire all islands (but Ionian Islands only from 1479-	14th/ 15th C.	Development of Mistra as Byzantine centre.
						1453	Fall of Constantinople.

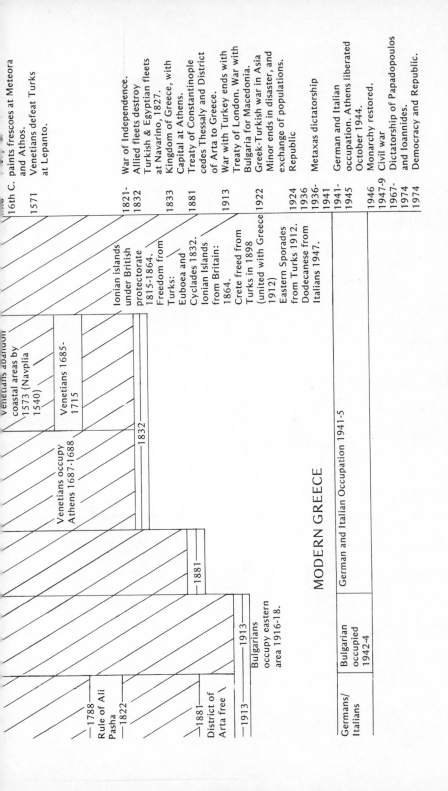

16th C. paints frescoes at Meteora and Athos.
1571 Venetians defeat Turks at Lepanto.

Venetians abandon coastal areas by 1573 (Navplia 1540)
Venetians 1685-1715
Venetians occupy Athens 1687-1688

Ionian islands under British protectorate 1815-1864.
Freedom from Turks:
Euboea and Cyclades 1832.
Ionian Islands from Britain: 1864.
Crete freed from Turks in 1898 (united with Greece 1912)
Eastern Sporades from Turks 1912.
Dodecanese from Italians 1947.

1821-1832 War of Independence. Allied fleets destroy Turkish & Egyptian fleets at Navarino, 1827.
1833 Kingdom of Greece, with Capital at Athens.
1881 Treaty of Constantinople cedes Thessaly and District of Arta to Greece.
1913 War with Turkey ends with Treaty of London. War with Bulgaria for Macedonia.
1922 Greek-Turkish war in Asia Minor ends in disaster, and exchange of populations.
1924 Republic
1936 Metaxas dictatorship
1936-1941
1941-1945 German and Italian occupation. Athens liberated October 1944.
1946 Monarchy restored.
1947-9 Civil war
1967- Dictatorship of Papadopoulos and Ioannides.
1974 Democracy and Republic.

1788 Rule of Ali Pasha
1822
1832
1881 District of Arta free
1913
1913 Bulgarians occupy eastern area 1916-18.

MODERN GREECE

Germans/Italians	German and Italian Occupation 1941-5
	Bulgarian occupied 1942-4

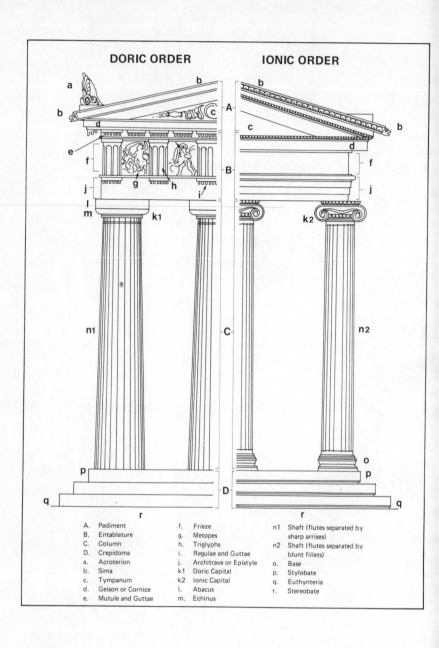

DORIC ORDER **IONIC ORDER**

A.	Pediment	f.	Frieze
B.	Entablature	g.	Metopes
C.	Column	h.	Triglyphs
D.	Crepidoma	i.	Regulae and Guttae
a.	Acroterion	j.	Architrave or Epistyle
b.	Sima	k1	Doric Capital
c.	Tympanum	k2	Ionic Capital
d.	Geison or Cornice	l.	Abacus
e.	Mutule and Guttae	m.	Echinus

n1 Shaft (flutes separated by sharp arrises)
n2 Shaft (flutes separated by blunt fillets)
o. Base
p. Stylobate
q. Euthynteria
r. Stereobate

ATHENS

At the time of Greek independence, centuries of Turkish occupation had left Athens no more than an unhealthy village of narrow dirt alleyways, huts and jumbled houses huddled beneath the Acropolis. Ruins poked out of the ground like broken bottles in a rubbish dump, of no interest to the mixture of its few thousand Greek, Turkish, Slavic and Levantine inhabitants. It was left to foreigners like Byron and Chateaubriand to see or care or know anything of Athens' glorious past, and probably only in deference to this outside feeling was the city chosen as the capital of the new kingdom.

The adopted capital was almost entirely contained within that tiny area which today is the Plaka, and at a distance was surrounded by wild hills and mountains infested with brigands. But in the past century and a half, and especially since the Second World War, the city has advanced against the mountains themselves and marches down to the sea at Piraeus: modern, hard, concrete, a sprawling whiteness shimmering in the heat of the day, glaring with lights at night. Henry Miller described it as a city which will not ungrasp the light of day. "The Greek is just as enamoured of electric light as he is of sunlight. No soft shades, but every window ablaze with light, as if the inhabitants had just discovered the marvels of electricity. Athens sparkles like a chandelier; it sparkles like a chandelier in a bare room lined with tiles."

Athens is one of the major growth points of the Mediterranean: not a pretty town, and historical monuments apart it could almost be described as an architectural disaster area. But the Greeks are not a fastidious people, and the excitement of Athens, like the beauty of Greece, lies in the way its people confront its starkness (and even seem to find such starkness necessary) with an elaborate hodgepodge of fast deals, ornate religion, kamikaze driving, slumbering cafes, flower stalls, markets, exploding tavernas, rudeness, generosity — all of which goes on theatrically, endlessly, a 24 hour non-stop show. Athens, like Paris or New York, has the amphetamine buzz of an insomniac's dreams.

Orientation   Athens has two major squares, Syntagma (known also, in English, as Constitution Square) and Omonia, with Stadiou Street running from one to the other. *Syntagma Square* is the international centre of the city, enclosed by luxury hotels like the Grande Bretagne, by airline offices (the airport bus arrives and departs from nearby Leoforos

31

Amalias), a late-night post office and the American Express. On the east side, Syntagma is faced by the Parliament building, while in the centre of the square and on the pavements all around its edge are numerous expensive cafes, crammed with tourists throughout the day and night.

Omonia Square is entirely different. What it lacks in class it makes up for in raw vigour. A fall-out zone for the late-night cinema crowd, it's the sort of place, like Piccadilly or Times Square, which has a fascination for people who like to stand amidst the traffic, noise and neon lights and watch the seamier side of the world go by. It's the Greek centre of the city, surrounded by small shops and open-fronted chicken and kebab joints, less fashionable hotels, hawkers selling lottery tickets, with escalators pouring thousands of workers on to the streets from the Athens-Piraeus underground station down below.

Stadiou Street and the two broad streets running parallel to it, *Venizelou* (popularly called Panepistimiou) and *Akadimias,* are lined with shops, cinemas, more cafes, and halfway down Venizelou the mock-classical facades of Athens University, the Academy and the National Library.

The two high landmarks by which you can never lose your way are Lykavittos hill to the east of Stadiou and the Acropolis to the southwest of Syntagma. *Lykavittos* is the higher of the two, a sudden eruption of ground with a small chapel like a cherry on the top. At night, with the base of the hill in darkness, the upper half is illuminated with floodlights and seems to hover above Athens like a giant dome-topped flying saucer.

On the planed-off top of the *Acropolis* sits the Parthenon, in daylight or floodlight gleaming like a yellow moon over Athens, no more noticed sometimes than the thousands of postcards on which it appears throughout the city. But then you stare at it and seem to see it smile, silent and demure, and 2,400 years of time bolt across your imagination. At the base of the Acropolis is *Plaka,* the old quarter of Athens with its steep, stepped and winding streets, quiet by day, frantic with nightclubs, tavernas and discotheques at night.

More or less within the bounds of these four points — Syntagma, Omonia, Lykavittos and the Acropolis — will the visitor find all the sights and activities of greatest interest, as well as scores of places to eat and stay within his price range.

Lykavittos   The best introduction to Athens is from the top of Lykavittos hill from where all of the city, the hills and mountains around it and the Saronic Gulf unroll in a

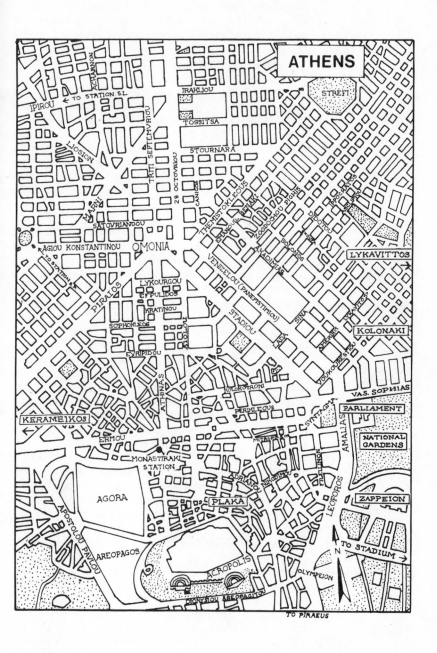

ATHENS

magnificent 360° panorama. The light of Attica favours seeing the city from Lykavittos in the late afternoon, while the early morning is the best time for gazing about from the Acropolis.

The No. 4 bus takes you to Kleomenous St., from where you walk up the steps one block for the funicular station at the base of the hill at the corner of Aristipou and Ploutarchou Sts. If you want to walk up, take the path from the corner of Kleomenous and Loukianou Sts.

Atop Lykavittos is the small 19th C Agios Georgios and an expensive restaurant/cafe where it's nevertheless worth sitting on the terrace, drink in hand, watching the sun go down. Also there's an observation platform which can get pretty windy. Below you is Athens, a city of white. White marble, white painted houses, and at night white lights, with Syntagma and Omonia picked out in red, blue and green neon. To the left is the Olympic Stadium and beyond that, further to the left, is the airport with its white and green beacon flashing in the evening. To the centre, Syntagma, the National Gardens and the Zappeion, and behind Syntagma is the Acropolis, around its base the close-packed twinkling of Plaka. And beyond that is Piraeus with off-lying ships lit up from bow to stern. To the right of Syntagma you can follow the lights of Stadiou down to Omonia.

Yes, it's best to come as the sun goes down, to catch Athens going from white to gold, and then enveloped by darkness, barely anything discernible but the ribbons of lights in streets and squares. Watch the Acropolis light up (through this is most impressive from the lower elevation of Plaka). The night sky above is only slightly touched by city smoke and haze, the stars and moon shine clearly. Though you've already paid (if you took the funicular) to go both up and down, make your way down Lykavittos by the pathway, Athens' lovers lane. Halfway down is a taverna; the views are not so spectcular as from the top, but then neither are the prices.

The Acropolis and Athens' Golden Age

Athens' Golden Age followed her defeat of Darius' army at Marathon (490 BC) and the defeat by combined Greek forces of the second Persian invasion, under Xerxes, at Salamis (480 BC) and Plataea (479 BC). Her extensive maritime empire made her wealthy and gave her the means to brilliantly celebrate her achievements. And celebrate, rather than commemorate, is the right word. For the victory was not just an isolated military event whose place could be marked by the usual stone pylon. Marathon has been called the birth cry of Europe; and after 479 BC,

Athens, full-grown, consciously took upon herself the task of laying the foundations of Western civilisation. "Men seemed to rise at once to the sense of the high historical importance of their experience. The great poets of the day wrought it into their song; the great plastic artists alluded to it in their sculptures." And under Pericles the temples on the Acropolis which had been destroyed by the Persians were rebuilt with an historical sense and as a sacred duty. "He recognised that the city by ennobling the houses of her gods would ennoble herself." (J.B. Bury, *History of Greece.*)

It's best to resist the temptation to climb the Acropolis right away, instead to circle it, view it from many angles and elevations at different times of night and day. View it from the hill of Ardettos, over the columns of the Temple of Zeus against the setting sun; or from Lykavittos, with Phaleron and Salamis as an historical panorama beyond; or from the Kerameikos by the Dipylon Gate, where travellers in ancient times would most likely have entered the city, proceeding towards the Agora and Acropolis along the Panathenaic Way. The rock itself is fascinating, abrupt and ragged, an upraised underworld in whose caves and fissures dwelt the earliest chthonic gods; the sheer masonry walls encircling its heights extending and refining its primitive form; and then the temples, delicate crystal flowers that blossomed in the sunlight of historical consciousness. For a while I worked near Omonia and lived on the far side of Philopappou, so that on my way home on those spring nights I would walk along Odos Thrassilou in Plaka, right under the eastern brow of the Acropolis where the great walls join at an acute angle atop the towering limestone cliffs. The rock would ride against the starry sky like some spectral ship ploughing through eternity to engulf me in its wake.

Early history of the Acropolis The Acropolis was inhabited at least as far back as 5000 BC. Men were attracted by its natural springs and the defence provided by its precipitous 300-foot height. The Mycenaeans fortified it; later tyrants imposed their rule from here. The Acropolis has these associations of primitive succour and power. But with the fall of the Peisistratid dictatorship in 510 BC the Athenians resigned the Acropolis to the exclusive inhabitation of their gods. It was an act of respect both to the deities and to the rock itself. And perhaps a shrewd political move by a people bent on democracy. Without tyrants over them and with their gods provided for, down below the citizens could say let us, let Man, be the measure of all things. In the century that followed, Athens achieved her apotheosis.

Restoration of the Acropolis

That moment of apotheosis has now in a manner been resurrected atop the Acropolis. When the defeated Turks finally surrendered the rock in 1833, the Classical structures, converted and embroidered over the centuries to serve the needs of the day, were obscured in a jumble of dwellings and alleyways, Frankish towers and Turkish minarets, that must have looked like a crowded quarter of Old Stamboul. Demolition of these encrustations began at once, though not without protest. One of the regents of the young Greek king complained that "the archaeologists would destroy all the picturesque additions of the Middle Ages in their zeal to lay bare and restore the ancient monuments". Of course it is not the living past the archaeologists have presented to us, but the bleached bones of antiquity. It has been more of an exhumation than a resurrection. A fifth century Athenian, used to seeing his Acropolis crammed with statues, dedications, monuments and sanctuaries; busy with workmen, officials, acolytes and worshippers; used to sniffing the burning incense, hearing the cries of animals slaughtered in sacrifice, seeing the temples luridly painted and indeed, then too, half obscured behind the jumble, might well find this present-day skeleton at least as alien as "the picturesque additions of the Middle Ages" that the archaeologists have torn down.

Pericles was an unabashed imperialist: "We have compelled every land and every sea to open a path for our valour, and have everywhere planted eternal memorials of our friendship and of our enmity"; but his imperialism was guided by his sincere belief that Athenian power was Greece's best defence against Persia, its best hope for unification, and that culturally Athens was "the school of Hellas". He could be merciless in time of war (see under Aegina), but could also argue at the end of his life that "no Athenian ever put on black for an act of mine". It was in this context that the Acropolis temples were raised: "We shall assuredly not be without witnesses; there are mighty monuments of our power which will make us the wonder of this and of succeeding ages". And the fact is that our own age has chosen to enshrine both Pericles' rhetoric and his monuments. But this has not always been so through all ages, and something needs briefly to be said about the more than 2000 years of intervening history that has been swept off the face of the Acropolis.

The Romans

The Romans were great respecters of the Classical achievement and modestly embroidered the Acropolis with a few contributions of their own: the Beule Gate through which we now first enter the site before making the final sharp ascent towards the Propylaia (the gate takes its name from the 19th C. French archaeologist who discovered it embedded in a Turkish wall); a small circular Temple of Rome and Augustus between the modern museum and the Parthenon, now slowly being reconstructed; and the enrichment, under Hadrian in particular, of many of the original shrines. Athens as a whole flourished during this period. But when the Roman Empire divided in two, the

The Byzantines Eastern or Byzantine Empire — resurgently Greek though no longer Classical — looked towards its new capital at Constantinople and Athens became increasingly a backwater. The Acropolis, as the home of pagan gods, lost its significance except as a citadel to be fortified as it had been in Archaic times, and the temples were converted to Orthodox Christian churches. The Parthenon became the metropolitan church of Athens; a barrel-vaulted roof replacing the coffered ceiling, frescoes added to the walls, the eastern entrance of Classical times turned into an apse to receive the altar, and the inner sanctum of Athena's priestess at the western end opened up to become the narthex or entrance to the Church of the Virgin Mother of God. Even a bell-tower was added to the Parthenon's southwest corner.

The Franks and Turks After the sack of Constantinople in 1204 by the Fourth Crusade, Greece was divided up in the western European manner amongst feudal barons, and under the Frankish dukes of Athens the Parthenon became a cathedral and followed the Latin rite. It was then predictable, with the coming of the Turks, that it should finally be converted into a mosque, the bell-tower conveniently transformed into a minaret.

Similarly with the Propylaia: the Byzantines used it as an episcopal residence; the dukes transformed it into a Florentine palace; while the Turks employed it as the commandant's headquarters and as a powder magazine.

Even so, right through to the mid-17th C. the Classical structures remained almost entirely intact beneath their cosmetic overlays. It was the advent of gunpowder that wrought the greatest changes to the Acropolis. Sometime near the middle of that century lightning struck the Propylaia, igniting the powder and blasting away much of

The Parthenon explosion the east portico. In 1684, as part of the running conflict between Venetians and Turks, the Turkish defenders demolished the Temple of Athena Nike to better counter improved Venetian gunfire with a battery of their own. And in 1687 a Venetian cannon on Philopappou hill lobbed a ball at the Parthenon, touching off the munitions within, sundering the temple nearly in half and causing a fire which raged for 48 hours. The Venetians also trained their guns on the Propylaia, wrecking the west facade and bringing down the famous ceiling.

Lord Elgin   In that context, Lord Elgin's removal at the beginning of the 19th C. of most of the bas-reliefs from the Parthenon's frieze and its pedimental sculptures (essential viewing at the British Museum before or after visiting the Acropolis) can only be applauded. Whether they should be given back, as the Greeks demand, is another matter — though as recently as the civil war in the 1940s the fighting in Athens again put the temples at risk, while at the outset of their coup in 1967 the Colonels placed guns on Philapappou once more, not ones to miss a lesson in tactics from the Venetians. And now that Athens has attained the distinction of becoming the second most polluted city in the world after Tokyo, with the sulfur dioxide in the atmosphere rotting away the marble stones, there's a real possibility that the Parthenon will fall down before the sculptures can be put back up.

The Propylaia   The zigzag ramp leading up from the *Beule gate* (1) to the *Propylaia* (2) is similar to the Acropolis approach of Mycenaean and medieval times; in Classical times the ramp was straight and extremely steep with an incline of one in four. In either case, one toils towards the Propylaia from below, its elevation and monumentality inducing a sense of humility in the visitor.

The ancients greatly admired the Propylaia and even in its state of partial ruin there are many who think it rivals the Parthenon itself. The structure, built entirely of Pentelic marble except for a few architectural details in blue Eleusinian stone, comprises a *central hall* with north and south *wings* flanking the approach. At the west (approach) and east ends of the central hall are Doric hexastyle *porticoes*, the sharp-fluted columns spaced to correspond to the five gateways (hence Propylaia, plural of propylon meaning gateway) of the *portal* which transects the hall two-thirds of the way in from the west portico.

The central hall   Running through the central hall was a *coffered ceiling* of marble sections, painted blue and gilt with stars, and held aloft by 18-ft long, 11 ton marble *beams*, its effect "still incomparable", said Pausanias in the 2nd C. AD, and indeed probably still so 1500 years later until the Turks and Venetians conspired in its collapse. As marvellous as the ceiling and its beams were, it is the overall harmony of the building, despite the difficult circumstances of its siting, that is most impressive. For not only does the Propylaia rise above the visitor's approach to the Acropolis, but it itself rises up the final scarp of the rock in two stages. This means that the beams supporting the ceiling in the higher east

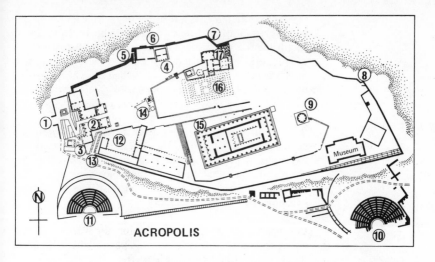

ACROPOLIS

portico can rest upon the architrave, but that some additional lift is required in the lower west portico and the vestibule. This can only be supplied by an *interior colonnade* running through the vestibule, its columns necessarily taller than the columns of either portico. But Mnesikles the architect was working within the Doric order and certain proportions had to be observed: taller Doric columns would mean fatter Doric columns, and the columns of the portico were already massive enough. Instead he took the original step of mixing in the newly-introduced Ionic order, its taller yet more slender columns solving an awkward problem with lightness and grace. It was the central hall which suffered in the 17th C. so that only the two outer Doric columns of the west portico rise to their full height of 29 ft and retain their capitals and portions of their architrave. On the left as you near the portal, one of the 33½-ft high Ionic columns has been restored to position along with a section of the coffered ceiling.

The south and north wings
The south wing succeeds in balancing that of the north despite being smaller, as it had to be to avoid trespassing on the Sanctuary of Artemis Vravronia. In the north wing the *Pinakotheke* (picture gallery) displayed the works of Polygnotos, the first great Greek painter (c450 BC), including one, says Pausanias, of "Odysseus at the river meeting the girls who were washing clothes with Nausikaa, in just the way Homer describes it". Going round the back, one can see that the outside walls remain unfinished, the rough stone lugs which gave a hold to the ropes still in evidence. The Propylaia was begun immediately upon completion of

39

the Parthenon and cost a fortune; the exigencies of the war with Sparta prevented its completion in detail; and when at length the war was lost the desire or wherewithal to pick up where work had been left off seems to have disappeared.

Nevertheless, Mnesikles succeeded in his essential purpose; the Propylaia in its almost Egyptian monumentality yet its Greek lightness and genius of harmony perfectly humbles and then uplifts — as it must have done those in the Panathenaic Procession as they passed from the profane world below to the sacred precincts atop the Acropolis — preparing the celebrants, as it prepares the visitor now, for that first close and best view of the Parthenon, the whole of its north and west lines of columns sweeping towards the foreground.

But instead of making directly for the Parthenon, the visitor should first pause at the Temple of Athena Nike and then, the better to appreciate the plan and historical associations of the Acropolis, make a circuit of the Acropolis walls. There is the advantage, too, of registering the impression the Parthenon makes at every degree.

Temple of Athena Nike
At the precipitous southwest corner of the rock, to the right of the Propylaia, is the rebuilt *Temple of Athena Nike* (3) — Athena, bringer of victory. From below the Acropolis, the temple blossoms from its bastion (see the cover photograph of this Guide); from the height of the rock it lends its charm to the marvellous panorama of the Saronic Gulf. But there is a tragic story associated with this very position, for it was said that from here King Aigeus kept watch for the return of his son Theseus from his expedition against the Cretan Minotaur. If he returned alive, Theseus was to lower his sail of black and raise a sail of white; but he forgot, and Aigeus, thinking his son was dead, threw himself over the edge.

It is striking that the temple specifically dedicated to Athena Victorious should be so unpretentious, even so minor. It stands on a stylobate only 12 by 18 ft, the nearly square cella graced to east and west by Ionic porticoes, the columns slender monoliths. The *frieze* is badly worn: on three sides the Athenians struggle against their enemies on the battlefield of Plateia; on the east side 22 (now headless) gods and goddesses seem oblivious to the commotion. The terrace was surrounded by a marble parapet adorned with high reliefs of Winged Victories attendant upon Athena. The lovely *Victory adjusting her sandal* is now in the Acropolis museum — a gesture symbolising the relaxed assurance of Athens at the very moment she plunged into the disasterous war with Sparta. For though the temple was already planned in 449 BC and assigned to the architect Kallikrates, it was only begun in 427 BC, two years after the death of Pericles, four years after the beginning of the war that was to last 26 years in all. There is irony and significance in the dates: Kallikrates was the architect chosen by Pericles' predecessor, Kimon, to build the Parthenon. But Pericles dismissed him after Kimon's death, the dismissal perhaps affecting Kallikrates' opportunity or desire to work on the victory temple too. Then with Pericles dead, Kallikrates got down to work on the Temple of Athena Nike; except that with Pericles dead, Athens substituted arrogance and blunder for a conservative war policy and was forced eventually to bow in surrender. At any rate, as the man who built the leaden 'Theseion' in the Agora and the light-weight Temple of Poseidon at Sounion, Kallikrates here acquitted himself well.

Following the walls

Heading past the Propylaia to the *north Acropolis wall* and a little along it to the right you come to the foundations of the *House of the Arrephorai* (4), the residence of the maids in waiting on Athena, noble girls of 7 to 11 years old who once every four years took part in the Panathenaic Procession. Annually, however, two of the girls, each carrying a parcel of unknown contents, would descend a *secret stairway* to the Sanctuary of Aphrodite, there exchange the parcels for others just as carefully wrapped to keep their contents secret, and return with these to the Acropolis surface. The meaning of this mysterious ritual is not clear: it could be that the parcels contained phalluses and loaves of salt, symbolising Aphrodite's birth from the sea, the god of which was Poseidon, worshipped nearby at the Erechtheion — and intended as a rite of fertility and renewal. The likely stairway used in the ritual is the one descending from south to north (5); though a bit to the right is another stairway descending from west to east (6) before turning under the wall: this is Turkish, but leads to a (now covered) Mycenaean stairway descending to a depth of 110 ft to a natural spring. From the platform here (the ball court of the Arrephoroi) there's an excellent view west to the Areopagus and below to the 'Theseion' in the Agora.

Fertility ritual

Reminders of the Persian sack

Further east another platform (7) behind the Erechtheion offers a view along a section of the north wall which was in part built from the *blocks and column drums* from an earlier Parthenon razed by the Persians (480 BC). The *Belvedere* (8) overlooks Plaka, Hadrian's Arch and the Temple of Olympian Zeus and also surveys the mountains enclosing the Attic plain. Once topped by statues of the gods, these mountains now, to the distress of Classicists, are

The mountains around Athens

topped by 'ugly' radar stations. But when darkness falls these radar peaks are illuminated and they sparkle above the city like jewels suspended from the night. And by day, the bulbous station nesting upon *Hymettos* to the southeast is easily imagined as a giant pterodactyl's egg, as stupefying a sight as any marble-breasted goddess and more likely to keep the Turks away. Since ancient times Hymettos has been famous for its twilight moods, favouring Athens with its violet crown at evening; and famous until recently, too, for its honey. The bees have now retreated to Pentelikon where the aromatic shrubs they love to browse upon still grow in abundance. Hymettos also produced a marble, but inferior to that exploited wholesale from the flanks of *Pentelikon*, to the northeast, from Pericles' day on. All the monuments on the Acropolis are of Pentelic marble, prized for its enduring edge yet, because of its iron oxide content, weathering to a soft golden glow. The coarser grained Parian marble — from Paros in the Cyclades — was still preferred, however, for sculpture. To the north is the *Parnes range*, wild, sparsely populated, crossed by only one paved road, still a barrier, as it always has been, between Attica and Boeotia. Finally, to the west running low behind Piraeus towards the Straits of Salamis is *Aigaleos* where Xerxes expectantly perched his throne, only to witness the destruction of his fleet (480 BC).

Between the Belvedere and the museum, directly before the east portico of the Parthenon, stood the circular *Temple of Rome and Augustus* (9), now being reconstructed. Looking over the south wall of the Acropolis you can see below two ancient threatres. The one on the left is the *Theatre of Dionysos* (10), rebuilt in stone in the 4th C. BC to replace the earlier theatre in which the plays of Aeschylus, Sophocles, Euripides and Aristophanes were first performed before audiences on wooden benches; while that on the right is the *Odeon of Herodos Atticus* (11), a Roman construction, where the Festival of Athens is held. Lifting your gaze, the hill opposite is *Philopappou*, named after a Syrian landowner, Roman consul and benefactor of Athens — though the Athenians seem to have lost all sense of proportion in honouring him (AD 115) with the overly-large and now broken-tooth monument dominating the summit. It was from that point in 1687 that the shot which blew up the Parthenon was fired.

Near the southwest corner of the Parthenon are two deep *pits* revealing earlier — at the bottom, Mycenaean — walls. The surface area along this south side of the Acropolis was extended only in the mid-5th C. by the

Theatres at the base of the Acropolis

Kimon's wall

construction of Kimon's massive *retaining wall*, providing the space required for the Parthenon foundations. Further

Sanctuary of Artemis on is the *Sanctuary of Artemis Vravronia* (12) where rituals expressing some connection between the Huntress, bears and childbirth were performed, but are not now understood. Between the sanctuary, the Temple of

Mycenaean wall Athena Nike and the Propylaia is a prominent section of *Mycenaean wall* (13) dating from about 1400 BC; large boulders piled upon one another, the interstices filled with smaller stones. Defences such as these walls and the deep well on the north side saved Athens from being overrun by the Dorian invaders who sacked Mycenae itself at the end of the second millenium. Though the Dark Ages followed, Athens led the reawakening in pottery, sculpture and literature; quite possibly because she had preserved some thread of culture from the previous Mycenaean and Minoan civilisations.

The approach to the Parthenon Back at the Propylaia: the ground rises about 40 ft between here and the Parthenon, so that the ascent towards and through the Propylaia is continued now, though less steeply. As you approach the Parthenon on the crown of the Acropolis, notice that the surface of the rock was cut with *transverse corrugations* in Classical times to afford a better foothold; and that along either side of the path *rectangular notches* have been cut into the rock to receive the pedestals of statues. One of the first of these statues to be seen upon entering was of Pericles, erected sometime after his death and certainly still standing when Pausanias

Athena Promachos visited the Acropolis. Much larger was the bronze *Athena Promachos* (14) by Phidias. Standing 30 ft high, the sunlight flashing off her gold-tipped spear and helmet could be seen from ships sailing up the coast from Sounion as soon as they rounded Cape Zoster where Hymettos runs into the sea. At some point this statue, which commemorated the Athenian defeat of the Persians at Marathon, was removed to Constantinople where it survived until 1203 when it was torn down by a mob, drunk, angry and distressed over the imminent sack of their city by the Fourth Crusade, "unable", wrote one Greek at the time, "to bear even a symbol of courage and of wisdom".

The Parthenon But the *Parthenon* (15) was not entered from this west side, although since the explosion the west pediment is more complete than the east and is the more imposing facade. The Sacred Way ran along the north colonnade to the pronaos. The cella at this end exists only in foundation, but at the west end much of its walls still stand. The name Parthenon means virgins' apartment, originally applied to the chamber at the west end of the temple, occupied by the priestesses of Athena whose chryselephantine cult statue towered in the cella. (There is a miniature Roman copy of the statue in the National Archaeological Museum; it looks hideous, but apparently the giant original was awesome and comparable to Phidias' similar cult statue of Zeus at Olympia which was reckoned one of the seven wonders of the ancient world.) The Doric temple was completed in 438 BC, built entirely of Pentelic marble except for a wooden roof, though this too was tiled with marble. Despite its avowed religious purpose, the Parthenon was principally regarded as a work of art and used as the state treasury, the Erechtheion remaining the holy place sanctified by tradition.

The friezes
Although Pausanias comments on the pedimental sculptures, he says nothing of the exterior Doric frieze surmounting the peristyle, or the interior Ionic frieze around the outer wall of the cella, both so high off the ground that they could hardly have been appreciated as more than incidental decoration. Indeed the interior frieze, deep within the shadows of the colonnade, would have been yet more difficult to make out; with the roof blown off, this, at least, is no longer the case. Nearly the entire *west interior frieze* is *in situ* and shows Athenian knights preparing for the Panathenaic Procession which, when the frieze was complete, would have paraded off from the southwest corner in opposite directions, meeting at the centre of the east frieze over the main door. A portion of the remaining frieze is in the Acropolis museum; most is in the British Museum. The *exterior frieze*, symbolising struggles against the forces of barbarism — Giants, Amazons, Centaurs — has either been carted off to various museums (the Lapiths and Centaurs are in the British Museum; fragments in the Acropolis museum) or remains, badly damaged, in place.

The pedimental sculptures
The *east pediment*, being over the entrance, was the most important but is nearly all gone. The sculptural theme was the birth of Athena but all we can see here are the figures (mostly casts of the originals in London) at the furthest angles: on the left, the four horses of Helios' chariot, representing dawn, and the reclining figure of Dionysos; on the right, the horses of Selene sinking out of sight. The *west pediment* pictured the contest between Athena and Poseidon for possession of Athens. What remains is original: Kekrops, the legendary first king of Athens and his daughter on the left; a reclining woman representing the Kallirrhoe spring on the right. It is likely that Phidias himself carved several of the pedimental statues.

The Parthenon employs certain optical refinements, like the gentle convexity applied to the stylobate to counter any illusion that it is sagging under its own massiveness; the swelling of the columns (entasis) part way up to correct a trick of the eye by which straight shafts appear pinched; the inclination of the columns inwards lest the burden of their entablature seems to press them outwards. And it is to these refinements, involving high mathematical precision, that credit is often given for the perfection of the Parthenon. Yet their use was general in all the better temples of the period, including the 'Theseion' or Hephaisteion in the Agora, and even the much earlier Peisistratid foundations of the Temple of Olympian Zeus display a convexity. Yet the Parthenon remains in a class of its own, at once combining power yet unleashed with bouyant lightness, the optical refinements doing more than correcting illusions, rather creating a tension that makes one believe that the Parthenon might just at any moment levitate if not cut loose from the gravitational bonds of earth entirely.

There is perfection, but it was born of the intuitive genius of the architect rather than in the precision of his mathematical calculations. In fact the Parthenon is Iktinos' brilliant *ad hoc* solution to the problem of having to build a new Parthenon upon the foundations and largely out of the materials of an only slightly older, unfinished Parthenon. Anyone interested in the fascinating details of this story should read Rhys Carpenter's *The Architects of the Parthenon*. The previous architect had been Kallikrates, commissioned by Kimon of the aristocratic party. When the populist Pericles came to power, Kallikrates was dismissed, Iktinos put in his place. The switch might have been political, but that the artistic implications were profound there can be no doubt. Kallikrates had been the architect of the Hephaisteion, still excellently preserved in the Agora. Compare it to the Parthenon. It is on lower ground, admittedly, and though constructed of exactly the same marble has inexplicably weathered badly, turning dull where the Parthenon glows. Even so, a comparison is possible and fair. The Hephaisteion is flat-footed. The Parthenon soars.

To the north of the Parthenon are the *foundations of the Old Temple of Athena* (16), thought to have been built in 529 BC (deduced by astronomical calculations from its alignment) during the rule of Peisistratos. It is therefore the only building in Athens whose foundations survive entirely exposed and intact from the years preceding the Persian sack. Immediately adjacent is its successor temple, the *Erechtheion* (17), completed around 394 BC. The particular veneration accorded to both temples was due to their location upon the spot where, it was believed, Poseidon and Athena contested for possession of the Acropolis. The myth probably records a struggle between patrilineal and matrilineal tribes in prehistoric Athens: the city was already Athena's, but Poseidon struck his claim by hurling his trident or a thunderbolt at this spot and causing a gush of sea-water (called Erechtheis); Athena responded by producing an olive tree. By a vote of the gods (in another version, by a plebiscite of the citizens) it was judged that Athena's was the better gift and the city remained hers, though at least one concession was made to the patrilineal claim — from then onwards Athenians took their fathers' not their mothers' names. The crevice caused by Poseidon's blow is exposed through the flooring of the north porch and a section of the coffered ceiling above was left agape in the belief that where once lightning has struck nothing should be built. Pausanias put his ear to the crevice and said that when the south wind blew he could hear the waves of the sea. He also reported seeing Athena's olive tree; and Herodotos, 600 years earlier, tells the story of how Xerxes, punctuating the prophesy that all mainland Greece would be overrun by the Persians, stormed the Acropolis and burnt its temples: "Now this olive was destroyed by fire together with the rest of the sanctuary; nevertheless on the very next day, when the Athenians, who were ordered by Xerxes to offer the sacrifice, went up to that sacred place, they saw that a new shoot 18 inches long had sprung from the stump. They told the king of this"; an omen of Xerxes' defeat at Salamis not long after. The tree now growing against the west wall of the temple was planted in 1917 by an American archaeologist.

The temple's need to house two deities and probably to encompass still older sanctuaries, and the prohibition on levelling the sacred rock on which it stands, accounts for the Erechtheion's unique, highly irregular plan and elevation. This is difficult to appreciate without walking through it (now forbidden), or at least several times around it.

The shallow *east portico*, with five of its original six columns in place (Lord Elgin made off with the north column), and its cella stand nearly 9 ft higher than the north porch fronted by four columns plus one at either side. It is the *north porch* that is particularly elegant, with its tall columns, coffered ceiling, its doorway decorated with rosettes, and its frieze of blue Eleusinian marble.

There is debate as to which cella served Poseidon and which Athena, though it would seem odd if the cella immediately behind the spot where Poseidon's trident or thunderbolt cleft the rock were not Poseidon's own. On the south side is the famous *Porch of the Caryatids*, the entablature here supported by maidens rather than columns, though their long Ionic tunics drape about their legs like flutings. The second from the left is a cast of the original now in the British Museum; the one at the back right is modern, the original having been destroyed in the War of Independence. Perhaps it was these maidens that gave the Turks the idea of turning this most harmonious and feminine of temples into a harem.

Porch of the Caryatids

The Areopagus To the northwest, between the Acropolis and the Agora, is the rocky outcrop of the Areopagus where cases of murder were heard, the accuser standing on the stone of Insolence, the accused on the stone of Recklessness. It was to this spot that Orestes, after killing his mother Klytemnestra, ran pursued by the Furies, and their chthonic demand of a life for a life was rejected by the new laws of Apollo and Athena. Southwest of here is the Pnyx, a hill into which a semi-circular terrace was cut as the meeting place for the Athenian Assembly, and where during the 5th C. and 4th C. BC Themistokles, Pericles and Demosthenes addressed their audience.

The Pnyx

The Agora The Agora may be entered from the southwest off Leof Apostolou, on free days from the base of the Acropolis, but is entered more usually from the north over the railway cutting from the flea market west of Monastiraki. At this entry there is a plan of the site from which you can get your bearings.

The broad pathway ahead of you, with the colonnaded Stoa of Attalos on the left, is the *Panathenaic Way* which ran from the Kerameikos, through the Agora, up to the Acropolis. Its gutters are noticeable, and further up some of its paving remains. To the right, the facade marked by sculptures of two Tritons, are the overlapping remains of the *Odeon of Agrippa* (1st C. BC) and the *Gymnasium* (5th C. AD), the latter the probable centre of the university which when finally closed in 529 by the Byzantine emperor Justinian marked the eclipse of Athens until modern times.

What now looks like a carefully tended bombsite was once the entertainment, cultural, commercial and legal centre of Athens. Then as now, the Athenians were an open-air people and here life was in full swing: "You will find everything sold together in the same place at Athens;

figs, witnesses to summonses, bunches of grapes, turnips, pears, apples, givers of evidence, roses, medlars, porridge, honey-combs, chick-peas, lawsuits, beestings, beestings-puddings, myrtle, allotment-machines, irises, lambs, water-clocks, laws, indictments". Now it is quiet and fragrant with jasmine.

The Stoa of Attalos is a faithful reconstruction built on the foundations of the 2nd C. BC original. Casting bars of cool shadow across your path, Doric columns which would have been colourfully painted support the ceiling of an open arcade, once lined by shops and a gallery above. The stoa houses a *museum* of finds from all periods made on the Agora site, including Mycenaean artefacts, coins, vases, even a child's chamber pot. Most interesting are the potsherds (ostraka) used in ballots which decided whether a particular citizen should be ostracised. Among the names appearing on the sherds are two of Athens' greatest citizens: Themistokles, victor at Salamis, who was ostracised, and Pericles, who was not. At one end of the building is an interesting set of photographs taken in 1931 and 1959. The earlier shows how even that recently the Agora site was covered by hundreds of little houses and alleys; the latter shows them cleared away, and under as much as 40 ft of soil the ancient masonry laid bare. The *upper gallery* has plans showing the topography of ancient Athens and stages in the development of the Agora, as well as scale models of the Acropolis and of the Agora at its greatest extent (2nd C. AD).

Again surveying the Agora, this time from the upper gallery of the stoa, you can see the Byzantine *Church of the Holy Apostles*, stripped of later embellishments to its 10th C. form, the narthex decorated with 17th C. wall-paintings from another, demolished, church. Just to the northeast of the church and extending westwards were the *Middle* and *Second South Stoas* of Hellenistic times, subsequently obliterated by the Roman Gymnasium. Beyond them, below the knoll of Kolonos on which the 'Theseion' or Temple of Hephaistos stands, were the major governmental buildings of 5th C. BC Athens. To the left are the circular foundations of the *Tholos* where the Prytaneis, the executive officials, were on duty day and night, easily alerted by a beacon fire or found by a runner and able to respond at once to an emergency. And a bit further left — the foundations are barely traceable — was the *Strategeion*, the headquarters of the ten annually elected generals. (Apart from his prominent role in the Assembly, Pericles was elected strategos — general — each year from 443 to his death in 429, this contributing to his unique authority.)

The Stoa of Attalos

Agora museum

Scale reconstruction of the Agora

Governmental buildings

The Prytaneis, who served on the executive by rota, were drawn from the elected tribal deputies who made up the Council of Five Hundred which thrashed out state policy before it was put to the Assembly for approval or rejection. The Council met in the *Bouleuterion*, to the right of the Tholos. Immediately in front of the Bouleuterion was the *Metroon* which contained the state archives.

The Hephaisteion   The *Temple of Hephaistos* owes its renown to being the best-preserved of any Greek temple; only the roof is missing, and the sculptures, of Parian marble (finer but less hard than the Pentelic marble of the blocks and column drums), are badly worn. The interior suffered some damage from the 7th C. when it was adapted to Christian worship and an apse, and later a concrete vault, were added. Set into a side wall is the tombstone of George Watson with an epitaph by Byron.

The metopes above the east entrance to the cella depict eight exploits of the legendary hero Theseus to whose worship the temple was wrongly ascribed in the Middle Ages. Indeed, there is a Theseion yet to be unearthed, probably beneath Plaka; for in 475 BC Kimon, discovering some gigantic bones (of a prehistoric animal probably) equal to Theseus' heroic stature, deposited them in a specially-built temple. But the Hephaisteion also bears metopes of Herakles' Labours, was sited appropriately in the metalworkers' quarter, and has been accurately dated to 449 BC.

The Hephaisteion opened Pericles' great building programme; its architect was Kallikrates, who later built the temples at Sounion and Rhamnous, and the Athena Nike. It is Doric hexastyle to the Parthenon's octastyle; its columns are more slender, but the entablature is heavier, while the stylobate seems to impart no verticle thrust. But overlooking the Agora as the ground rises towards the Acropolis, the Hephaisteion does provide welcome shade from where to gaze on greater works.

Odos Ermou, running westwards from Syntagma Square, is the fashionable shopping street of Athens, at least until it
The flea market   approaches Monastiraki. The flea market extends along Ifestou and Astingos streets parallel to and south of Ermou. The bargains are often more imaginary than real, though it can be surprising to see what unlikely curiosities have found their way here. Ermou continues past shabby workshops towards the light industrial area along Odos Piraios and just here, between the angle of the two intersecting roads, lies one of the most pleasant, fascinating yet unfrequented
The Kerameikos   archaeological sites in Athens. The part of the Kerameikos within the city walls was the quarter of potters and smiths,

while beyond the walls it was the major Athenian cemetery, where beautiful headstones and statues of the worthy dead and monuments to those who fell in battle were placed, the roads from Piraeus, Elefsis and Thebes converging here, the great processions of the Panathenaia and Eleusinian Mystery cult passing by. The site has been excavated to its ancient level. Ermou and Piraios are hot and dusty above, but below along the Sacred Way, along the walls, amongst the marble tombstones, the air is fresh and cooler, grass and flowers grow, and frogs and tortoises move amongst the water plants of the Eridanos stream. The Sacred Gate spans both the Sacred Way and the stream; a few paces north of it is the larger Dipylon (double gateway), most of the city's traffic entering through here and on into the Agora. Between the two are the foundatons of the Pompeion, a place of preparation for the processions.

Standing back from the walls, on the terrace overlooking the Street of the Tombs, you can imagine these roads rising towards the Agora, lined by colonnades, as Pausanias described, "with bronze statues along the front, of men and women whose stories are glorious", and you can see the Acropolis and its marble monuments as visitors to Athens would first have seen it as they entered here. And from here too, amongst the graves of those who died in the first year of the Peloponnesian War, Pericles asked the mourners to **Pericles' funeral** lift their gaze: "I would have you day by day fix your eyes **oration** upon the greatness of Athens, until you become filled with the love of her; and when you are impressed by the spectacle of her glory, reflect that this empire has been acquired by men who knew their duty and had the courage to do it, who in the hour of conflict had the fear of dishonour always present to them, and who, if ever they failed in an enterprise, would not allow their virtues to be lost to their country, but freely gave their lives to her as the fairest offering which they could present at her feast. The sacrifice which they collectively made was individually repaid to them; for they received again and again each one for himself a praise which grows not old and the noblest of all sepulchres — I speak not of that in which their remains are laid, but of that in which their glory survives and is proclaimed always and on every fitting occasion both in word and deed. For the whole earth is the sepulchre of famous men; not only are they commemorated by columns and inscriptions in their own country, but in foreign lands there dwells also an unwritten memorial of them, graven not on stone but in the hearts of men. Make them your examples".

A museum exhibits sculpture and vases from the site.

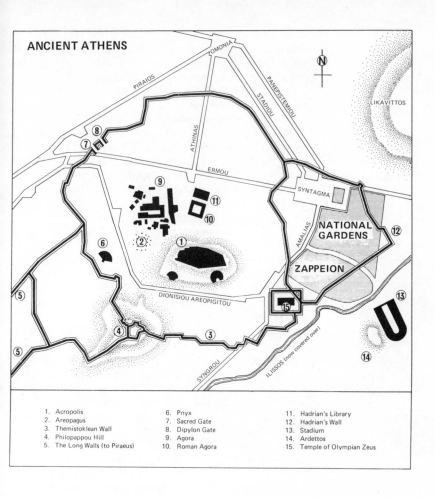

ANCIENT ATHENS

1. Acropolis	6. Pnyx	11. Hadrian's Library
2. Areopagus	7. Sacred Gate	12. Hadrian's Wall
3. Themistoklean Wall	8. Dipylon Gate	13. Stadium
4. Philopappou Hill	9. Agora	14. Ardettos
5. The Long Walls (to Piraeus)	10. Roman Agora	15. Temple of Olympian Zeus

Between 8 pm and 2 am Plaka blazes and blares as the nightlife centre of Athens. During the day it's silent and nearly dead except for the tourists wending their way up to the Acropolis or an occasional cat slipping along like a shadow against whitewashed walls. Nevertheless, this is the time, during these quiet hours, to walk around and fix the plan of Plaka and its many curious details in your mind.

Plaka   Plaka gets its name from a white stone slab once at the junction of Adrianou, Tripodon and Kydathenaion streets near the monument of Lysikrates. About the size of Soho and only one-third the size of Greenwich Village or Montmartre, its maze of narrow streets and steeply climbing

51

steps seem to make it bigger. Plaka is the oldest part of Athens, in plan and architecture little different from how it was before Greek independence except that it has lost what must have been a more Eastern flavour: some of the streets are less narrow than they were, its mosques are gone or in ruins or have been adapted to other purposes, and its bazaars have all but vanished.

The one vestige of a bazaar is Odos Pandrossou running along the north wall of Hadrian's Library and extending from the Mitropolis (cathedral) to Monastiraki, chocka-block with antique dealers and sandal-makers. In the south-east corner of Monastiraki Square is the 18th C. former Mosque of Tzistarakis, its minaret brought down in 1821, now used as the Museum of Greek Popular Art. The west and east walls of Hadrian's Library still stand on Areos and Aiolou Sts; it takes a moment to realise that all the distance between the two was taken up with a vast building, pool and courtyard in the centre (where the foundations of a 7th C. church can be noticed), reading rooms all around, and in nine niches along the east wall bookshelves from floor to high ceiling.

Museum of Greek Popular Art

Hadrian's Library

Roman Forum and Tower of the Winds

South along Aiolou is the Roman Forum, an eastward extension of the older Agora paid for by Julius Caesar, the graceful octagonal Tower of the Winds the most complete and interesting building to be seen here, built in the 1st C. BC as a combined weather-vane and clock. Though it had sundials round its walls, it more ingeniously employed an Acropolis spring to fill an upper chamber which then dripped water into a lower chamber in exactly twenty-four hours, indicating on the outside the level and therefore the time to passers-by. The name and symbol of the cardinal winds adorn each face: Boreas the north wind, bearded and heavily dressed; Zephyros the west wind, young and hand-some, scattering flowers; Notos the south wind who brings rain, emptying an urn; Apeliotes the east wind, carrying in his cloak the fullness of the harvest; the themes continued

with each of the intermediate winds. In the 18th C. it became a tekke, the home of an order of Turkish dervishes, whose strange rhythmic cries and whirling dances convinced the Greeks that both frieze reliefs and inhabitants were the embodiment of evil spirits. Apparently the Turks felt the same way about the Greeks: one 18th C. English traveller reported seeing 16 ostrich eggs hung outside to avert the evil eye. In the northwest corner of the forum is the former **Fetichie Mosque**, dedicated to Mehmet II, conqueror of Constantinople, and the only surviving large mosque of the early Turkish occupation (15th C.). It is now used as an archaeological laboratory. Just to the south of the Tower of the Winds is the sadly all but destroyed Mendreses, an 18th C. Islamic seminary, its cells once lining two sides of an enclosed garden, now only the gateway with its Turkish inscription surviving. When in 1821 the Greeks in the Peloponnese rose against Turkish rule, a cadi addressing his people here dissuaded them from massacring the entire male Greek population of Attica.

The Byzantine churches of Athens are modest in comparison to those of Thessaloniki; and certainly modest in size but fascinating in detail is Agios Eleftherios in the lee of the ugly 19th C. Mitropolis (cathedral). It dates from the 12th C. but is entirely constructed of reliefs from a 6th C. church and from blocks and reliefs from earlier pagan buildings. Eagles, angels, Maltese crosses, signs of the zodiac and a calendar of Attic state festivals contribute to the gingerbread effect. That is on the northern 'lowland' fringe of Plaka; climbing higher are numerous little churches and chapels, some passed unnoticed at first and discovered later with surprise and pleasure. Agios Ioannis Theologos, halfway up a flight of steps at the corner of Erechtheos and Erotokritou Sts, is a 9th or 10th C. church tucked away in the most medieval part of Plaka with its thicket of twisting lanes and sudden flights of steps interspersed with little squares and courtyards. At night the tables of two tavernas spill into the street where Erechtheos and Erotokritou meet and run up the steps like ivy. The sound of bazouki from down the way is not too deafening and the mood is congenial, unlike the cacophony and touting along Odos Mnesikleous, Plaka's taverna strip.

Off Odos Theorias which runs along the top of Plaka and towards the Acropolis entrance is the newly-opened Kanellopoulos Museum, a diverse family collection of jewellery, church plate, ikons, antiquities and everyday objects. On the northeast slope of the Acropolis and higher still, is what could as well be an island village. It is called Anafiotika after Anafi from where its inhabitants came in

Margin notes:
Fetichie Mosque
Gate of the Mendreses
Agios Eleftherios
Kanellopoulos Museum
Anafiotika

the late 19th and earth 20th C., bringing their traditional Cycladic style of church and house building with them. The islanders came to Athens as building workers, but unable to afford living in the houses they built they took advantage of a Greek law saying if you can build your house in the space of the night it's yours, their houses springing up like mushrooms on the Acropolis itself.

Choregic monument

At the southestern end of Plaka along Odos Tripodon is the Monument of Lysikrates, put up in 335 BC after the chorus that gentleman sponsored had won the Dionysos competition. It is preserved because it became part of a Capuchin Convent in which both Byron and Chateaubriand later stayed. Byron wrote home: "I am living in the Capuchin Convent, Hymettus before me, the Acropolis behind, the Temple of Jove to my right, the Stadium in front, the town to the left; eh, Sir, there's a situation, there's your picturesque! nothing like that, Sir, in Lunnun, no not even the Mansion House. And I feed upon Wood-cocks and Red Mullet every day, and I ride to Piraeus, and Phalerum, and Munychia." Before the monastery burnt down in 1821, the last abbot introduced tomatoes to Athens, the population at first using them as decorative

Shadow Theatre

plants. Opposite this is the Haridemos Greek Shadow Theatre, a traditional entertainment with origins in the East, the theme however invariably that of opposition to Turkish oppression. Now it competes against television and the cinema and only the faithful attend.

Gardens

Half surrounding the Parliament by Syntagma Square are the National Gardens, lush, fragrant and shady with a maze of paths winding through the palms, evergreens and orange trees where people stroll, children play, lovers neck. It is marvellously well-tended, almost continuously irrigated, and sure to be at least ten degrees cooler than anywhere else in the city. It was laid out by Queen Amalia in the 19th C. when the Parliament was still the Royal Palace and these were the Royal Gardens. Peacocks and swans make their

homes here, and there is also a small zoo. Adjacent is the Zappeion with its more formal layout and broad promenades like the Tuilleries, but also a bandstand where an amplified Greek sings popular songs to a cafe audience (pushing up the price of a coffee five-fold), and there's a free children's playground. The splendid neo-Classical rotunda was built towards the end of the last century as a national exhibition hall. Its interior colonnade, encircling an open court, is very fine and the painted walls and ceiling give a good impression of how the Classical temples were decorated. At the southern end of the Zappeion where Leof Amalias and Leof Olgas meet is a statue of Hellas, a posturing Byron at her bosom, and behind the two a cringing baldheaded figure who could be a wicked Turk or humble Greek, but looking more like he's about to pick Byron's pocket.

Hadrian's Arch   Across Leof Olgas is Hadrian's Arch marking the extension of the city in AD 132: on one side it reads "This is Athens, the ancient city of Theseus"; on the other "This is the city of Hadrian and not of Theseus". Towering behind like giant reeds growing along the banks of the Ilissos are **The Olympeion** the 15 standing Corinthian columns of the Temple of Olympian Zeus. A plentifully-shafted octastyle with three rows of eight columns at each end, two rows of twenty along either side, it had 104 columns in all and rose to a height of 90 ft, more than half again high as its columns.

The foundations of this largest of temples in Greece were laid by Peisistratos and some of the column drums were cut before work stopped with the fall of the Peisistratids and the growing Persian menace. Themistokles incorporated the drums in his wall, now exposed at the north end of the site. The temple was only completed under Hadrian, 700 years later — "a great victory of time". In the Middle Ages a stylite considerably increased the distance between himself and this world, and marginally lessened the distance between himself and God, by spending his life atop the architrave of the two westernmost columns of the southeast corner group.

The Ilissos   Just south of the Olympeion is the bed of a dried up river, the Ilissos, which once flowed down from Hymettos but is now reduced to an underground seasonal trickle and around the bottom of the tennis courts and swimming pool is covered over by a new road. Plato expresses his love for the countryside that was here in his *Phaedrus*. Odos Anapafseos runs up from here to the gate of the Proto Nekrotafeion Athinon, Athens' major cemetery, where many famous heroes of the War of Independence, writers, artists, politicians and archaeologists lie buried, often within sumptuous, sometimes outlandish, tombs. It is the modern kitsch counterpart to the Kerameikos and well worth a visit. The Greeks see little in death other than the reminder that life is to be enjoyed, and visitors to the graves and tombs often come in family groups with picnic baskets and bottles of wine, spending many hours talking and laughing, hosing down the sparkling marble and watering the flowers. Even on less cheerful occasions the injunction to enjoy is there: I live near the cemetery and again visited it today, the day I am writing this, and came upon a woman in black, sobbing and tearing at her hair and breasts. She was at the grave of her son, a handsome young man (his enamelled photograph was on the stone) who died a few years ago at the age of 22. She saw me and came weeping to me, and though her grief after these several years must have been bandaged in ritual mourning, her loss was real and sad enough that I embraced her. And when I did so, she slipped 100 drachmas into my shirt pocket. I was astonished and gave it back but she stuffed it into my pocket again and said "buy some wine". A third time I gave it back and a third time she insisted: "Drink some wine tonight for Theodoros (her son) and the boys". So tonight I am a little drunk and I have bought drinks for everyone at my local kafeneion for Theodoros, who couldn't make it, and for those of us who could.

The Stadium   The Stadium is opposite the eastern side of the Zappeion. "A thing not so attractive to hear about, but wonderful to see", said Pausanias, though I'm not so sure it's wonderful to see, either. It is, after all, just a stadium; impressive in its Pentelic whiteness and symmetry and boring for the same reason. It is an accurate reconstruction of, and built on the same foundations as, the AD 144 stadium of Herodos Atticus — born at Marathon, a Roman senator and benefactor of Athens — who decided to replace the earlier wooden and somewhat dilapidated original. George Averoff, an Alexandrian Greek, decided to do the same thing 1750 years later to provide a venue in 1896 for the revived **Ardettos**   Olympic Games. Excellent but entirely ignored is Ardettos, the hill in whose slope the Stadium nestles. It is a minor hill; not nearly so high as Lykavittos nor so high as the Acropolis, but the view from the top is the best in all Athens. The city and the plain climb away towards the mountains; the landscape is gently tipped towards you as a restaurant waiter might slightly tip a bowl of fruit to permit a better view without the apples, peaches and oranges spilling out onto the table.

The royal palace   Odos Herodos Atticus runs up along the eastern side of the National Gardens and passes the *new* former royal palace, as Greece, not for the first time in its modern history, has declared itself a republic. But the huge evzones in their War of Independence uniforms still stand and stamp about outside. This road meets with Leoforos Vasilissis Sofias; turning right leads you to the Byzantine Museum. Or crossing over to Odos Koumbari there is the Benaki Museum on the corner.

Byzantine Museum
Early Christian, Byzantine and post-Byzantine work, including sculpture, architectural specimens from churches and bits of their decoration, religious vestments, jewellery, manuscripts, mosaics and ikons, are on display in the Florentine-style villa that is now the Byzantine Museum. After so much Classical art in Athens, it is refreshing here to sense the animism of the natural world, a world in which snakes and eagles, deer, rams, vines and trees entwine to express and enfold God's mysteries. In Byzantine art the ornate and spectacular, even the grotesque, are given full rein.

Church interiors
The *ground floor* of the main building chronologically presents sculpture and reproduces a 5th to 6th C. basilica (*Room II*), an 11th C. Byzantine cruciform church with cupola (*Room IV*), and a flat-ceilinged post-Byzantine church of plain square design but 18th C. rococco decoration (*Room V*) including a sculptured and gilded ikonostasis from the Ionian islands, a choros, the huge circle of sculptured plaques suspended from the ceiling, and one especially marvellous ikon of St George killing an outrageously spiney dragon. *Upstairs* are ikons, frescoes and vestments, *Room II* containing a fine selection of ikons from the 14th and 15th C. Byzantine renaissance. The double-sided Crucifixion (169) is particularly noteworthy, as is another Crucifixion (246), showing Venetian or Florentine influence though amply retaining Greek literalness: Mary Magdalen, long hair flowing, reaches her hands up to the nailed feet of Christ; blood squirts from his side as from a garden hose and is caught by an angel in a cup of gold.

Ikons: embodiments of spiritual truth
To the *right* of the main building a detached wing presents ikons chronologically; while the exhibits in the *left wing* seem always to be changing but usually include some popular ikons, sometimes a whole joyful room of them: amateur and refreshing for their lightness (almost lightheartedness) of touch after the more formal and sombre ikons elsewhere; more idiomatic, often like comic strips, and with a strong Eastern influence. In the Orthodox Church the ikon is an attempt to portray, but also to capture, Christian truths and so is itself sacred.

Popular ikons

The Benaki Museum
The Benaki Museum contains the personal and eclectic impedimenta of Antoine Benaki, a man of evident wealth

and catholic taste, whose town house this was until he presented it, lock, stock and barrel, to the state in 1931: ancient Greek and Roman art; Byzantine, Moslem, Chinese, Coptic and Western European art; plus jewellery, historical souvenirs, a unique collection of Greek regional costumes and assorted bric-a-brac. Just up Odos Koumbari is Kolonaki Square, the centre of the most fashionable part of Athens with its pavement cafes and tributary streets lined with smart and expensive shops.

Kolonaki

In contrast to Kolonaki is the area west of Stadiou and north of Plaka running up to Omonia. The reconstructed Stoa of Attalos was meant to give some impression of what the ancient Agora was like but denies the essence of agora life in its own lifelessness. It is better to walk along Athinas, Sofokleous, Praxitelous or any of the smaller streets running between them to feel the pulse of Athens today. Nor along these sometimes sleazy, usually fascinating streets would you get an impression of Athens any worse than you would have got in Periclean days: "The streets are nothing but miserable old lanes, the houses mean with few better ones among them. On seeing the town for the first time the stranger would hardly believe that this is Athens of which he has heard so much" (the philosopher Dikaiarchos, 3rd C. BC). The flower market is in the square of Agia Irini Church along Aiolou; nuts, bolts and whores are for sale down Athinas; the meat and fish market is at the intersection of Athinas and Sofokleous, a series of iron-framed halls covered with glass, live rabbits hopping about, whole animals hanging from giant hooks above, four-foot-long sharks stretched out, their noses lopped off and then their skins ripped right to their tails; and the cornucopian vegetable market is just across the road.

The market and tradesmen's quarter

Every province, or nome, in Greece has its archaeological museum housing local finds. The museum in Athens not only has the city as a prize, but in the past has had the pick of the crop, wherever it may have come from. Though this is no longer the case (the museum has hardly any Cretan antiquities; the Heraklion museum has prior claim), the collection here is superb and includes much of the finest and most famous Classical sculpture not already shipped off to London, Paris or Berlin. In particular, its Mycenaean collection is probably the best to be found anywhere in the world. The National Archaeological Museum is located north of Omonia on Odos 28th October (invariably known as Patission) at Odos Tositsa. A guide to the sculpture and an illustrated souvenir booklet covering the

The National Archaeological Museum

entire collection are available in the foyer. Reference is made here only to a selection of the finer or more curious exhibits.

The Mycenaean exhibits

The Mycenaean collection is in the *central salon* on the ground floor and contains gold jewellery, frequent bull images and at the back, frescoes dating from 1550 BC, not unsimilar to those from Thera (upstairs) as the Mycenaeans were the successors to the Minoan empire. The first exhibit to strike you as you enter is the gold *'Mask of Agamemnon'*, as Schliemann excitedly and erroneously believed it to be (see under Mycenae). To the left in a case are three *bronze daggers* (394, 395) inlaid in black niello alloy, silver and gold; and further back in separate cases are the gold *Vaphio cups*, one depicting the capture of wild bulls with nets (1758), the other the trapping of bulls with a decoy cow (1759). All of these objects evidence exquisite technique, but the cups in particular, full of movement and drama, are wonderful.

In *Room 6*, off to the right, are objects from the Cycladic islands, many of them having the spare, abstract form of the most modern sculpture, though they are almost all pre-Mycenaean and the statuettes of *male figures playing musical instruments* date from 2400 BC.

Cycladic sculpture

Geometric pottery

With the Dorian invasion and the collapse of Mycenaean civilisation around the 11th C. BC, artistic expression in Greece was chiefly limited to abstractly decorated pottery. At first concentric circles — derived from Mycenaean spirals — and then rectangular patterns were employed in this 'Geometric' period. By the 8th C. BC the human form, in the shape of spindly figures, had made a come-back, and an impressive example of this is the *scepulchral amphora* (804) in *Room 7* (to the left of the museum entrance) with its stylised depiction of the laying-out and lamentation over the dead. This vase was found in the Kerameikos cemetery and dates from c760 BC. It is a century later that free-standing sculpture makes its appearance and then in the formalised kouros (nude youth) and kore (draped maiden), both employed as funerary monuments. The arms of each were held stiffly to the sides; the left leg of the kouros was advanced. The restriction was dictated originally by the timber from which they were carved, but carried through, with less reason, to stone. These sculptures of the Archaic period (rooms 7 to 13) have a zombie lifelessness or at least impassivity. The fine *kouros from Melos* (1558) in *Room 9* seems heir to the Cycladic miniatures of 1500 years before, with a slenderness and delicacy still owing more to the abstract than to reality: if he started moving it would probably take him half an hour to slouch across

Archaic sculpture

the room. It was Attica, perhaps because it avoided the brunt of the Dorian dislocation, that first excelled both in pottery and sculpture: in *Room 10A* the *Attic kouros* (1906) from the mid-6th C. is also delicate and charming, but has more substance than his island cousin.

The great period of Athenian power and civilisation followed the defeat of the Persians; but the mettle required to beat back the invader had been forged in earlier genera-

The Anavissos Kouros

tions. What was to come was implicit in what had gone before. For that reason, to look upon the *Anavissos Kouros* (540-520 BC) in *Room 13* (3851) is to look upon the awakening youth of the man that was to come. Though the arms are still at the sides, they are no longer at rest; nor is the advanced left leg rooted there by tradition. The beautiful contour between arms and body, the slight leaning forward of the entire statue, impart a tension to the figure — no longer timber or stone, but an aggrandise-ment of space. When that right leg steps forward, as it must, as it already seems to do, all Greece strides forward into

The Poseidon

greatness. The brilliant *Poseidon* (15161) in *Room 15* is the Anavissos Kouros grown to manhood: tried and tested strength and relaxed mastery of circumstance.

Eleusinian relief

Also in *Room 15* is a *low relief from Elefsis* showing Demeter presenting the seed corn to Triptolemos and behind him Kore (Persephone) crowning him with a garland. It's a famous work, capturing the majesty, one imagines, of the Mysteries. Many of the sculptures in these rooms are funerary monuments and often have the capacity to move us today. In *Room 16* there's a *tombstone* (715) dating from c430 BC showing a dead youth waving farewell while his grieving slave leans sadly on a pillar — and where life goes on, the cat eyeing the bird in its cage.

Continuing clockwise, the rooms progress through the Hellenic, Hellenistic and Roman periods. *Room 20* (leading off from Room 17) should be visited for the copy (129),

Athena Parthenos

one-twelfth of original size, of Phidias' chryselephantine *Athena* that stood in the Parthenon. It gives a clear idea of the details of the original, but is uninspiring and fails to convey the essence of Phidias' presumably great statue.

Race horse and jockey

Room 21: As a technical tour de force, few statues can compare with the *bronze race horse with boy jockey* (15177) found in the sea with the Poseidon statue. The horse leaps forward as though to take a hurdle, nostrils flared, ears bent back, muscles and vessels standing out, adding tension to the vigorous posture. The boy leans forward into the leap, his left hand holding the reins, his right (now empty) probably grasping a whip.

Bronze youth

The finest piece in *Room 28* is the bronze *athlete*

(13396) — though he is possibly Paris clutching the now missing golden apple — with inlaid eyes, bronze plate lashes and superb musculature, dating from c340 BC. In *Room 30, Aphrodite* threatens to clout Pan in the face with her sandal (3335). But judging by the smile on her face, this is one last formal gesture of resistance before she enthusiastically succumbs to this grinning archetypal sex maniac. Though from Delos, 1st C. BC, it's hard to believe that the statue is Greek at all; it looks naughtily French 18th C., an inartistic but entertaining bit of neoclassicism.

The 'Slipper Slapper'

Vase rooms

The *upstairs gallery* is full of vases, a feast for the aficionado; though even the least interested person must delight in the *white vases* of *Room VII*, where three in particular (17916, 1818, 1935) depict in the most delicate line and colour Hermes conducting a young woman to the banks of the Styx while Charon waits in his boat, and a woman making offerings at a tomb while the dead man stands in a blazing red cloak to one side.

The Thera exhibition

Also upstairs is the 'temporary' *exhibition of Minoan findings on Thera.* This is a must. The outstanding features of Minoan art are the use of brilliant colours and the great freedom of line. There is a fine pagan feeling for nature in the decorations and a frequent recourse to marine motifs. Here there are vases and other pottery with undulating octopus, dolphin and seaweed designs. And wall *frescoes* of monkeys, antelopes, flowers, birds and bare-breasted aristocratic women.

Piraeus

PIRAEUS is, as it was in ancient times, the port of Athens. The fortunes of the two have been bound together inextricably. When Themistokles determined upon the construction of a great Athenian fleet, he simultaneously chose triple-harboured Piraeus as its base over the nearer but exposed roadstead at Phaleron, and set about constructing the mighty walls that linked the two cities throughout the 5th C. Phaleron lies 6 kms southwest of the Temple of Olympian Zeus, Leoforos Syngrou running between the two and more less following the course of the Phaleric Wall. Odos Piraios covers about 8 kms from the Kerameikos to Piraeus and over most of that distance follows the course of the North Wall. Between these two, a Middle Wall, often no more than 200 metres from the North Wall, ran from city to port on a line now followed by the electric railway. When Athens declined to barely more than a backwater with the rise of Constantinople, Piraeus lost all importance. At the moment of Greek independence, not a single house was to be found here and it was only the choice of Athens as the capital of Greece that brought Piraeus back into

The Long Walls

existence. It swelled with refugees in 1922 following the Anatolian disaster, and is now the busiest port in the Eastern Mediterranean, overtaking, some decades ago, Istanbul.

You will come to Piraeus enroute to the Saronic or Aegean islands, and despite the port's history there is next to nothing in the way of surviving monuments to cause you to linger. (Enthusiasts, however, can see sections of both the North and Middle Walls between the Karaiskaki Stadium and Odos Piraios — or Odos Athinon as it there becomes — a short walk from the Nea Phaleron electric train station. Also, it was said by Demosthenes that the ship-sheds housing the Athenian fleet were worthy of mention in company with the Parthenon and Propylaia, and the remains of some of these may still be seen in the basement of a block of flats on the east side of Zea harbour. Finally, a new Maritime Museum has opened along Akte Themisto-kleous to the west of Zea's mouth.)

Traces of the past

The pleasure of the port lies not in its past, nor in the imagined *joie de vivre* claimed for it in *Never On Sunday*, but in the routine of its commercial harbour, boats shuttling between the islands, cruise ships awaiting the return of their passengers from day-trips to the Parthenon, if you're lucky the QE2 dwarfing every hull and highrise in sight, and always, beyond the moles, a dozen or more freighters and giant tankers grazing mindlessly like sea-cows. Also a walk around the Akte peninsula is recommended for its changing views across the Saronic, especially at sundown when Hymettos fades from honey-gold to violet and the mountains of the Peloponnese stand out in cobalt silhouette. The circular harbour of Zea, crammed with yachts, is hemmed by charmless modern apartment blocks; but the smaller yacht basin of Turkolimano (Mikrolimano to chauvinistic Greeks) lies cosily in the arms of Munychia, terraces of lovely houses falling back upon the hill, cafe and taverna tables round the quay, and amongst the elegant sailing boats, sturdy fishing craft, large and small, piled with nets, chandeliered with night lamps. It's a good place to come to from summer-sweltering Athens for a cooler, sea-fragrant evening. From the top of Munychia there's a marvellous view of all three harbours, the entire Saronic, and Athens spilling down the plain.

Yacht harbours

AROUND ATTICA

Kaisariani Only about 5 kms from the centre of Athens, up the slopes of Hymettos and near the source of the Ilissos, the 11th C. monastery of Kaisariani sits tucked away amidst the shade of plane and cypress trees at the head of a ravine. A fountain just above was reputed in Classical times to cure sterility, and the spot was made famous by Ovid in his *Ars Amatoria*. The Germans favoured the ravine during the Second World War for executing hostages; Athenians favour the fountain today for washing their cars. The well-restored convent buildings and the church with its 17th and 18th C. frescoes are now a national monument.

Daphni The more famous monastery near Athens is DAPHNI, 10 kms west on the way to Elefsis, following the route of the ancient Sacred Way and passing the litter of 20th C. life: motels, snack bars, gas stations; also, more endurably, a leper colony where oddly (I thought) I was once confined on suspicion of cholera. The surprise is that in its leafy gardens behind battlemented walls the monastery entirely eludes the encroaching present. Founded in the 5th or 6th C., it stands on the site of a sanctuary of Apollo (deriving its name from the laurels — daphnai — sacred to the god). The very pleasant flagged courtyard is lined by low cloisters dating from the 13th to 15th C; the entrance to the excellent 11th C. Byzantine church is just beyond, its exonarthex especially satisfying for its uncommon incorporation not just of ancient fragments but of entire architectural features such as Ionic columns into the overall design of pointed arches and crenellations.

The mosaics The mosaics within, jewels of this supreme art of Byzantium, are rivalled in Greece only by those at Osios Loukas and Thessaloniki. In the dome the *Pantokrator*, Christ Almighty, glares to the right and a great gap yawns between his fore and middle fingers as though with mind and body he is struggling to keep the cosmos from cracking apart. The *Baptism* is delicately worked to show Christ's body shimmering through the translucent waters of the Jordan; and Mary, in the *Annunciation* and in the *Nativity*, is at once graceful and resplendent in her night-blue robe illuminated in gold. The four mosaics on the pendatives show Christ as meek and mild; as an infant, as a young man — as incomplete. The Pantokrator, then, comes as a great whack: Christ with the gloves off; terrible and awesome in his revelation and power.

Apart from these, the finest mosaics are in the choruses: the *Entry into Jerusalem*, the *Crucifixion*, the *Resurrection*, and *Thomas*.

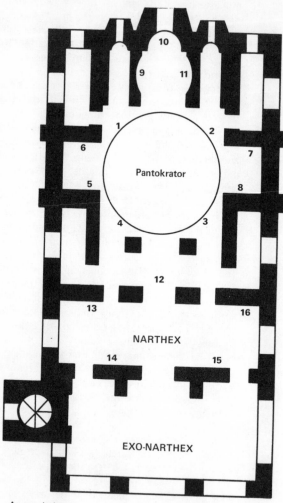

DAPHNI CHURCH

1. Annunciation
2. Nativity
3. Baptism
4. Transfiguration
5. Entry into Jerusalem
6. Crucifixion
7. Resurrection
8. Thomas
9. Michael
10. Virgin with child
11. Gabriel
12. Assumption of the Virgin
13. Last Supper
14. Judas' betrayal
15. Prayer of Joachim and Anna
16. Presentation of the Virgin

Elefsis   From Mycenaean through Roman times ELEFSIS (Eleusis) was the goal of millions of pilgrims who came here to be initiated into the Mysteries. Today the mystery is gone. The town, 22 kms from Athens, anciently the birthplace of Aeschylus, is now a centre of heavy industry, occasionally dramatic when blazing gas erupts from tall pipes into the night sky. The site, on a low rocky hill, is a jumble of excavations of interest to the archaeologist but baffling and without charm for the layman.

The Mysteries   A lesser Eleusinia took place in Athens, on the banks of the Ilissos, in late February and early March, the celebrants then being accepted as initiates, or Mystai, to the Greater Eleusinia held in September. In the course of the nine days' proceedings of the Greater Eleusinia, the Mystai walked from Athens to Elefsis the first day, returning to Athens on the last. This part of the ceremony was public and full of pomp. But at Elefsis, in the high-walled and windowless Telesterion within Demeter's sanctuary, 'the holy things' were shown and 'the unutterable words' were enacted, and the Mystai were pledged to a secrecy so faithfully kept that in the course of 1700 years nothing of the culminating revelation found its way into record.

Yet it is possible to guess at the form of the ceremony and to appreciate its import. It was probably like a medieval Passion play but performed mute and therefore all the more engaging to the imagination. The level at which it was taken, and the precise interpretation put upon it, would have been a matter of individual response. Certainly the response could be profound. Pindar wrote that "he who has seen the holy things and goes in death beneath the earth is happy: for he knows life's end and he knows too the new divine beginning"; while Cicero, 400 years later, said "the greatest gift of Athens to mankind and the holiest is the Eleusinian Mysteries". Peisistratos, Kimon, Pericles, Hadrian and Marcus Aurelius all contributed to the magnificence of the sanctuary with new and greater walls and buildings.

Legend of Demeter and Persephone   It was anciently accepted that the cult was founded by Demeter (literally Earth Mother), goddess of agriculture in the Olympian scheme. While searching for her abducted daughter Kore (Persephone), she paused at Elefsis and was told by the king's son Triptolemos that Kore had been carried off to the underworld by Hades. Demeter at once put a curse upon the land, forbidding trees to bear fruit, crops to grow, until mankind was extinguished. Zeus intervened with his brother, commanding Hades to return Kore. But she had eaten a pomegranate beneath the earth; she had tasted the food of the dead, Hades said, and must stay. A compromise was reached: Kore would live nine months in the world with her mother, three months underground with Hades as his queen, and life would flourish, then wither, and then be born again in turn. To Triptolemos, Demeter gave wheat seeds, a wooden plough and a winged chariot to travel about the earth teaching mankind the blessings of agriculture.

In Homer both Persephone and Demeter are mentioned but not linked. That the queen of the underworld should be brought back to the land of the living by a grieving mother was a later invention, answering a growing need amongst Greeks for a doctrine of the soul otherwise lacking in the Olympian religion. The late Egyptian myth of Isis and Osiris grappled with the same question, and finally when a young man was crucified outside Jerusalem's walls, a doctrine incorporating and satisfying this Eastern Mediterranean quest was launched with considerable success upon the world.

Beaches The coast road from Athens to Sounion passes the airport and just beyond comes to Glyfada (17 kms) with numerous hotels and sandy beaches crammed with Athenians escaping the stifling city heat. At 20 kms is Voula, also a seaside resort, though smaller. Vouliagmeni, at 25 kms, has the finest beaches, well-developed by the NTOG with all facilities. It's a fashionable place for wealthier Athenians to summer with many luxury flats to rent. There are no hotels under B class. All of these beaches can be reached from Leof Olgas at the Zappeion by bus.

The road winds along the rocky and beautiful coastline, passing the bay and (2 kms inland) village of Anavissos where the marvellous kouros now in the National Archaeological Museum was found. At 70 kms at the southeastern extremity of Attica the Temple of Poseidon perches high on its cliff and outstares the sea.

Cape Sounion CAPE SOUNION was a lookout post for the Athenian navy; the temple dedicated to the god of the sea. For sailors running wheat down from the Black Sea or from Egypt across the open Mediterranean, Poseidon's gleaming columns were the final landfall with a last tack along the sheltered Attic coast to home. The temple was built by Kallikrates in 444 BC, immediately after the Hephaistion. Twelve Doric columns still stand: back in the days when a man could carve his name where he damn well pleased, these columns were a favourite target; they are wormed with lettering, including BYRON by that arch-grafitti artist of the Mediterranean.

Apart from grafitti, Byron also wrote poetry:

Place me on Sunium's marbled steep,
Where nothing, save the waves and I,
May hear our mutual murmurs sweep;
There, swan-like, let me sing and die:
A land of slaves shall ne'er be mine —
Dash down yon cup of Samian wine!

Silver Mines The land, however, or rather the mines beneath it, toiled with slaves throughout the 5th C. BC: just up the coast is Lavrion whose silver mines earned Athens the surplus that financed the construction of its fleet in time to counter the Persian attack; the fleet that then ensured Athens' imperial grandeur. During the period of their greatest output, the mines are estimated to have employed the labour of 30,000 slaves.

The road north from Sounion and Lavrion passes through Markopoulou, a market town with vineyards surrounding and a reputation for good retsina. The Sanctuary of Artemis Vravrona on the Athenian acropolis has its origins 5 kms **Vravron** towards the coast from here, at Vravron. Iphigeneia and Orestes were said to have fled from Tauris in the Crimea with a primitive wooden statue of Artemis, and founded her cult here. It seems that an earlier bear-goddess cult was incorporated; at any rate, every four years girls of Attica between five and ten years old came here dressed in saffron robes and impersonated bears. The foundations of the sanctuary of Artemis and near it a cave venerated as the tomb of Iphigeneia are evident, and below them several columns of a Doric temple.

The Plain of At dawn on 12 September 490 BC, 9000 Athenians and **Marathon** 1000 Plataians attacked 30,000 Persian soldiers on the Plain of MARATHON. Within a few hours 6400 Persians lay dead at the loss of only 192 Athenians. Athenian courage gave the lie to Persian invincibility and decided the fate of Europe **Athenian burial** for the next 2400 years. The mound under which the **mound** Athenian dead were buried is scratchily covered with grass in spring; by summer it is a bare brown pile of dirt worn by tourists. But from the top there is a fine view over the plain, green and cultivated with olives and probably not so different now than it was. Behind are the mountains.

The battle The Athenians showed daring from the start. They had left their fortified Acropolis to fight on the beaches, though now waited four days on the mountain slopes for Spartan reinforcements. The Persian cavalry and archers, combining with their larger infantry, would have proved fatal to an Athenian attack across level ground. Thinking the issue would not be resolved here, on the fifth day the Persians

67

embarked their cavalry to advance on Athens by sea, sending their infantry forward to cover the operation. At that moment Miltiades, Spartan help or no, sent his men racing down the slopes and quickly under the Persian arrows to engage in close combat. The Athenian centre was kept purposely weak while the wings were reinforced. The Persians resisted the Athenian centre but the momentum of the wings soon engulfed them on either side and to the rear. The Persians panicked, scattered, and were beaten into the marshes and the sea.

The remainder of the Persian force now sailed round Sounion to land at Phaleron, but Miltiades had brought his army back to Athens by forced march and stood ready to meet the enemy again for the second time. Courage, intelligence, and that astonishing burst of energy — 10,000 men marching 37 kms in full armour after fighting one battle to fight, if need be, another — overwhelmed the Persian numbers and announced the spirit of the civilisation that entered into manhood that day. Aeschylus was one of the soldiers at Marathon; it was the moment in his life of which he was most proud.

Rhamnous   Difficult of access and unviolated, Rhamnous is the most delightful of the minor archaeological sites in Attica. It lies 26 kms further up the coast from Marathon, the ruins of its two temples romantically lost upon an overgrown plateau above the sea, with good swimming below the site. It's the sort of place an early 19th C. adventurer would have had to himself before a million tourists each year would follow in his footsteps, reciting his mawkish poetry. The smaller temple was dedicated to Themis, goddess of law, custom and equity; the larger temple, built by Kallikrates in 436 BC, dedicated to Nemesis, the goddess who doled out happiness to the miserable and misery to the happy.

THE ISLANDS OF THE ARGO-SARONIC

As well as visiting some of the places easily reached by land from Athens, consider the islands which lie, at most, just a few hours' sailing time south of Piraeus: Aegina, Poros, Hydra and Spetsai. Any of them are suitable for day-trips or longer stays and just the voyage itself, through the narrow blue waters separating the islands from the stark mountains of the Argolid, is an eye-filling experience.

Aegina

An unpretentious island and the nearest of the four to Athens, AEGINA (Aigina) is on the tourist route for its Temple of Aphaia but is otherwise commonly underrated. But I lived here for six months and think of it with fondness. Shaped on the map like an upside down triangle, its southern point is marked by the magnificent cone of Mt Oros, the highest peak in these islands and of volcanic origin, visible on a clear day from the Athenian acropolis. The centre and eastern side of the island is mountainous; a gently-sloping fertile plain runs down to the western extremity where Aegina town overlays in part the ancient capital of the island. Pericles, brooding out across the Saronic Gulf, called Aegina "the eyesore of Piraeus", a purely political rather than aesthetic judgement, for in contour and variety the island is well-endowed, and plentiful today in pines, pistachios, olives and citrus fruits. Pindar celebrated this "beloved city", this "city thronged with strangers, the Dorian island, Aegina", which kept "glory perfect from the beginning and is sung of many for her shaping of heroes".

When the world was small and a city or an island could aspire to be a Great Power, Aegina, strategically situated between the Peloponnese and Attica, looking out upon the Aegean and all the Mediterranean beyond, became a great and wealthy trading state, with shipyards, fleets and a sophisticated banking system, outstanding athletes, sculptors and temple-builders. In the 7th C. BC Aegina was the first place in Europe to use coinage, and such was the prestige of its currency that its silver coins stamped with a tortoise were readily accepted throughout the known world. Its merchants set up a temple on the Nile and sailed as far west as Spain. The island was a centre of Greek art and was renowned for its pottery and bronze-founding. At Salamis in 480 BC it was the Aeginetan fleet that was awarded the laurels after the Persian rout.

A Mediterranean power

But Pericles saw Aegina, her fleet and her Dorian ties with Sparta, as a threat to Athens' burgeoning maritime empire. In 457 BC and again at the beginning of the Peloponnesian War the Athenians defeated the Aeginetans at sea, on the second occasion ruthlessly expelling the island's entire population after first hacking off their thumbs lest even from exile the Aeginetans might return upon their enemies with spears and bows.

Just as little remains of ancient Aegina, so it is difficult on this pleasant island to imagine the air once filled with the clamour of battle and the screams and weeping of defeat. But in the most silent hour of Aegina's scented nights I have heard those sounds echoing between the harbour and the mountains, incongruous, sad and startling, a civilisation ripped from the pages of history.

The voyage from Piraeus

Frequent ferries pass through Piraeus harbour and clear the Akte peninsula to port with the Bay of Phaleron — where the Persian fleet was beached the evening before the Battle of Salamis — sweeping away to the airport beyond. To starboard extends the long, scrubby island of SALAMIS itself and between it and the belching smokestacks of Elefsis is the narrow dog's leg channel where the Greek fleets lured and broke the pursuing Persians that August morning nearly 2500 years ago. Out in the open water, small silvery fish leap high in the air from the ferry's churning wake, some to be caught in the smiling beaks of seagulls wheeling, plunging and dancing behind. Aegina's coastline draws near and before rounding the southwesternmost spit of land, marked with a lighthouse, is the house where Kazantzakis lived during the German occupation and wrote *Zorba the Greek*.

Aegina's acropolis

Just before the port, atop a promontory which served as the acropolis of Aegina from Mycenaean through Classical times, stands a single snapped-off Doric column, all that remains above foundation level of the Temple of Apollo. From the sea the position is not impressive, but to stand on the very point of that promontory, especially as the sun is setting over the Peloponnese, is to enjoy one of the grandest views in Greece, Mt Oros behind you, the great mountains of the Argolid lying off to the left, and before them Anghistri, an island inhabited by Albanians which can be reached from Aegina port by motor launch. The sugarloaf of the Acro-corinth is just discernable ahead, while sweeping off to the right are the Megarid, the island of Salamis and the ring of mountains around Athens.

The harbour

There are harbours more pretty in Greece, but the port here is delightful for its busyness, its sailing boats in summer, brightly painted caiques, and on the quayside the tiny chapel of St Nicholas, beaming white in the sunshine. To the left as you sail in is the ancient military port, now a bathing area, dredged and protected by a breakwater built during the Greek War of Independence by the American Philhellene, Samuel Gridley Howe (later married to Julia Ward Howe, authoress of 'The Battle Hymn of the Republic'), in part to provide work for the starving Greek refugees from Egypt, Asia Minor and Turkish-occupied Greece who were pouring into the little town which briefly in the late 1820s was the capital of the new nation.

The town   Aegina town possesses a few undistinguished churches, lacking in rich Orthodox ornament and musty atmosphere (though left off the Aphaia road, 15 minutes out of town, is the 13th century Omorfi Ekklesia with well-preserved frescoes), and a small museum tucked a few streets back containing some broken and badly worn sculptures from the pediments of the Temple of Aphaia (the best were stolen from the temple and taken to Munich) and much smashed pottery — a collection which emphasises by its skimpiness what is evident elsewhere around the island: Athenian destruction, Venetian neglect, the butchery in 1537 by an Ottoman landing party under Barbarossa of the entire male population, the women and children carried off to slavery, and finally the depredations of 19th century culture vultures.

But though largely shorn of visible evidence of its history, there is the island itself, its rich cultivation, varied topography, and a hardworking, prosperous population of fishermen, farmers and merchants who feel near enough to the bright lights of Athens not to want to abandon their homes as has happened on so many other islands. And in the security of their well-being they are not obliged to fawn upon the tourist trade for their living, though in summertime Aegina is a favourite day-trip for Athenians wanting an afternoon swim and an evening meal on the harbour front before catching the last crowded ferry home. Aegina is a workaday place with fishermen back from a night at their nets selling their catches at the covered fish market, caiques over from the Peloponnese loaded with melons and courgettes for sale, bed and furniture makers, grocers and butchers in the backstreets, and bored guards puffing cigarettes outside the prison, formerly a museum, and originally an orphanage built by Capodistria, the first president of Greece, which stands hot and white beyond the town.

Visitors to the island intent on improving themselves make for either the Monastery of Agios Nectarios or the Temple of Aphaia. It's Greeks who make for the former, some of them while still on the boat already thumbing through their Bibles and mumbling prayers, leaving it to foreigners to consult mere guide books for revelations on

Monastery of Agios Nectarios

the pagan temple. Nectarios is the most recent of Orthodox saints, though how he became one is unclear as the Orthodox church has not canonised anyone for hundreds of years and the procedure for doing so has been forgotton. Still, just one look at old Nectarios (he only died in the 1920s) on any local postcard or lapel button, his stern features and magnificent white beard, is enough to convince anyone that this was a man to be reckoned with, as now some reckon with God through him. Following the Aphaia road out of town you slowly climb into the mountains and halfway across the island alight by a taverna and a souvenir shop, and a large hotel and yet larger church still under construction. The Nectarios business is booming. I paid a visit to the monastery under the mistaken impression that there was an embalmed body to see, but Nectarios is well concealed within a stone sarcophagus. An old woman takes you round his rooms, left as they were when he passed on to better things, leaving his collection of seashells behind. I never saw a monk while I was there, but numerous women in black washing monkish underwear, cooking, and drawing water from the wells.

Palaiochora

The monastery stands on a hill across from another littered with the remains of more than twenty churches and monasteries. These once dotted the precipitous streets of the old chora, the capital of the island from the 9th century to 1826, built high and inland as a fruitless defence against attack, for it was twice destroyed by Barbarossa and once by the Venetians. When the Turks were thrown off the island in the 1820s the inhabitants of Palaiochora came down to the port, lugging the stones of their houses with them but leaving their churches behind.

Monastery of Panagia Chrysoleontissa

Every year the islanders celebrate the Assumption of the Virgin (15 August) by climbing, either from here or further back from Agioi Asomatoi, the mountain (on the right-hand side of the road as you come from town) rising above Palaiochora. On its peak is a small white chapel. Beyond, set in a bowl green or gold with wheat and ringed by peaks,

is the Monastery of Panagia Chrysoleontissa. Goats, chickens and peacocks wander peacefully in its grounds; a Shangri-La entirely removed from sight and everyday contact with the world around. The church should be visited for its remarkable ikonostasis. The monastery once owned a third of the island; since 1935 it has been inhabited by no more than 14 nuns who on any day of the year will offer you accommodation for the night.

Temple of Aphaia

Further along the road, amidst fragrant pinewoods at the northeast point of the island high above the Saronic is the Temple of Aphaia, comparable to Sounion and Lindos in its magnificent confrontation with the sea. Built in celebration of the victory at Salamis, the temple was dedicated to the protector of women who presumably realised that need after narrowly escaping the clutches of lustful Minos, fleeing Crete, and reasserting herself as a local goddess on Aegina. She seems to have been a version of the goddess Artemis and was worshipped in Sparta under that name, elsewhere as Dictynna or Britomart, figuring in Edmund Spenser's 'The Faerie Queene' as "Britomartis a Lady knight, in whome I picture Chastity". Her nine-month pursuit by Minos, says Robert Graves in *The White Goddess*, is "the basis of the Coventry legend of Lady Godiva. The clue is provided by a miserere-seat in Coventry Cathedral, paralleled elsewhere in Early English grotesque woodcarving which shows what the guide-books call 'a figure emblematic of lechery': a long-haired woman wrapped in a net," — Dictynna means a net — "riding sideways on a goat and preceded by a hare". For all that, or perhaps because of that, the feeling of the temple is masculine, with the heaviness and power of late Archaic architecture and unusual for its two storeys. The pedimental sculptures depicting combats before the walls of Troy are now in Munich's Glyptothek, while an earlier group discovered buried are in the National Archaeological Museum in Athens.

Agia Marina

The road twists down to what was once the little village of Agia Marina on a beautiful bay, now fast becoming a German package holiday centre, a thick film of Ambre Solaire upon the water.

Perdika

Mt Oros

More secluded swimming is to be had at Marathon, on the road between Aegina town and the fishing village of Perdika, or off the rocks of the islet of Moni reached from Perdika by launch. Also from Marathon, or from Agioi Asomatoi (on the Aphaia road), the 3-hour ascent of Mt Oros (1742 feet) can be made. The remains of Mycenaean and later settlements fringe the summit from where there is a commanding view of the island seemingly rising from a vast lake almost entirely encircled by coastline.

The Methana peninsula The next port of call is at Methana, frequented (if at all) for its sulphur springs, huddled beneath the terraced hillsides of a bulbous extension of the Peloponnese. From here, or further on from Galata, opposite Poros, you can backtrack along the north coast of the Argolid to Epidavros (though with some difficulty if journeying by bus as the schedules are not always convenient), or more easily you **Troezen** can visit the traces of ancient Troezen, birthplace of Theseus, whose wife Phaedra fell in love with his bastard son Hippolytos as told in the tragedies of Euripides and Racine.

Poros The boat now threads its way through a hairpin strait and puts in at the island of POROS, linked by proximity but often contrasted to the island of Hydra, like unidentical twins. Poros is less commercialised than Hydra, less trendy, more visited by vacationing Greeks. Less commercialised it may be, but as you step off the boat a bustle of waiters pounce upon you (the waiters on Hydra have enough business already!), and the presence of motor cars comes as a mild shock after days of seeing only donkeys clambering up the steep stepped streets of Hydra. The internal combustion engine and Galata only a stone's throw away on the Poloponnese shoreline create also the impression that Poros is not quite an island.

On the other hand you can climb to the Monastery of Zoodochos Pigi on the pine-covered hill behind the town, and above it, in a saddle between the two hilltops, is the ruined Temple of Poseidon: Galata is opposite, olive trees cover the mainland hills, dark mountains rise behind them; the red-tiled houses of Poros, always in need of paint, fan out below. The colours are not shattering, but are warm, old and give you a cosy feeling.

Hydra If HYDRA (Idra) is to be faulted, it can only be for the large number of tourists who show up over Easter and during the summer. The town itself and the landscape all around it is strikingly beautiful. One of the peculiarities of tourists is that they charge about *en masse* like lemmings, and here they are very trendy lemmings indeed: elegant French boys reeking of *eau de Cologne*; English yacht-owners who never go to sea, conspicuously drinking Martinis on their poops; sunburnt Swedish girls painfully ensconced at cafe tables; Adonis-like artists displaying themselves before wretched canvases; armies of Americans disembarking from cruise ships; all of them compacted along the harbour front lined with commercial gyp-joints, catered to by humourless waiters. Not as bad as St Tropez, but going that way.

But the higher reaches of the town and the hills beyond remain surprisingly untouched, charming and full of colour. Walking up through the maze of steep lanes, the clean air is filled with the varying scents of flowers, dung, the sea and cooking. Donkeys' hooves grip the cobbled streets; vistas of harbour, town and surrounding hillsides change at every pause. Doorways of mahogany or brilliant blue, marble architraves, brass hand-shape knockers, and in springtime flowers everywhere, sometimes growing right out of the walls and rock.

The Hydra you see today was settled by Greeks escaping from the Turkish occupation of the Peloponnese. Her maritime power guaranteed her wealth and independence: Little England she was called, and flourished into the 19th century with a population of 16,000. Approaching from **The harbour** Poros through the narrow stretch of water dividing the island from the Peloponnese, the town is invisible until the last moment when a break in the coastline reveals her horseshoe harbour between two headlands mounted with gun emplacements. Climbing sharply back against the hillsides are the glistening houses, the occasional windmill, cubes of white, but also dashes of red, ochre, pale blue, green and turquoise. Now with a population of only 3000, many of them foreign writers and artists, you notice old abandoned houses crumbling in the vegetation above the town.

The island of Hydra is quite large, but as it's mountainous and without roads, the only settlement is the small port of Hydra. So it's very easy to get away from it all just by turning your back on the harbour and walking uphill. It's typical of the Greek mania for putting a church on every likely spot of land that on this depopulated island there **Easter on Hydra** are 366 churches and monasteries! Easter is a marvellous time to be here, when the island takes on the sombre mood of the Passion and then explodes with joy and festivity at the Resurrection.

Walking up the hillside directly away from the town along a steep and rocky path I came to a grey-walled, red-tiled church atop the hillcrest; a strenuous walk in the heat of the day: do it in the morning or late afternoon, but not so late that you're forced to inch your way uncertainly down in the darkness. Climbing these hills I was surrounded by the sound of a thousand ringing bells attached to unseen donkeys, lambs, horses and goats, loudest in the evening as the flocks were brought in, an ancient music as though the hillsides themselves were singing in the still air. From the church I could see the open sea across the far side of the island, and to the left on a low hill sat the Monastery of Agia Tria, its white walls surrounded by huddled stables

75

in which the musical flocks spent the night. A sign on the door read: "Women and improperly dressed men are utterly refused admission to the monastery". It was the Saturday before Easter Sunday that I came here and the monastery hummed with chanting. Dry with thirst, I knocked, was greeted silently by two startled monks who disappeared, one returning with a cold glass of water and a Turkish delight handed to me on a silver tray. I drank, watched the sun set over the black mountains of the Peloponnese, listened to the last tinkling of the goats and stumbled in the darkness down the thorny hillsides back into Hydra where the smell of roast lamb and a sense of expectancy announced the imminent celebration of a miracle.

On Good Friday the church bells had tolled and all of Hydra settled into quiet mourning. The atmosphere went deeper than convention. The pain of thorns, the sour taste of vinegar, the slow heaving death upon the Cross were worn into people's countenances. Now on Saturday a subtle shift in mood and mounting activity as red Easter eggs and long white candles disappeared from shops and stalls while tavernas prepared lambs over bright wood fires. Black-robed priests came down from hilltop monasteries carrying bundles of palm fronds which were arched across the streets and interwoven with coloured lights. Mourning had been supplanted by tense expectation, crowds gathered around the churches, and I made my way into the stark white courtyard of Panagia Faneromeni, the church that stands right on the harbour front.

The night was black and still but here warm chants rolled along the dark-timbered nave, richly carved and bossed with gold, a final midwifery of Easter. As midnight chimed from the tall clocktower the bishop emerged into the courtyard and from a bower of palms called out "Christ is risen!" and every face in the gathering flushed with joy at the miracle renewed. A single candle brought from the alter lit another and each in turn carried the message of rebirth from candle to candle in outstretched hands until throughout the courtyard and its stairs and balconies and out into the harbour front itself thousands of candles flickered and reflected in shining eyes.

Fireworks exploded above the waters, ships' sirens blasted through the starry night, people cried and kissed each other and laughed — and some just stared into their candle flames, at the birth of life, for the three-day ritual had impressed its meaning deeply on people's minds.

Spetsai SPETSAI is the furthest and smallest island of the group, bare except for a few olive groves, distinctly cooler than elsewhere in the Argo-Saronic. For this reason it is a favoured retreat of wealthy Athenian families who in summertime occupy spacious mansions in the pretty town. Cars are non-existent, locomotion being by carriage, bicycle or scooter, all of them rentable for jaunts round the island. Around the far side of the island is one fine sandy beach, Bekiri; the beaches nearer the town are skimpy. Even so, the island has become a popular holiday resort and has a modest nightlife.

Spetsai is distinguished for being the first in the archipelago to revolt against the Turks in April, 1821, and the fortified point, still bristling with cannon, now forms the town's plateia, with many cafes. A museum contains relics of the Revolution and the town's four churches are worth a visit.

THE ARGOLID

The Peloponnese, a giant hand of which the Argolid is the thumb, is rich in ancient associations, and for the Greeks at the time of the Persian invasions it was the heartland to which they would have withdrawn and made their stand had not Themistokles just barely convinced them that Athens could not be sacrificed. And today it is the least developed part of the mainland, with poor roads, formidable mountains, magnificent scenery, untouched traditional villages and friendly people.

Some of the ancient sites, like Mycenae and Olympia, are on the tourist circuit, and certain coastal towns, like Nafplion and Kalamata, are established resorts. But the beauty and interest of the Peloponnese is not confined to beaches and antiquities, even though the tourists are. A meander through the interior is highly recommended for the more adventurous.

The road to the Peloponnese

Approaching the Peloponnese from Athens you follow in reverse the route that Theseus took when he left Troezen. Past Elefsis and Megara (mother-city of Byzantium) the road mounts a corniche above the waters of the Argo-Saronic. It was here that Theseus vanquished Skiron who, demanding that passers-by should wash his feet, would kick them over the precipice into the waiting jaws of a huge tortoise. In ancient times this path was known as the *Kaki Skala*, or Bad Stairway, and though the modern road cut into the sheer rock face presents no danger, the way remains awesome, with stunning views of the gulf below from all along its 700-foot high, 10-kilometre stretch.

The isthmus

The road descends to the isthmus, the narrow hinge connecting the Peloponnese to the rest of Greece, cut by the Corinthian Canal. The first attempts to cut a canal were made by the Romans, with even Nero delivering an imperial blow with a golden pickaxe. But it took the technology of the Industrial Age to do the job, and the canal only became a reality in 1893. The achievement is most impressive when you glide through aboard a ship; from the wobbling roadway that crosses over it you have no perspective and therefore no sense of scale. Even if a ship passes through far below you, it's not until you notice how incredibly small the passengers are and how very large the ship must be that you become amazed.

Loutraki

But before crossing over the canal you might turn right and, running north along the Gulf of Corinth, come to Loutraki (80 kms from Athens), an old watering place into which new life has been breathed by recent development and prosperity. It's a pleasant place to idle, for its hot springs, its sunsets over the gulf, and the charm of its pre-war hotels with balconies, elaborate entrances and staircases, and occasional circular rooms. The swimming, too, is good. Thirteen kilometres north of Loutraki (and 25 kms from Corinth) is the village of Perachora. There are fine views all along the route. With the rise in the price of resin, the village, set on a small plateau about half a kilometre from the sea, is emerging from its historical poverty. Between the village and the sea is a lake, a few tavernas on its north shore. Paths continue towards the western tip of the pine-covered peninsula where, amidst jagged tumbling rocks, the site of ancient Perachora commands a magnificent view down the entire length of the Corinthian Gulf. An agora and stoa surround the modest harbour (strong currents and the occasional shark make it unwise to swim beyond it), while a sanctuary of Hera and the remains of an 8th C. temple lie on higher ground. There is a museum back in the village. Barely more than a stone's throw from the cross-roads of Greece and beautifully described by Dilys Powell in *An Affair of the Heart*, Perachora is rarely visited.

Corinth Modern CORINTH (81 kms from Athens), just across the isthmus, is in that category of towns which includes Troy, New York and Athens, Georgia: the place bears no relation to the original. It is lifeless, unattractive, with wide empty streets and box-like houses. This is at least partly because the modern town, which was built at at distance from the Classical site to avoid earthquakes, was itself flattened by an earthquake in 1928. The living in old Corinth inhabit a small village which occupies part of the ancient site upon a rocky plateau 6 kms southwest of the modern town. A coffee in it little plateia with plane-tree and fountain is the only self-indulgence available. The Classical city of at least 300,000 owed its wealth and power to its strategic position at the isthmus, but owed its fame to its life of indolent luxury. St Paul ranted agaanst Corinthian whores and was answered with a riot. The Roman ruins of the city Paul visited—refounded by Julius Caesar one hundred years after the Greek city had been razed to the ground for participating in a revolt against Roman rule—are extensive, but of Greek Corinth nothing remains except the seven **Temple of** columns of the Temple of Apollo, one of the oldest in **Apollo** Greece (c550 BC), with monolithic Doric Archaic columns and a squatness about it that reflects the uncertainty of early architects when building with heavy stone instead of wood.

It was at Corinth that Alexander the Great encountered Diogenes, the Cynic philosopher who, shunning worldly pleasures, chose to live inside a barrel. Taking pity on this abject figure, Alexander asked if there was anything he wanted. "Yes", replied Diogenes, "stand aside a little, for you are blocking the sun". "If I had not been Alexander, I would have wanted to be Diogenes," came the reply.

The Acrocorinth

The fantastic ACRO-CORINTH which looms on the sunset horizon like an Aztec mesa red with sacrifice was originally topped with a temple to Aphrodite and serviced by a thousand sacred prostitutes. It rises precipitously 1885 feet above the ruins of the Classical city, a 1½ hour walk to the top or a drive along the road from the museum. From a distance there's a hint of fortifications along the top, and now as you climb closer the enormous crenellated walls and towers of the medieval fortress loom sombrely above you. Corinth was so often sacked that successive Byzantine, Frankish, Venetian and Turkish rulers retired to the Acro-corinth and built up one of the most imposing medieval monuments in Greece.

One set of gargantuan walls sits within another, seemingly impregnable, with commanding, magnificent views of Corinth on the plain below, the isthmus and the two gulfs it divides and the far shores of Attica. Yet the fortress was several times taken in desperate battles by lunatic warriors who heaved up the steep hill and battered against its stones, their blood and screams still lingering, tangible, in the atmosphere. Here myth prefigures history:

Myth of Sisyphos

Zeus ravished Aegina, daughter of the river-god Asophus, and Sisyphos, for exposing Zeus to her father, was condemned by the gods to ceaselessly roll a rock to the top of the Acro-corinth, whence the stone would fall back of its own weight. The gods had thought with some reason that there was no more dreadful punishment than futile and hopeless labour.

The road and railway weave across one another all the way to Argos; the railway narrow gauge, single track, the trains themselves like trolleys, wobbling with suburban complacency through the fierce landscape as if conveying you for an afternoon's picnic to the Vienna Woods. To the west are the ruins of Nemea where Herakles slew the Nemean lion.

Nemea

Mycenae

Not far off the Corinth-Argos road or railway line (from Corinth 42 kms), almost lost in a fold between the twin hills of Zara and Agios Elias, is the low mound on which MYCENAE (Mikinai) stands. Drawing closer, the mound rises steeply and spread upon it like broken shingles are the grey, brooding ruins of Agamemnon's citadel. On the bare curtain of mountains behind it, a watchman sighted the beacon signalling his lord's return from Troy and cried, "All hail, bright father of joy and dance in Argos", while bitter Klytemnestra and her lover Aegisthes set the stage among these stones for murder.

From this ground and in this light grew the civilisation which followed upon the collapse of Minoan Crete. In all such places, primordial in aspect and associations, there's a sense of timelessness, of dream-history. Once in through the Lion Gate and standing on the Cyclopean walls over-looking the richly-patterned Argive Plain fanning out below, you feel funnelling in upon you shards of time and legend, of warriors, kings and gods, of tourist buses, cold orange drinks and finely-beaten masks of gold.

Origins of Mycenaean civilisation

From 1600 to 1200 BC, Mycenae was the leading city in Greece, its highly hierarchical society dominating the Argolid and exercising some kind of feudal control or influence over other Mycenaean kingdoms such as Iolkos in Thessaly, Thebes and Orchomenos in Boeotia, Athens in Attica, Pylos in Messenia and perhaps a kingdom (though a Mycenaean settlement has yet to be found there) in Laconia. The origins of Mycenaean civilisation are obscure: for some decades it was thought to have derived from the Minoan, though now Crete is thought only to have moderated and refined an independent and already vigorous culture; the prevalent theory is that Mycenaean civilisation was introduced by invaders coming from the East, across Anatolia and to Greece via Troy around 1900—1800 BC. But just as the very notion of outstanding Bronze Age civilisations in Greece and Crete did not exist until Schliemann in 1876 and Evans in 1900 revealed fable as fact, so soon serious consideration will have to be given to the startling possibility of ancient Britain playing a critical role: fresh radio-carbon and tree ring dating has established that Stonehenge, which bears marked similarities in construction to Mycenae, is in fact *older* than Mycenae.

The world that Homer describes in his epics is the Mycenaean world, the tales and oral history of an expansive 400 years dramatically focused on the Trojan expedition and encapsulated within the 10-year span of the *Iliad* and the following 10-year span of the *Odyssey*. Many of the great figures of Greek literature — Theseus, Jason, Kadmos, as well as Agamemnon — were born of this period, as was the Greek language itself and the elements of later Greek religion. To the extent that Western civilisation has developed from that of Greece, it is to Mycenae, if no further, that we must look for the foundations of 3500 years of culture.

The Lion Gate

From the village you can walk the final kilometre up a gradual hill to the citadel. You enter the citadel by passing through the *Lion Gate* (1), so named for the massive triangular relief over the lintel of two rampant lions on either side of a downward tapering column probably once surmounted by a double-headed axe, reminiscent of Knossos. The Cyclopean unmortared stones making up the adjoining walls are cleanly cut and well fitted into place, and the execution of the relief above all adds up to the intended impression of architectural mastery and cultural achievement.

The grave circle

Forty feet in from the Lion Gate is the *grave circle* (2) originally excavated by Schliemann. In the last shaft he excavated, he found the well-preserved body of a high-ranking man who appeared to have died in his thirties. He wore a gold mask. Schliemann removed it, found the eyes, the mouth, the flesh still intact, and sent a telegram to the King of Hellenes: "I have gazed upon the face of Agamemnon".

Beehive tombs

In fact, the actual burial spot of Agamemnon is not known and the mask, now dated with some accuracy, must have belonged to a still more ancient personage. Apart from the shaft Schliemann excavated, there is the beehive-shaped *Tomb of Agamemnon,* also known as the Treasury of Atreus, and while the possibility is open that it could be the former, it is certainly not the latter. It was Pausanias who passed on the misinformation that the tholos was Atreus' treasury, for by his time (2nd C. AD) such tombs had been plundered; only in the late 19th C. was a tholos tomb found near Athens containing remains of the dead and so confirming their use. At the burial ceremony, the mourners laid the body—if he were a king—on a carpet of gold, with vessels of food and flagons of wine around him. Weapons of war were added too. Rams and other animals were slayed within the tholos itself, while outside, beyond the great bronze doors, the horses that had drawn the funeral chariot were slaughtered within the dromos — the cut leading to the tomb — before this was filled in with

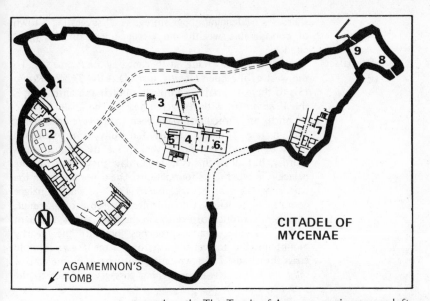

CITADEL OF
MYCENAE

AGAMEMNON'S
TOMB

stones and earth. The Tomb of Agamemnon is on your left as you come up the road out of the village and are approaching the citadel. Passing along the *dromos* running into the side of a hill, you enter an enormous, cool, dark interior where all echoes converge with great force at the centre. Looking back at the doorway (the bronze doors long since plundered), notice the curved *lintel* above it. It's about 30 ft long, 16 ft wide and 3 ft high, weighs 120 tons and is made from a single piece of limestone. The Mycenaeans put this in place around 1300 BC, without aid of jacks, pulleys or other mechanical inventions. All the stones making up the curved interior surface are beautifully fitted and smooth. Closer to the citadel and to the right of the road are the so-called tombs of Klytemnestra and Aegisthes, both smaller than the tomb of Agamemnon, though the *Tomb of Klytemnestra* is of superior workmanship and so probably of later date, while the poorly constructed *Tomb of Aegisthes* is earlier (c1470 BC).

Mycenae "rich in gold" was Homer's phrase, and he need not have been referring only to the panoply of dead kings: near the tombs of Klytemnestra and Aegisthes are **Houses** the *remains of merchants' houses*, the House of the Oil Merchant with a dozen rooms on its lowest floor alone, the House of the Sphinxes and that of the Shields (the names derive from the objects discovered within) found with carved ivory inlays for furniture, fragments of frescoes, fine pottery, vases of serpentine, Linear B tablets recording a variety of spices for scenting the oils and, architecturally, staircases evidencing upper storeys — all suggesting a town of considerable wealth and elegance beneath the royal citadel.

The palace

Back atop the citadel at its centre is the *Palace* (3). To the west of the open *Great Court* (4) is the *Throne Room* (5); to the east , passing through a porch and anteroom, is the *Megaron* (6) with its sacred hearth. The small rooms to its north are thought to have been the *private apartments* and in one of them, rather fancifully, a red-stuccoed bathtub is said to be the very place of Agamemnon's murder. But all of this is in broad daylight as much of the palace is levelled to its foundations. The panorama from the palace or the *House of Columns* (7) — a smaller palace complex — provides a complementary sense of grandeur, and there's a touch of evil too in the associations, the giant stones, as the citadel crouches beneath the nearby mountains. But to feel the intensity of menace you should cross the citadel to its western point where, by the narrow *sally port* (8), a twisting, falling passageway leads to the *secret cistern* (9).

The secret cistern

The first time I came to Mycenae I tried to find my way inside, lighting one match after another, but the feeble illumination was swallowed by the darkness. The second time I brought a flashlight. Where daylight ends, just a stone's throw from the entrance, you turn left and descend the stairs into time-erasing blackness. There are no pitfalls and you can guide yourself by running your hands along the damp stone walls pressing in from either side. Only claustrophobia and the growing conviction that this will be the moment, after thousands of years, that this ancient engineering marvel will collapse and entomb you as surely as Agamemnon need deter you. The vaulted passageway turns right for a last long descent to a high-roofed cistern deep underground, well beyond the citadel walls, the guarantee of a water supply at times of siege.

Argive Heraion

A path runs 3 kms south along the mountainside and then east from Mycenae to the Argive Heraion, or Sanctuary of Hera, queen of the Olympian gods, which stands upon a promontory by the village of Konika with a fine view down to the Argolikos Gulf. The extensive ruins date from Archaic and Classical times, though the site had been in use much earlier than that. It was here that the Greek chiefs gathered to pledge loyalty to Agamemnon in the great expedition against Troy. Pausanias describes the chryselephantine cult statue of Hera, famous for its grandeur and beauty, which stood (but no more) in the New Temple in his day. He also mentions a gold peacock dedicated by Hadrian and Nero's golden crown and purple robe, testimony to the longevity of the cult. The New Temple is at the centre of the site, the Old Temple, believed to be the first example in the Peloponnese of a temple built of stone as well as wood, to the north east. The Heraion is rarely visited today and so can be unusually enjoyed in some solitude.

Argos The prosperous but otherwise unexciting town of Argos (from Corinth 48 kms) occupies the site of the ancient city and is possibly the oldest continuously inhabited town in Europe. It does have a lively market and a good museum, some excavations revealing its Greek and Roman past, and a fine medieval kastro cobbled together by Byzantines, Franks, Venetians and Turks on more ancient foundations.

Tiryns At Argos the road forks, the left fork leading to Nafplion (12 kms) and, 4 kms before Nafplion, Tiryns, a considerable Mycenaean citadel though always subject either to Mycenae itself or to Argos. This is one of the two reputed birthplaces (Thebes the other) of Herakles and served as the base of operations for many of his labours. The citadel surmounts a hill which rises like an island from the surrounding plain, the sea only a kilometre or two distant. Though lacking the imposing position and atmospherics of Mycenae, Tiryns offers a better preserved and more extensive palace complex, surrounded by walls famous as the finest specimens of Mycenaean military architecture.

Nafplion With Mycenae, Tiryns and Epidavros all within easy reach, NAFPLION (Nauplia) makes a good centre for travelling around this part of the Peloponnese. It's a lovely and stylish resort, hugging the base of a steep headland atop which the great Venetian fortress of Palamidi gazes out across the Argolikos Gulf. This was the residence of the new King of the Hellenes during the first few years of independence, and so the better hotels have an old European elegance while the placid harbour front is set with tables for afternoon teas and views of the diminutive kastro on the close-by island of Bourdzi. The climbing streets are overhung with iron balconies overgrown with flowers, with always a delicate combination of salt and scent in the air. There is good swimming off the West Mole towards the point of the peninsula.

Mycenaean collection The museum, on the upper floors of an early 18th C. Venetian building, is one of three in Greece (Athens and Heraklion are the others) with an important Mycenaean collection. On the first floor are stelai from Grave Circle B at Mycenae (a grave circle found outside the citadel), one with what is possibly the oldest bas-relief in Greece; pottery from sites around the Argolid, showing marked Minoan influences; and most remarkable (also unique), a complete suit of bronze Mycenaean armour. On the second floor there is a Mycenaean helmet from Tiryns.

Tolon and Asine

The beautiful bay of Tolon, now a popular resort, is 10 kms behind Nafplion. On the rocky headland above are the remains of prehistoric Asine, with Helladic houses, Hellenistic ramparts, Roman baths and Venetian fortifications.

Epidavros

Forty-one kms north of either Nafplion or Tolon, on the north coast of the Argolid, is the Sanctuary of EPIDAVROS. A new highway now runs from the Isthmus of Corinth permitting direct and speedy access from Athens and also the possibility of touring right round the Argolid without retracing your route. The site is most famous for its theatre, the best preserved and most beautiful in Greece. During the last two weekends of June and the first three weekends of July the celebrated festival of drama at the theatre ensures that Epidavros (Epidaurus) is still more easily reached by the special boats that are laid on from Piraeus.

Annual drama festival

The sanctuary was once a religious centre and fashionable spa associated with the cult of Asklepios. Set in a broad and (tourists permitting) lonely valley, it rivals in extent the sanctuaries of Olympia and Delphi, though its interest for the layman lies entirely in its theatre. To Henry Miller, "Mycenae, like Epidaurus, swims in light. But Epidaurus is all open, exposed, irrevocably devoted to the spirit. Mycenae folds in upon itself, like a fresh-cut navel, dragging its glory down into the bowels of the earth where the bats and lizards feed upon it gloatingly. Epidaurus is a bowl from which to drink the pure spirit; the blue of the sky is in it and the stars and the winged creatures who fly between, scattering song and melody".

THE CENTRAL PELOPONNESE

Taking the southwards road out of Argos with the hilltop medieval kastro on your right you follow the coastline for a few miles and then abruptly turn west into the Ktenias range, carried aloft by steep, thrilling but well-engineered hairpin turns, the Argolikos Gulf across to Nafplion a sheet of brilliant blue below. During the descent through pines on the other side of the range a road sign announces that this is Arcadia and you are to enjoy it.

Tripolis But the flat, monotonous, treeless plain on which Tripolis squats, wracked by the extremes of punishing heat and violent hail and thunderstorms in summer, enclosed within an amphitheatre of barren mountains, is anything but Arcadian. A modern manufacturing town, noted for its tanneries and carpet factories, Tripolis (60 kms from Argos) is the communications centre of the Peloponnese. Three attractive plateias enlivened by cafes belie the atrocities that were committed here in 1821 by the besieging Greeks during the first months of their revolt against Ottoman rule. Previous failed revolts led to barbarous retaliation by the Turks; this time the Greeks determined to kill every Turk in the Peloponnese, and here within the now vanished walls of this fortified capital of the Pasha of the Morea the Turks made their final stand when all of the remaining Peloponnese had been ripped from their grasp. While supposedly negotiating with the inhabitants for their safety, the Greek brigand-general Kolokotronis suddenly led his men in a storm of the town: in two terrible days they put ten thousand Turks to death, often cutting off their arms and legs and roasting their living bodies over fires.

Tegea Eight kms southeast of Tripolis at the village of Alea are the scattered remains of ancient Tegea, once the largest city in the plain and an early enemy of Sparta. There's a museum in which are gathered finds from the site. Fifteen kms north of Tripolis are the ruins of **Mantinea** Mantinea, age-long rival of Tegea. During the Peloponnesian War, Tegea, which had been subjected to Sparta nearly two centuries before, fought on the side of its masters against Athenian-allied Mantinea. Mantinea was again to become a front-line state when the Theban general Epaminondas built the walls (the ones now visible) as part of his Arcadian strategy against a Spartan revival following Sparta's defeat at his hands at Leuktra in 371 BC. Epaminondas was in fact killed here at the moment of triumph in his last battle against Sparta in 362 BC.

Megalopolis

The perfection of the theatre at Epidavros rightly attracts the many, but for the few there is the theatre and buried city of MEGALOPOLIS, 34 kms southwest of Tripolis. The site is barely excavated and infrequently visited and looks like a painting of an idealized Arcadia hung in a Paris salon. This was in fact a planned city, built in 371 BC by Epaminondas as a buffer between recently defeated but always threatening Sparta to the southeast and the Arcadian states, of which it was meant to be the federal capital. But the city never took root and by 194 BC it was destroyed and left to be covered by earth, grass and trees.

The theatre

When you arrive you see an attendant sitting on a chair in a field in the sun; you can see nothing of the city. He smiles, pulls out his one and only plan of the site, and in Greek, or broken English, French or German, takes you on a private guided tour, leading you first around a hill and, *voila*, set into the side of it is the largest amphitheatre in Greece, built to hold 20,000. Only the first half-dozen rows have been excavated. The rest of the theatre climbs the hillside as a series of ridges under the grass, with a crescent of tall pines occupying the upper circle seats. The acoustics are still marvellous. When you take your seat with the trees at the top you can hear very clearly the normal conversation of people on the stage below.

And spread out before is the rest of the city. Immediately behind the stage is the Thersilion or federal assembly hall which had a capacity of 16,000. The attendant points to a row of cypresses, an electricity pylon, leading your eye to ridges and mounds of earth across the river where stoas and temples once stood, where indeed their foundations, perhaps more, are still in place below the cloak of a few feet of earth. It's a lovely and relaxing place; birds chirp, pines creak in the breeze, otherwise not a sound and it may be an hour before another visitor comes.

Karitaina

Some of the loveliest countryside in the Peloponnese lies west of Megalopolis: rich, grassy valleys, dark pine-clad hills, cypress groves and irregular mountain outlines. About 16 kms along the road there's a steep hill with a village wrapped round like a shawl beneath the Frankish kastro at the peak. This is Karitaina, a part of medieval Greece, looking like a hill village in the South of France, or even like a Tibetan lamasery. It's reached by a switchback road which finally brings you amidst houses attached to the hillside like clams, where old men with enormous waxed moustachios puff along the alleyways to meet at one of the two cafes by the statue in the village centre, where the view of the surrounding plain is magnificent and the feeling is one of being cut off totally from the 20th century.

Coming away from Karitaina you now start along a mountain road with a deep gorge to the right, the crystal-green Alpheios splashing along its rocky bed. You pass through a succession of beautiful villages, like Andritsaina for instance, where more moustachioed old men sit about in chairs watching the younger rakes drinking ouzo, playing backgammon. A still more mountainous road cuts off after the church in Andritsaina and bounces you upwards to the wild spot where incredibly the Greeks built a temple to Apollo. This is VASSAI (Bassae), and like Delphi it soars above a primitive landscape; a temple of sombre grey stone upon a mountain surrounded by mountains, small goat-herding villages in the distance, the sound of bells and whistling and dogs barking their flocks in, a blast of wind against your eardrums.

Nearly 4000 feet above sea level on a mountain scored by ravines (*vassai* in Greek, hence the modern name), the Temple of Apollo Epikourios is missing its roof, while its superb frieze is now in the British Museum, but the general structure is well preserved due to the temple's inaccessibility. Built by Iktinos, architect of the Parthenon and almost certainly at a later date (probably 420 BC), the unusually aligned temple, facing north, with its outer Doric columns is particularly interesting for its use of three-face Ionic columns within and, making its first appearance in architectural history, at least one Corinthian column (the capital no longer extant) at the sanctuary end of the cella.

Starting in 776 BC, five midsummer days were set aside every four years for the Games at OLYMPIA (101 kms from Megalopolis). Contestants came from all over Greece, and eventually from throughout the Mediterranean; hostilities ceased, arms were forbidden and athletes competed peacefully for the highest honour, the olive wreath. Social and even diplomatic intercourse were also features of the gathering, with the evenings taken up in philosophical debate, music and song, feasting and the signing of treaties. Initially the Games had a religious content, but increasingly they became more secular and open to commercialism and corruption, especially under Roman influence. The absurd Nero once came and entered the lists, the judges prudently declaring him the victor in every competition, even when, as in the case of the chariot race, the Emperor was thrown and failed to finish.

Andritsaina

Vassai

Temple of Apollo Epikourios

Olympia

Its history

89

Nero also imposed upon the Games contests in singing and playing on the lyre. During his interminable performances he would permit no one to leave, so that men feigned death in order to escape. Those Games contaminated by Nero, however, were struck off the sacred register after the Emperor's death.

The Games continued here for a thousand years in all and were only wound up at the command of the Roman Emperor Theodosios I, whose new-found Christian sensibility objected to these "pagan rites". The site itself was then brought to ruin by succeeding emperors, barbarian invasion, earthquake and the rising of the river. Excavations were undertaken in the 19th C. by the French and Germans, and it was Baron de Coubertin who initiated the modern Olympic Games in 1896.

Legendary origins

The athletic contests probably developed from the funeral games of a local hero, Pelops (whence Peloponnese). It was prophesied that King Oinomaos would be killed by the man who married his daughter. So the King challenged each suitor to a chariot race and stabbed his rival in the back before reaching the finishing line. Thirteen suitors were killed in this way and Oinomaos was already talking of building a temple of skulls by the time Pelops came along. Pelops' lover, Poseidon, gave him a team of fast horses, but not satisfied with that, Pelops also replaced the lynchpin from the King's chariot with one of wax. Needless to say, the King took a fall and was killed while Pelops got the girl. It's not how you play the game that counts, but whether you win or lose.

Temples of Zeus and Hera

The museums

The major ruins are the foundations of the Temple of Zeus with its columns tumbled to one side, the Temple of Hera and the various Treasuries of the Greek states. The New Museum contains artefacts found on the site; the Old Museum displaying the outstanding statues from the east and west pediments of the Temple of Zeus, the Nike of Paionios, and the statue of Hermes carrying the infant Dionysos by Praxiteles (c340 BC).

The pleasure of the site is in its leafy, cool, pastoral setting, but if you come in the summer heat you'll probably get only dust (though the Games were indeed held in August). And even in springtime when the pines are smelling fresh, the number of visitors disturbs the tranquillity of the spot. (As recently as the late 1950s only 500 tourists came here each year; now the figure is over a million.) I confess I have never been more put off by a ruin as at Olympia, partly because of the crowds, but partly too because the site even in its own time was a monument instead of a place to be lived in, and monuments are always

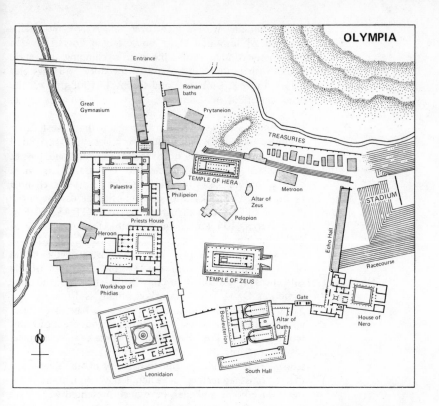

OLYMPIA

Entrance

Roman baths

Great Gymnasium

Prytaneion

TREASURIES

Palaestra

TEMPLE OF HERA

Metroon

STADIUM

Philipeion

Altar of Zeus

Priests House

Pelopion

Heroon

Echo Hall

Racecourse

Workshop of Phidias

TEMPLE OF ZEUS

Gate

N

Bouleuterion

Altar of Oaths

House of Nero

Leonidaion

South Hall

Stadium   more boring than people. But there is the Stadium, approached from the Temple of Hera through a tunnel. Now this seems real. The starting and finishing lines, the judge's stand and the dedication to Demeter are still evident. You can make out the rows of seats under their covering of earth and grass. You can run back and forth along the length of the track, cheer from the sidelines, wait for the judge to clear his throat. Here at least there is action. You can get the feel of the place and play it all out (though purists should do so stark naked).

Driving out of Olympia on the rough road to Lalas you climb into the mountains and get a good view of the ancient site below. Beyond this you are wandering about in a Peloponnese which could have been like this one hundred **Mountain villages** years ago. The villages are isolated; some of them are plain and rough, like Foloi and Koumanis on the edges of a great forest with a fern-covered floor. Here it comes almost as a shock to see men working with timber instead of herding goats. Other villages are like flowers on the mountainsides. Labia is such a village, in a niche between

91

two mountains with a view over valleys and mountains beyond. Whitewashed stone houses, blue doors, wooden balconies, red-tiled roofs, the houses climbing up gentle slopes with terraces above and below thick with figs and grapes, flowers, fruit trees and shrubs. In 1948 this was the headquarters of the Communist forces in the Peloponnese.

Pirgos Had you instead followed the main road west from Olympia you would find yourself in Pirgos (22 kms) a dull market town. Travelling north from here you would pass at **Frankish castle** some distance the Frankish castle of Chlemoutsi on a high cape with fine views in one direction across the channel to the island of Zakynthos, in the other across the entire **Patras** plain of Elis. The road carries on to PATRAS (96 kms from Pirgos, 135 kms from Corinth), the largest city of the Peloponnese and western gateway to Greece. I have left Greece from here in sadness, and have arrived here full of anticipation; but with the possible exception of the **Head of St** gold-encased head of St Andrew in the church of the same **Andrew** name on Odos Trion Navarkon, there is little here of particular interest. The church is said to have been built on the site of Andrew's martyrdom and the head was returned here by Pope Paul VI from Rome as an ecumenical gesture towards the Orthodox Church after 900 years of schism. It is the civility and generosity of the inhabitants that is most appealing, as when I have bought food for the voyage home and then have been presented with more as a gift: the heart is touched, the separation so much harder, the need to return and somehow to repay so much stronger. Patras, characteristically, is the one **Carnival** city in Greece which still enjoys its pre-Lenten carnival in the traditional, colourful manner, unlike Athens, for example, where the season has become no more than an excuse for knocking strangers over the head with plastic hammers.

Kalavrita From mountain villages like Labia or from coastal Patras, the roads towards Kalavrita (95 kms from Patras), wind higher, the mountains now capped with snow even early in June. This is a resort town, summer and especially winter, and though not very pretty itself its situation is marvellous. (In 1943 the Germans here massacred 1436 males over the age of 15 and burnt the town. The schools have since been endowed by the government of the German Federal Republic.) It lies in a valley which when approached from the south is broad, well-cultivated, with waves of wheat along its floor and brilliant spots of poppies and jonquils.

When approached from the north, the road slips through a powerful gorge which cuts directly through the mountains, massive outcrops of worn, rounded, oddly-shaped rock shoved to either side like unwanted dough. But rather than take the road, treat yourself to a ride on the Kalavrita Railway, engineered in 1885-95, which creeps up the gorge, sometimes pushed, sometimes pulled by little 75cm gauge diesels, along gradients as much as 1 in 7 from Diakofto on the Corinthian Gulf.

The gorge and the rack-and-pinion railway

The Monastery of Megaspeleion is 10 kms north on the road out of Kalavrita, or a long donkey ride out of the gorge at Zaklorou, one of the railway stops. The old monastery was destroyed by fire in the 1930s and the new one, built into the cliff face, looks like a cross between a hotel and a prison. Nevertheless, it's worth trudging up here for the view over the gorge and the valley beyond. Inside is the Treasury containing sacred relics, including a miraculous ikon, 9th to 11th C. Gospels, the heads of the monks Theodore and Symeon, founders of the monastery, and assorted hands of martyrs and saints, while hanging out the windows monks in their underwear call to one another or brush their beards into the wind.

Megaspeleion monastery

Seven kms south of Kalavrita is Agia Lavra, the monastery where Bishop Germanos was first to raise the standard of revolt on 21 March 1821.

Agia Lavra monastery

The National Highway from Athens runs along the littoral of the northern Peloponnese from Corinth to Patras, a good fast road for those in a hurry, but the older road meandering along the coastline from village to village past vineyards and olive groves, cypresses and willows, is more pleasant. Coming from Patras, or after the descent from Kalavrita to the coast near Diakofto, you can cross the Gulf of Corinth at Rion by car ferry, landing at Andirrion on the other side (see *Road to Delphi* chapter).

Along the Gulf of Corinth

From Diakofto, 41 kms east is Xilokastro, a major resort with a sandy beach and camping site, the mountains behind almost tumbling into the gulf. Another 13 kms towards Corinth is Kiato, the name derived from Sikyon, one of the most ancient of Greek cities famous for its cultivation of the arts and extolled by Homer as "a lovely and fruitful city, adapted to every recreation". The original settlement was on the shore, but following its destruction by the Macedonians in 303 BC it was rebuilt on an acropolis 3 kms inland from which there are fine views. There is a two-level gymnasium with fountain and, the most obvious feature of the site, a large 3rd C. BC theatre cut into the hillside.

Xilokastro

Sikyon

THE SOUTHERN PELOPONNESE

I was not expecting the excitement that grew within me on my way towards SPARTA (Sparti). Thucydides said, "Posterity will find it difficult to believe its power corresponded to its fame", as unlike Athens Sparta made little effort to glorify itself with monuments, and I was prepared to be suitably dismissive. Defended by a great wedge of mountains, the Parnon range to the east, the Taigetos to the west, the Laconian plain narrows to a spear point at its northern end. The 63-kilometre road from Tripolis runs through a long defile through Parnon and hesitates along a ridge with spectacular views of mountains all around. At this moment, as the road begins to twist down into the plain, you realise that Thucydides was not a man for describing superlative scenery, nor did he care to suggest the mystery of penetrating these mountain walls as though entering a secret garden, this extensive and bountiful Laconian plain shimmering with olive groves and thick with the scent of oranges, watered by the Evrotas, and cooled by late afternoon breezes as the sun sets early beyond the high Taigetos. At no place in Greece have I so suddenly and completely appreciated the strategic location and hence the power of an ancient city.

The Laconian plain

Homeric Sparta

In Homeric legend, this was the home of Menelaos, husband of Helen, brother of Agamemnon of Mycenae. According to the *Iliad* Menelaos exercised control or influence over most of the Greek principalities, though archaeologists — perhaps only through oversight — have failed to turn up evidence of a settlement here comparable to Mycenae at the same period. In any case, Menelaos is likely to have been based at Amyklai, 8 kms south of Sparta, where the not very illuminating remains of a Sanctuary of Hyakinthos (accidentally killed by his friend Apollo — a flower grew on the spot) have been discovered. But as with Classical Sparta, the true fortifications of the Mycenaean settlement here were probably the mountains themselves.

Spartan character and history

The latter-day Spartans, however, did not look back upon the Mycenaean inhabitants of the Laconian plain as their ancestors. The Dorians, a tribe which had previously lived in northern Greece on the edge of the civilised world, overran the Mycenaean cities of the Peloponnese in two waves, the first about 1200 BC, the second about two hundred years later. Whether the Spartans were pure Dorians or some mixture of conquered and conquerors cannot be ascertained, but the Spartans themselves claimed a pure descent from the rugged newcomers, spoke their dialect and lived by their austere traditions. Good conversation, particularly the sharply witty though not ungraceful retort, leavened their hard lives. Plutarch records that one Spartan, being asked to go hear a man who exactly counterfeited the voice of a nightingale, answered, "Sir, I have heard the nightingale itself". Nor, despite their restraint, were they without fine poetry and sculpture or mastery in the art of pottery. Sparta was even infamous for the freedom of its women and did not acquire its reputation for philistinism and repression until the 6th C. when state anxiety strangled culture at home as surely as its military juggernaut crushed the real or imaginary threats of external rivals.

Sparta's problem was that as a land-based power locked away in the Peloponnese she failed to take advantage of the expanding commercial horizons which were being exploited by 6th and 5th C. maritime states like Athens. Agriculture was the basis of her conservative economy. The use of a freely-exchangable currency was forbidden. Territory was the measure of wealth and power. The inner core of Spartan villages came to an accommodation with the peripheral villages of the Laconian plain, the perioikoi ('dwellers around'), whom they dominated but declined to conquer. This master-client relationship was later extended where convenient to other states in the Peloponnese. The Spartans kept to the duties of their estates and of government, leaving commerce and crafts to the perioikoi, who lived as freemen (though without voting rights in the mother city).

Perioikoi

As Sparta's needs and ambitions grew, so necessarily did her hunger for land. Towards the end of the 8th C. BC Sparta attacked the fertile plain of Messenia across the Taigetos to the west, then moved north against Tegea (c600 BC), and finally defeated Argos (494 BC), her only serious rival in the Peloponnese. The peoples she defeated and did not supervise as client states she reduced to the condition of helots, enslaved populations whose only function was to cultivate the Spartan estates now too extensive for personal attention.

Helots

But Sparta was caught up in a vicious circle. With a population jealous of its own privileges and never exceeding 10,000, instead of extending rights, sharing prosperity and evolving towards a more liberal society as were many other Greek states, the fear that one of her 'allies' might prefer greater independence, or that the vastly outnumbering helot masses might revolt — as did the Messenians in the 7th and again in the 5th C. — led her into oppressive reaction on the one hand and on the other still further

The Messenian revolt

95

aggression abroad to acquire the resources needed to hold down what she already brutally possessed.

The 'reforms' of Lykourgos which put power in the hands of a gerontocracy may have come either immediately before or immediately after the Messenian revolt, that is, either in anticipation of efficiently governing an extending land empire or in fear of losing it. Their effect was to repress individual initiative and vagaries. Weak and deformed children were left to die on Taigetos; the stronger surviving males being taken from their mothers at seven to be educated in camps where privacy was denied, flogging employed to develop fortitude, and stealing encouraged towards the attainment of self-reliance. At the age of 20 these young men joined the army or perhaps the Krypteia, the secret police who from time to time were let loose on the helots. From these few thousand highly disciplined Spartans was forged the most powerful army of pre-Hellenistic Greece.

The mountains magnificently impose and provide the reminder of Spartan power even if their own lack of monuments, as Thucydides said, do not. But the harsh reality of that power is lost amidst the luxuriance of this peaceful plain and it is with some satisfaction that one scuffles through this banal, provincial modern town and thinks how nicely it commemorates the anonymity Spartans strove for.

The modern town, in fact, occupies only the southern third of the full extent of the ancient city. A short walk northwards through olive groves brings you to the 66-foot high acropolis surrounded by the remains of Byzantine walls. Just to the west, built into the side of a hill, is a 2nd or 1st C. BC theatre, second in size only to that at Megalopolis, but unimpressive as most of its masonry was put to use in the building of Mistra. Leaving the acropolis by the north gate and turning right along this side of the Evrotas brings you to some remains of the city walls, a feature of Sparta's decline, as in her heyday she claimed that her fighting men were her best defence. About a kilometre further along this course is the sanctuary of Artemis Orthia, where Spartan boys were flogged. The Romans, perverse where the Spartans were merely brutal, built a theatre here for spectators to witness what had by then become a folk entertainment. Back in town, the museum contains a marble bust of Leonidas, commander of the Spartan troops at Thermopylae, and some Roman mosaics.

Mistra Six kms to the west of Sparta and hard beside the flank of Taigetos, the ruined Byzantine city of MISTRA ascends a steep hill crowned at the summit by a Frankish fortress. Fascinating in itself, Mistra is not least worth visiting for its enchanting position overlooking the Laconian plain. The fortress was built by William de Villehardouin in 1249 to protect medieval Sparta from marauding Slavs coming down from Taigetos and after several alternations in ownership became firmly Byzantine in the early 14th C. By this time the plain had been deserted by its inhabitants who clustered beneath the citadel for security, and for the next hundred years and more the city flourished as the seat of the Despotate of the Morea — governed by either sons or brothers of the emperor in Constantinople — and nurtured the last Byzantine renaissance. The philospher Plethon, rediscoverer of Plato, lived here during the first half of the 15th C. Constantine XI Paleologos was Despot of Mistra from 1443 to 1448 before succeeding to the Imperial throne at Constantinople.

The Lower Town Entering the gate to the Lower Town and turning right, the Metropolis, built in 1309, stands in a spacious court from which there is an agreeable view across the valley of the Evrotas. Along with the paintings and intricately carved marble ikonostasis inside, also interesting is the double-headed eagle in the floor, possibly commemorating the coronation of the last emperor, Constantine XI. The museum, containing decorative fragments from the churches, is next door. A bit further uphill is the Vrontikion, monastery and cultural centre, and burial place of the Despots. Of the two churches within this complex, the Aphentiko, furthest on, is outstanding for its interior proportions and boldly coloured frescoes depicting the Miracles of Christ. Had you turned left at the entrance gate you would after some distance along the path have come to the Monastery of the Perivleptos and its 14th C. church with excellent frescoes and a Pantokrator glowering down from the dome. But it's most convenient to stop here on the return journey down.

The Upper Town Passing through the Monemvasia Gate into the Upper Town you come upon the Palace of the Despots, a rare and impressive example of a Byzantine civic building. Though roofless and crumbling, its facade now spare of ornamentation, its vast hall and gaping windows convey a grandeur appropriate to the surrounding landscape. Left from the gate is the Pantanassa, in plan similar to the Aphentiko but more slender in its proportions and containing some of the finest examples of late Byzantine fresco. The church belongs to a convent, the nuns now the only inhabitants and guardians of a city which once had a population of 40,000. A breathtaking view of Mistra spilling back down the mountainside is the reward of those who sweat their way up to the fortified summit.

Often the humblest village in Greece will erect a proud statue to the local boy who went away and made good, and in the same way, a short walk down the road at the top end of the present village of Mistra, a statue has been put up to Constantine XI Paleologos. On a May night in 1453 a crescent of fire embraced the Land Walls of Constantinople as the overwhelming army of Sultan Mehmet prepared for the morning kill. This last emperor, named Constantine like the first, gathered his followers in Agia Sophia, the most magnificent church in Christendom, to celebrate a final mass amidst sobs and wailings and cries of *Kyrie eleison*. Calling "God forbid that I should live an Emperor without an Empire! As my city falls, I will fall with it!" he rode out against the Turks and was immediately cut down. Around the plateia, its plane tree and spring, are several small tavernas and kafeneions where you can refresh yourself after a hot day's climbing with a meal and some wine, Byzantium lingering in the evening light.

The Langada Pass to Kalamata

The steep and twisting road from Sparta to Kalamata (63 kms) cuts by way of the 5000-foot high Langada Pass through the Taigetos range, providing some of the most spectacular mountain views in Greece. Goat-footed nymphs and the goddess Artemis were said to frequent this high-alpine country.

KALAMATA is known for its silk and its olives, and is flanked by good beaches. The modern city was constructed by the French in 1829 after they landed 14,000 troops here to encourage the army of Ibrahim Pasha, which was assisting Turkish efforts at crushing the Greek revolt, to return to Egypt. But it lacks French charm, and Greek charm too for that matter. The Messenian plain extends northwards, but the modern town of Messeni just to the west of Kalamata is in no way related to the ancient object

Messene

of Spartan rapaciousness. That site, now partly occupied by the attractive village of Mavromati, lies 20 kms to the north. The colossal walls of Messene, once encompassing the city's farmlands within their 10-kilometre length, are the most complete extant from the Hellenic period. They too owe their construction in 369 BC to Epaminondas and his anti-Spartan strategy (see Megalopolis and Mantinea). The foundations of a fine temple have very recently been excavated on the site which wraps about the southwest slope of Mt Ithome, 2600 ft high, where from its summit Messenian helots, during their final rebellion against Spartan humiliation, held their besieging oppressors at bay for five years, from 464 to 459 BC. The view from here takes in most of the Messenian plain, rich in cotton, wheat, dates and bananas.

Battle of
Navarino

Fifty-one kms west of Kalamata is PYLOS, doubly famous for the Palace of Nestor and, under the more familiar name of Navarino, for the spectacular destruction of the Turkish and Egyptian fleets at the hands of the combined British, French and Russian squadrons under the command of Admiral Codrington. Without the loss of a single one of their own 26 ships, the European allies on 20 October, 1827 sailed into the bay and sank 53 enemy ships, killed 16,000 men and, by breaking the Ottoman Empire's control of the seas around Greece, ensured Greek independence. The magnificent natural harbour closed to the Ionian Sea by the long and undulating island of Sphakteria, the surrounding pine woods, a Turkish castle and good swimming, make Pylos the most pleasant place to stay when exploring this area.

Palace of
Nestor

Nestor's Palace is in fact about 15 kms up the coast from modern Pylos which sits at the southern end of the bay. The panorama befits a great king, and Nestor, according to Homer, provided the Greeks with their second largest fleet in their expedition against Troy. In searching for his father Odysseus, Telemachos, in company with Athena (disguised as Mentor), was received here with generous hospitality. "The travellers now came to Pylos, where they found the people on the sea-beach sacrificing jet-black bulls to Poseidon, Lord of the Earthquake, god of the sable locks. There sat Nestor with his sons, while their followers around them were piercing meat with skewers or roasting it in preparation for the banquet. But as soon as they caught sight of the strangers they all made a move in their direction waving their hands in welcome, and beckoning the newcomers to join them. Nestor's son, Peisistratos, who was the first to reach them, took them both by the hand and gave them places at the banquet on downy fleeces spread over the sandy beach".

The best preserved of all Mycenaean palaces, and now largely under a protective roof, the walls of Pylos still stand 3 ft high over a considerable area. Excavations under the direction of the American Carl Blegen took place in 1939 and from 1952 to 1965, revealing vast rooms with lofty, probably 11-foot high ceilings, brilliant frescoes (now in the museum 2 kms away in Chora), and numerous

Linear B tablets, the first to be found on the Greek mainland.

Venetian
castle Worth the journey 11 kms from modern Pylos in the opposite direction is the great Venetian castle at Methoni, its vast walls mingling with the sea, a way-station for pilgrims to the Holy Land and merchants engaged in the Levantine trade, towers and crenellations wavering in the heat, a dream-image of the East.

Mani The road south from Kalamata to Areopolis winds along the ruggedly beautiful western coast of Mani, the central peninsula of the Peloponnese formed by the arching backbone of the Taigetos which plunges finally into the sea at Cape Matapan, famous for wrecks and feared by sailors for centuries.

The peninsula is traditionally divided into Outer Mani, less mountainous and relieved by the large plain of olives, figs and grain running down from Kalamata to Kardamyli, and Inner Mani which begins just above Areopolis, rocky and treeless, mountain pressed against mountain, where villages grapple seemingly inaccessible ledges and stone towerhouses, built in defence against vendettas, accentuate the forbidding but exciting landscape. The Maniots claim direct descent from the ancient Spartans and are a stern though hospitable people.

Its history Certainly, with the decline of Sparta the Maniots organised themselves into the Confederation of Free-Laconians, whose independence was recognised even by Augustus after he had subjected the rest of the Peloponnese to Rome. The great Byzantine general Belisaurius reported only pagans when he landed in Mani in AD 333, and the Maniots as a whole probably only converted to Christianity during the reign of the Emperor Basil I (867-886), though four churches dating back to the 6th, possibly to the 5th C. have been identified. The Slavs made only minor inroads and the Turks had to content themselves with nominal allegiance of the principal clan chieftan, the Bey of the Mani. Petrobey Mavromichalis, the last such title-holder, ensured his place in the pantheon of Greek heroes by leading his people in rebellion against the Turks in 1821, his home town of Tzimova being renamed Areopolis, city of the war-god Ares, at the outset of the revolt. The scarce soil of Mani never afforded much livelihood; the attraction of Mani was as a last rugged sanctuary from where Greeks could resist foreign invasion. With that purpose gone after independence the region suffered from depopulation and improverishment which is only now being reversed as the Greek government is encouraging the first trickle of tourism into the area. Anyone wishing to familiarise himself with this least explored part of Greece should read Patrick Leigh Fermor's classic *Mani*.

Kardamyli   A magnificent view of the entire western coast greets you as the road from Kalamata descends from the mountains above Kardamyli. Now a seaside village of barely more than 300 inhabitants, it was apparently once of sufficient significance to form part of an offer by Agamemnon to Achilles to appease his wrath. Set in its little plain of olives, it's a very attractive resting place. The village of **Oitilo** Oitilo below the bare dun slopes of Profitas Elias is riven by a gorge which marks the boundary between Outer and Inner Mani. In Turkish times this was a slave market and Napoleon later put in here on his way to Egypt. At night the wind blows past the Turkish fort on the headland and chops at the water in the bay, so that a can or two of the potent local wine is usefully fortifying as the sun goes down. From here on the western coast is locally known as Shadow Mani, as opposed to Sunny Mani on the eastern side, the unclad land and half deserted villages exposed to the vagaries of the open Mediterranean. **Limenion** Limenion, the tiny port of Areopolis, lies in a shallow cove just further on, a silent, barely inhabited place of charm and superb views, fine for a swim and a simple meal off the two-burner stove of the little waterfront taverna.

Areopolis   On a headland high above is AREOPOLIS (76 kms from Kalamata), 700 inhabitants strong, the chief centre of Mani. Its towerhouses, twisting narrow lanes suddenly blooded by a flow of Bougainvillia and its stark churches, especially the Taxiarkis with a primitive panel of martial saints over its door, sets the atmosphere for the rest of Mani that lies beyond. It's possible to take a bus or drive along the continuingly dramatic coast as far as Yerolimin and the completion of an intended road to Soloteri will permit a circular tour of the lower peninsula without retracing your route to Areopolis. Ten kms south of Areopolis is the Bay of Diros, fine for swimming and with **Caves of Diros** illuminated caverns of stalactites and stalacmites viewed by boat on an underground lake. Below Yerolimin, an austere fishing village, is Alyka with its early Christian **Towerhouses at Alyka and Vatheia** basilica of Agios Andreas and scattering of towerhouses on the olive grove slopes running down to the sea. At Vatheia, a bit further south, the particularly numerous towerhouses erupt from the hilltop like a natural extension of the rocky landscape. Incorporated into the wall above the door of the Church of Agios Spyridon is a Roman relief of Athena.

But without travelling any further south it is possible to get an excellent impression of the landscape of Mani by cutting the 26 kms across from Areopolis to Gytheion on the Laconic Gulf. The best journeys in Greece are by bus, and on this early morning run we shot between bare mountains black with rock and scrub, past chapels and more towerhouses, propelled by screams of bazouki music, a frantic soundtrack oddly suiting the passing scenes of olive trees on arduously created terraces stunted and blown in a uniform direction by the hard frequent wind. It is a strangely beautiful land, the far side of Mars where life tenuously but tenaciously persists.

Gytheion

Gytheion, once the ancient port of Sparta and now the capital of the Mani, is hardly like the settlements of the interior. It lies on the edge of the Laconian plain where it spreads out before the gulf, and so the mountains are at some distance, the immediate landscape not rugged, the town itself a placid, wash-coloured place, agreeable rather than fiercely austere. The ancient city was on the low hills about a kilometre back from the present shoreline; the new town is built on reclaimed land. The very earliest settlement, however, was on the islet of Marathonisi, now reached by a causeway, and it was here that Helen and Paris were said to have spent their first night together before leaving Menelaos' kingdom and setting course for Troy.

Kithera

From Gytheion it's possible to catch a boat back to Piraeus, stopping at the island of Kithera off Cape Malea at the tip of the easternmost finger of the Peloponnese, and also at Monemvasia. Historically part of the Ionian islands but geographically an extension of the Peloponnese, KITHERA is fairly large (about 30 kms long by 18 kms across) and is rocky, largely uncultivated, and covered with low hills. A Minoan trading station was excavated here in 1964 and there are several beautiful monasteries. But its main charms are its simplicity and remoteness.

Around Sparta the Laconian plain is flat and luxuriously cultivated, but heading seawards there is a ridge of low rock-strewn hills assiduously deforested of their pine cover and planted with olives. The ridge marks the earliest limit of the Spartan villages and subordinate perioikoi. Perhaps the first drums were heard in Sparta's aggressive expansion when her army topped that ridge and bore down on the fan of land below. Making for Monemvasia along the main road from either Gytheion or Sparta takes you through the market town of Skala after passing over the Evrotas on its way to the sea. The coastal plain is flat and green, thickly cultivated with cotton and rice. There is an uneasy sense of exposure, of vulnerability, the security of the mountains being so far off on either side, yet with the knowledge that well-girded at the point where the mountains join to the north, but also girding itself for war, lies Sparta. For it is here, just below Skala, that ancient Helos stood, the first to be enslaved as 'helots', and you feel its doom, as though yet impending, as though the landscape is what it was 2700 years ago and the marsh-cultivating folk of Helos realise with terror their imminent subjection as the steady, growing sound of Spartan drums advances down the plain as certainly as the Evrotas itself.

Helos

An alternative and seldom followed route from Sparta to Monemvasia (about 90 kms) is along the rugged road which skirts the flanks of Parnon and passes through Geraki, a large village on the site of ancient Geronthrai, its towering 1940-foot acropolis still guarded by imposing Cyclopean walls, possibly pre-Mycenaean, in which case they have survived on a scale unique in Greece. Nearby, on a detached mountain rib, stands a Frankish kastro surrounded by several beautiful Byzantine churches with frescoes and mosaics dating from the 12th to the 16th C.

Ancient Geronthrai

Across the top of the Malea peninsula, the burning rocks and dry scrub of diminishing Parnon give way to an assuaging vista of blue Aegean. Except that almost at once your eye is caught by the sight of a giant rock rising forbiddingly from the sea. "At night it seemed to me a terrible beast lying in wait; today in the light of dawn it gleamed above the water like a monstrous anvil", as Kazantzakis records his first impressions of MONEMVASIA in *Travels in Greece*. My first more prosaic thought was that I had been misinformed, for though the bus now raced closer along the shoreline and my eyes searched the wading hulk, I could see nothing of the expected medieval town which flourished there as the commercial counterpart to Mistra, political capital of Byzantine Morea. Alighting at Gethira (90 kms from Gytheion), the modern nondescript sprawl at the mainland end of the causeway linking rock with shore, it seemed depressingly certain that the only prize for arriving at the end of the world was the realisation that I was better off where I had come from.

Monemvasia: the rock

The bus arrives at that blank and shadowless time of day when the sun is fiercest and the inhabitants of Gethira are sleeping off their noon-day meals in the cool of their shuttered homes. The streets are dead. The rock simmers uninvitingly through the heat haze. Nor does the sea approach from Piraeus reveal anything more of the

103

'Venice of the Peloponnese', as this invisible city on the rock has been called in comparison with that "great enchantress, magician of the seas", though after the six to eight hour voyage the sun is sinking, the great anvil glows red against the darkening mainland mountains and the atmosphere is wildly romantic.

Crossing the causeway, the sole landward access to Monemvasia *(moni emvasis,* single entrance), a road along the gentle shelving at the base of the rock runs round towards its far side but is suddenly halted by a great towered and crenellated wall reaching right down to the sea. Once through the crooked portal, broad enough for entry by foot or donkey only, the enchantment begins, though tantalisingly piecemeal as narrow stone-paved streets and still narrower alleyways diverge and twist in several directions, offering momentary perspectives of this beautiful and melancholy town.

The Byzantine town

Much of the Lower Town has fallen into decay and is permanently inhabited by only a few dozen people, though recently — like Hydra, but on a far lesser scale — it has attracted Athenians and foreigners, particularly writers and artists, who have bought and are repairing old houses, whitewashing their steps and tiling their roofs, bringing some vitality and bold colour back to the town and modestly enlivening the main street which runs into the Cathedral square with some late night dining and laughter. During the day there's a pleasurable routine of descending via steps and paths through tunnels and under arches to the narrow ledge of rocks under the seawall and diving into the fresh deep sea.

Its history

Like Mistra, the rock began as a refuge against the Slav invasion and thereafter was nearly always the last outpost of the Morea to fall to the succeeding waves of conquerors. Until 1464, Monemvasia was Byzantine and it is the Byzantine atmosphere that pervades it today. Subsequently it several times changed hands between the Venetians, the Pope and the Turks; the last, after four months of siege and hunger — alleviated by a diet of oats and mice, asses' ears and, occasionally, Greek children — surrendering it in 1821 to Maniots under the command of Mavromichalis. Malmsey, a corruption of the Greek Monemvasia, was how the English knew the rock in medieval times and was the name of the sweet wine imported from here. There's an apocryphal story that the Duke of Clarence, sentenced to death by Edward IV, asked to be drowned in a cask of it.

Churches   At the height of its prosperity when the rock sheltered 30,000 people, the Lower Town alone had as many as 40 churches (though it defies the imagination that such a number could have been crammed within the fortifications along with so many houses which even now seem piled upon one another for want of space). Now only 5 remain, though another 9 are said to be discernable, either as ruins or walled up in gardens. The Cathedral dedicated to Elkomenos Christos (Christ in chains) forms one side of a charming central square where a cannon points out to sea. It dates from the 13th C., though the portal was rebuilt by the Venetians in 1697 and a typically Venetian bell tower added. Services are still held here. Next door a marble relief of the Lion of St Mark decorates the doorway of the priest's house. Across the square under a low dome that is visible only from higher in the town is Agios Pavlos, built in 956, transformed by the Turks into a mosque, by the Greeks into a cafe after independence, and now a locked sometime-museum. Through an archway at the north end of the square is the Myrtidiotissa with a fine drum and dome, and inside a 13th C. ikonostasis taken from the Cathedral. East out of the square along the main street, the gaunt 18th C. Agios Nikolaos, now used as a schoolhouse, is an example of the Greek cruciform reduced to its bare essentials, a remarkable expression of structural form without the distraction of a decorated facade. Beyond this and towards the parapet overlooking the sea is the whitewashed Panagia Chrysaphitissa from the 16th C.

As can only really be appreciated once you get here, the Lower Town is a complete though miniature medieval city, rewarding your exploration of its churches and houses, and delightful as you wander its intricacy of streets and alleyways, passing from patches of broiling sun into deep sharp shadows along your way, and at night, in a pitch blackness only here and there illuminated by paraffin lamps hung from walls in glass boxes, ghostly and evocative. From higher in the town you can look down upon roofs of Moorish tile, sensitive to contrasts of light and shade, and peer into walled gardens of figs, pomegranates and oranges, and blazing bougainvillias.

The citadel   Climbing up the steep lane past the Myrtidiotissa towards the seemingly sheer wall of rock you fall in with a path which switches upwards through an iron-clad gate and tunnel (conveniently open here and there at the roof to permit boiling oil or molten lead to be poured upon the heads of attackers) to the Upper Town, levelled and formless, with occasional gaping holes and underground cisterns for the careless tourist to fall into — the visit is

Agia Sophia certainly not recommended at night. The one exception to the desolation upon this 'fortress in the clouds' is Agia Sophia, a superb 13th C. church with a plan similar to that at Daphni, sculptured marble lintels above the doorways, frescoes adorning the squinches and a 16-sided drum supporting the considerable dome. Where it is comfortable and enclosing down below, up here it is eerie, with 800-foot vertiginous drops most of the way round, but also breath-taking views of the wrinkled sea and at sunset the outlines of mountains receding further into the violet spectrum under a brilliant pink and orange sky.

THE ROAD TO DELPHI

Boeotia Beyond the mountains of Kithairon and Parnes which form the northern boundary of Attica, the plains of Boeotia (Viotia) extend between Mt Helikon in the west and Klomon in the north to the feet of Parnassos. This is one of the most fertile areas in Greece. Enclosed by the distant hills, the pale fields of cotton and wheat appear to stretch endlessly ahead as you travel for 80 kms with hardly a gradient. In fact until the end of the last century there was a large marshy lake fed by the river Kephissos in the middle of the area directly east of Levadia, which was then drained and later cultivated by a British company. Boeotia is no stranger to foreigners: as the only land approach to Attica and the Isthmus of Corinth it has long known the march of armies through its fields, from the Persians in the 5th C. BC down to the Germans a generation ago. Its fertile land has supported the early civilisations at Orchomenos and Thebes, the numerous city-states of the Classical period, the Frankish dukes of Athens and Turkish pashas at Levadia. Now the Boeotian towns and villages enjoy a quiet prosperity, but their fortunes in the past illustrate the history of foreign interference in Greece and also the destructive rivalries amongst the Greeks themselves.

There are two main ways into Boeotia from Attica. The first is by the National Highway to the east, which is dull, although it offers fine views across to Euboea (Evvia); the railway goes this way also. The alternative is to take the old road over the mountains from Elefsis: at the entrance to the pass over Kithairon you can still see on a **Eleutherai** hillock on the right the fortress of Eleutherai which guarded the approach to Attica for the Athenians. Fine though its 4th C. BC walls remain in parts, they do not **Aigosthena** compare with the contemporary fortress of Aigosthena on the coast of the Corinthian Gulf, reached (in 20 kms) by a turning to the left about 2 kms before Eleutherai. Aigosthena is almost complete, with several huge towers still standing, and in the afternoon shadows, amidst the greenness of the holm-oak and olive trees, is almost Wagnerian. The nearby village of Porto Germano has good swimming, with several tavernas.

It was on Kithairon that Oedipus was said to have been exposed at birth: Pausanias the traveller of the 2nd C. AD naively writes, "no-one knows where this occurred in the way that we know the Schist Road to Phocis, where Oedipus killed his father", (more of which later). From the top of the pass, with Kithairon on the left, Boeotia spreads out below and Parnassos is visible beyond Helikon. From Erythrai it is 5 kms westwards to the ruins of PLATAEA, near where the famous battle took place in 479 BC when the Greeks defeated the Persians commanded by Mardonius.

Plataea

The ruined town is on a low triangular plateau above the plain, which is often muddy from the numerous watercourses. Its walls are in places well preserved but represent several different periods as the town was often destroyed and rebuilt. Probably the Classical city was in the southern part of the site while in the north there are ruins of various Byzantine churches, and also the foundations of a temple (perhaps that of Hera which stood outside the city in 479), and of a building called the Katagogion, an inn for visitors, built in the late 5th C. by the Thebans.

The battle

The importance of Plataea lies chiefly in the battle which finally decided the fate of the Persian invasion of 480 BC. It is still not agreed where exactly the battle took place (whatever the locals say) despite the almost contemporary account in Herodotos. There is something in the descriptions of topography both by the ancient and modern Greeks which often leads to uncertainty, a vagueness at odds with the hardness of the landscape's features in the bright light. The battle was fought in September when the fields must have been dry and stubbly: the Persians were camped near the river Asopos with their Boeotian allies (who had 'medised') and the eventual battle, which was fought in two separate areas, can generally be placed to the north and east of the town, between it and the river. The Spartans defeated the Persians and killed Mardonius, while the Athenians and Plataeans defeated the Boeotians and Thebans; the majority of the Greek allies took no part until the end when victory was clear. The treacherous Thebans had their revenge in 427 when, this time allied with the Spartans against the Athenians, they took the city of Plataea after a long seige, killed the gallant defenders and destroyed it for the first but not the last time.

Thebes

THEBES (Thivai), 73 kms from Athens and about 14 kms from Erythrai across the small Asopos stream, is a dull modern town belying its former importance. The town centre occupies a steep plateau, formerly the ancient acropolis known as the Kadmeia. The very name of Thebes conjures up many of the legendary figures of Greece. It was the birthplace of Dionysos (whose Bacchantes ran wild on the slopes of Kithairon) and, some say, of Herakles. Traditionally founded by Kadmos, who here sowed the

Legendary associations

dragon's teeth, Thebes was the city of Laius and Oedipus, Kreon and Antigone. The walls and towers of the 'seven-gated' city were said to have been built to the music of Amphion's harp. But the curse on Oedipus lived on long after the quarrels of his sons Polyneikes and Eteokles and there were repeated destructions of the city, of which the most notorious was that by Alexander the Great in 336 BC. Two years after the battle of Chaironeia he killed or enslaved all the inhabitants of Thebes, destroyed all the buildings save the house of the poet Pindar, and completed Thebes' humiliation by restoring its old rival, Plataea.

Consequently as the traveller William Mure said, having visited Thebes in 1838 and seen a jumble of ruined buildings after the fresh destruction of the War of Independence against the Turks, "there is no Greek city whose site and aspect are so little in unison with the associations either of poetical or historical celebrity that attach to them". Even after Mure's visit the town was twice damaged by earthquakes in the 19th C.

Its history   At several periods Thebes was of major consequence. Excavations below the regular modern streets in the centre of the acropolis have revealed two Mycenaean palaces, destroyed by fire. The stories of the descendants of Kadmos plainly recall this era, but little tangible remains to be seen. After the Trojan War Thebes was said to have taken from Orchomenos the leadership of the cities of the Boeotian League, which she retained — except for a period after the battle of Plataea — until the war between Athens and Sparta at the end of the 5th C: by allying with Sparta she helped in breaking the power of Athens. Then in 371 BC after a change of alliance, at the battle of Leuktra — "the most famous battle ever won by Greeks over Greeks" (Pausanias) — the Theban army led by Epaminondas defeated the Spartans and through the subsequent foundation of Megalopolis and Messene in the Peloponnese the Thebans achieved the permanent loss of authority by Sparta. For a few years until Epaminondas' death Thebes led the whole of Greece.

If Thebes contributed to the division and decline of the Greek city states, in 338 BC the Thebans redeemed their reputation from Plataea by allying with the Greek forces who faced the common enemy, Philip of Macedon, at Chaironeia: the Theban Sacred Band was annihilated. After the destruction by Alexander the city was restored in 316 by its allies, and despite the depredations of the Romans, Mummius (146) and Sulla (86 BC), Pausanias found its temples and sanctuaries intact. But it was taken by the Goths a century later, and in the Middle Ages was prey to the Bulgarians in 1040 and the Normans of Sicily in 1146, by which time the city was a centre of silk manufacture. In the 13th C. the Frankish dukes of Athens made Thebes their capital — their only monument is now a solitary tower in the courtyard of the museum. In the mid 15 C. the town, with most of Greece, fell under the torpid rule of the Turks, and became little more than a village.

The museum It is the museum alone, at the north end of Odos Pindarou (on the acropolis) which justifies a visit to the town. It is approached through a charming courtyard and is one of the best small museums in Greece. The collection includes 14th C. BC *cylinder seals* from Anatolia, *Linear B tablets* found in the Mycenaean palaces, 6th C. *statues from Ptoion*, and many *Tanagran-type clay statuettes* of the 5th C. — like the amusing figurine of a man apparently grating cheese. Above all there is a unique collection of painted Mycenaean *sarcophagi* from Tanagra: some show women mourning, others have bulls and some form of tree or double axe worship, reminiscent of objects from Minoan Crete.

The road from Thebes to Levadia (46 kms) passes a turning on the left to Thespiai, from where via Palaiopanagia you

Valley of the Muses can walk in about 1½ hours to the attractive Valley of the Muses which has scant remains of an altar and a theatre. On the right of the road after Aliartos, commences the area which was formerly Lake Kopais. Nearing Levadia you can see to the northeast the long finger of Akontion, 'the javelin', reaching into the plain, with the small acropolis fortress of Orchomenos just visible on the southern end.

Levadia LEVADIA is by contrast with Thebes a town whose past is not oppressive: it rises on a slope up against a northern spur of Helikon and although it doesn't impress much if you are merely passing through on the way to Delphi or Lamia, it is worth a visit. The town is a local centre of some importance, and the capital of the nome or county of Boeotia. If you go straight on at the traffic island rather than turn right for Delphi, you pass along a busy street

leading to the main plateia: beyond this the road narrows, and a right turn leads you over unexpected water rushing between crumbling stone buildings. The street which you then meet at right-angles is full of interest: old grocery shops, a cooper, shoemakers, a coffee-shop (which has both 'American' and Greek coffee — they are ground from the same Brazilian beans, but the Greek coffee far finer) and at the bottom of the street a shady square with several kafeneions, where old men sit in their dark suits; in the other direction (which you take) is another small plateia, with a bridge which is usually draped with colourful blankets. The water becomes more insistent as you go on past the old fulling factories and under a large tower which descends from the Catalan Castle above, and there amongst huge plane-trees are the springs of the Herkyna. The springs issue from the rocks to left and right but have now, alas, been channelled and landscaped below a new Xenia restaurant, the effect of which not even the attractive Turkish bridge with swans swimming underneath can completely mitigate.

Oracle of Trophonios

It is in this area that they direct you, incorrectly, to the oracle of Trophonios. On the right hand side there are holes in the rocks for votive offerings (in the largest of them the Turkish governor used to retire for a cool smoke of his pipe) but the oracle itself was elsewhere, although no one knows exactly where, despite Pausanias' personal visit to it. If you walk on from there, the cleft between the rocks opens out into an immense gorge with high cliffs on one side, and a rocky hill on the other crowned by the castle. It's a wild place only a few minutes from the town centre. High on the left hand side is a small Chapel of Jerusalem on the site of a small spring, to which you can climb by seemingly endless steps and obtain a good view of the countryside to Parnassos. It is also possible to scramble up to the castle from the gorge, but easier to walk up from the town side.

Levadia was a prosperous Classical city, largely owing to its oracle. Trophonios, by tradition the son of the King of Orchomenos and an architect, was according to Robert Graves lucky enough to be chosen as a sacrifice for the dedication of the very first stone temple of Apollo at Delphi, which he had helped to build; he was then rewarded with his own oracle at Levadia. The oracle was sufficiently important to be consulted by King Croesus and Mardonius, as well as Pausanias, who described the terrible experience: after drinking the waters of Forgetfulness and Memory, the first to forget what he'd been thinking previously, and the second to remember his later adventures (probably these

111

were the two springs of the Herkyna), the inquirer would descend into a hole, from which he would be shot out again, if fortunate, that day or several days later. When he'd been debriefed by the priests as to what he'd seen or learnt of the future, his relatives carried him off "paralysed with fear and unconscious of himself and everything around him".

The oracle was, it seems, somewhere on the hill between the sacred grove and sanctuary of Trophonios, and the unfinished Temple of Zeus. The sanctuary was probably on the site of the church of the Panagia in the town, where ancient inscriptions have been found — the Greek Church is rather clever at making pagan sites its own. The unfinished Temple of Zeus can still be seen on the hill of Agios Elias, some distance to the southwest of the town in a marvellous position surrounded by mountains. One possible site for the oracle is under the chapel at the top of the castle, but Frazer dismissed this as only a cistern. So the hole-in-the-ground oracle keeps its secret.

The castle was built by the Catalans during their brief rule, following victory over the Frankish knights in the marshes of Lake Kopais in 1311. Later under the Turks the town became the second city of Greece, and boasted "a gay assemblage of mosques, minarets, houses and gardens". Yet the Turks have left little other than the attractive bridge over the Herkyna: when Mure made his visit here, Levadia too was a mass of recent ruins, but somehow it still retains in its narrow streets an atmosphere quite missing at Thebes. (Mure stayed in the Turkish *khan* or inn, a square two-storeyed building around a central courtyard; this structure, he observes, was very similar both to buildings described by Homer and to the 5th C. BC Katagogion or inn at Plataea.)

From Levadia the modern route to Delphi goes westwards along a twisting, humpback road (50 kms). The ancient route went northwards via Chaironeia and Panopeos (above Agios Vlasios) and through a valley now called Tseresi, before arriving at the Schist Road. In this direction are several interesting places.

Orchomenos

About 6 kms out of Levadia on the Lamia road is a turning across the plain to Orchomenos (about as far again), a dull town full of shops looking like warehouses, lying at the bottom of a bare sloping hillside. But at one time Orchomenos was one of the richest cities in Greece and the slope above the modern town has yielded evidence of almost continuous occupation from the Neolithic to the Hellenistic periods. Its fame dates from the Mycenaean period when the Minyans (after a King Minyas) achieved great wealth and importance: they succeeded in draining Lake Kopais through canals and dikes, and may have placed the fortress at Gla to guard one of the lake's natural outlets. With the decline of the Minyans the area became a lake again — the story of the Theban Herakles blocking up the outlets suggests their deliberate obstruction by the Thebans — and remained so for two millenia. Their civilisation is comparable to that of Mycenae owing to the similarity of the so-called Treasuries, and also of the pottery (although at Orchomenos there is a distinctive wheel-made 'Minyan Ware', as the excavator Schliemann termed it).

Treasury of Minyas   The Treasury of Minyas is at the bottom of the hillside, down a short lane across the road from the Church of the Koimisis. Like the 'Treasury' of Atreus at Mycenae, the Treasury of Minyas is a beehive tomb but its roof has fallen in. There is a massive lintel of dark-grey marble and, inside, a long marble pedestal (for statues) which is a much later Macedonian intrusion. To the right is a doorway leading to a small chamber which was hewn out of the rock from above: the ceiling has slabs of greenish schist decorated with spirals and rosettes (take a flashlight with you).

The acropolis   You can walk up the slope to the acropolis fortress above by a path opposite the church: this was the acropolis of the Hellenic city which was enclosed by a triangular wall, remains of which can be seen on the north and south. The fortress, approached by about 90 steps in the cliff-face, has magnificent 4th C. walls on the south and west designed to combine with the natural defences of the cliffs to north and east. The Orchomenians needed their defences: Thebes which had anciently robbed Orchomenos of its pre-eminence destroyed the city twice in the 4th C.

Church of the Koimisis   The Byzantine Church of the Koimisis or Assumption of the Virgin Mary is another remarkable building. (If it's closed — and Greek churches often are, owing to the valuable clutter inside — the priest who lives in the old monastic buildings to one side has the keys.) The church was built in 872 and incorporates a lot of material from a Temple of the Graces previously on its site: circular column drums are clearly visible in the outside walls. The structure of the church is interesting: it was the first cross-in-square church built in Greece, although it retains basilical-style side aisles which are, however, blocked off from the central nave. The dome rests directly on the walls without the device of squinches such as at Osios Loukas. The frescoes are badly damaged.

Gla   The fortress of Gla can be approached by the road which runs eastwards from Orchomenos along the northern edge of the Kopais basin to Kastron (19 kms) — or of course via the National Highway if you're on it. The fortress occupies a low triangular rock, a short walk to the east side of the Highway (or it can be reached by car). It is surrounded by a wall of almost 3 kms long, and so is far bigger than Mycenae or Tiryns. Yet its precise role and even its date remain uncertain, although broadly speaking it is contemporary with Orchomenos and Mycenae. There are 4 gates of which the main gate is in the south: from there a street led to a 'market-place' in the middle of the fortress, which was linked in turn to a palace at the highest point towards the north. The palace had two wings and a court-yard within an enclosing wall. The whole place seems too large and important to have been only a fortress of Orchomenos — guarding an outlet of Lake Kopais.

Returning to the main road to Lamia it is not far to CHAIRONEIA (14 kms from Levadia). On the left of the road before the village you can still see in places on the hillside crude huts made from pine branches and reeds which are used by the Vlachs when they bring their flocks down from Thessaly for the winter. Many have now built only slightly less crude houses from brick, particularly around Thourion. The Vlachs who possibly derive from the Roman colonists of Dacia, north of the Danube, are tradi-tionally a pastoral people and provide one of the few remaining instances in Europe of long-distance trans-humance — that is, the feeding of flocks in summer on upland pastures and in winter on the plains.

Chaironeia battlefield "As you approach the city, there is a common grave of the Thebans who were killed in the struggle against Philip. It has no inscription but there is a lion on top, which probably refers to the spirit of the men" — that is Pausanias' succinct description of the lion of Chaironeia. The battle took place in the plain between the road and the river Kephissos, on the bank of which the young Alexander led the cavalry charge which destroyed the Theban Sacred Band. (The Sacred Band were a small force, some 300 strong, comprised of pairs of homosexual lovers — an older and a younger man, fighting side by side; their loyalty to each other ensured they would fight to the finish). Philip of Macedon had been able to use the pretext of the perennial squabbles over the plain of Krisa to invade Greece: the Macedonian victory over the Athenians and their allies including the Phocians and Thebans marked the end of the significant period of the Greek city-states, whose com-petitive ethos had contributed both to their previous importance and to their ultimate downfall.

114

The lion   The marble lion, 18 ft high, now sits bolt upright over the Theban grave but it had disappeared from view under the earth until discovered in 1818: shortly afterwards the ignorant Odysseus Androutsos, a bandit-general in the War of Independence, smashed it to pieces to see if it contained treasure. It is easy to forget that the statue was erected by the defeated, for in its face and through the tension in its body it expresses a quiet pride. The eyes look out towards the scene of the battle and the one token of defeat is its tail tucked between its legs. (I owe the last observation to a local farmer whom I met when walking in the area of the battlefield; there in the ripening corn the only sombre feature was the familiar magpie.)

Next to the lion is a small museum.

Acropolis and theatre   The acropolis of the old city of Chaironeia is on a rocky hill above the theatre: in the theatre once a year at the beginning of June there is a short festival in honour of its most famous citizen, Plutarch, the historian of the 1st C. AD, who taught there and became a priest at Delphi; for a couple of evenings the almost invisible grey stone seats are filled with colour as the spectators, after the conventional eulogistic addresses from local and national officials, watch traditional dancing and ancient tragedy, looking out over the innocent cornfields in the fading light.

Chaironeia which owed its wealth to the manufacture of ointments from flowers was only one of a number of city-states hereabouts. As you go on to the northwest you pass **Phocis**   into the old region of Phocis. Today Phocis (Fokis) has mysteriously shifted to the west and is the name of the nome or county west of Parnassos, but it once extended in a large semi-circle to the north, east and south of the mountain. Of Phocis' many cities, none was of first importance (except Delphi, and that was only because of the oracle) but collectively they assumed importance, particularly in the 4th C. BC.

Panopeos   There was Panopeos, for example, the ruins of which lie above Agios Vlasios, a small farming village of brown tiled roofs and whitewashed stone farmhouses, a short way on and to the left of the main road. Panopeos guarded the passes through the hills towards Delphi: on the hill above the village are well-preserved 4th C. walls, where you can wander alone amongst the tortoises and look across to Davlia and the nearer peaks of Parnassos. In the 2nd C. AD Pausanias was unimpressed by the city on his visit — he asks if one can call Panopeos a city when it possesses no government office, no gymnasium, no theatre and no market-place— but by then the city like the other Phocian towns had fallen low: both Daulis and Panopeos were destroyed by Xerxes in 480 and Philip in 348. In the small village plateia the farmers now sit and complain of the extortions of the middlemen, the merchants; perhaps near here laughter once came from the Thyiads, the Attic girls who, on their way to celebrate the Dionysian orgies at Delphi, paused at Panopeos to dance.

From Agios Vlasios it is possible to walk beside the Platania river through the beautiful, quiet valley of Tseresi to the main Levadia-Delphi road: this was the old route to Delphi and in the middle of the valley in a field on the left can be seen a few marble blocks which are all that remain

The Phocicon from the Phocicon, the old meeting place of the Phocians. (Some words of advice for walkers in Greece: get a good map if you can — the only readily available maps which are at all reliable are the 1:200,000 nome maps from the National Ministry of Statistics, 14 Likourgou, Athens, near Omonia Square: passport required; regard with scepticism any directions from a Greek, and at least double any estimates of time; wear a sturdy pair of boots or shoes; take water and if you meet any fierce dogs stoop as if to pick up a stone and if they still don't go away, throw it.)

Davlia Davlia is a walk of 1½ hours away across the plain (like Agios Vlasios, and Tithorea, below, it is off to the left of the Lamia road). The village is strung out on a hill at the feet of the steep, fir-dark slopes of Parnassos: half-way up the village is the plateia, where there is cold mountain water and the men sit outside under the shade of the planes. The old houses of stone or mud brick under clay tiles are two-storeyed, the living-rooms reached by an outside staircase and balcony over the store-rooms and animal quarters. Here and there a new concrete taratsa intrudes; it's hard to blame the villagers, because the old houses don't even have a tap inside and are infested with rats (I lived in such a house), but it's only a matter of time before the universal concrete dominates all the mountain villages.

If you travel up the vertiginous street above the plateia, you emerge at the top of the village. The view is spectacular back across the plain, towards the mountains near Thebes. To the south is Helikon and, under it, across a valley of olive trees, where water falls past old stone mills, is the old acropolis of Daulis, the city of Tereus. Only a few courses of wall ring the hill, and there is little there except wild flowers and a restless spirit.

Above the village high up in a cleft in the mountains can
Monastery of be seen the Monastery of Jerusalem, reached by a turning
Jerusalem off the new road which now runs through Parnassos from Davlia to join the road from Levadia to Delphi. The

116

monastery has become a summer resort, apart from being a place of pilgrimage for the Orthodox: you can camp outside amongst the firs. The monastery itself is a little disappointing — despite its colourful courtyard, the monastic buildings and the church are not particularly interesting.

Tithorea

It's possible to walk in about 3 hours along the lower slopes of the mountain from Davlia to another Phocian town, Tithorea: you pass through the small village of Agia Marina, in a tobacco-growing region, which has a small frescoed chapel dedicated to the saint. (The villagers believe that St Marina physically captured and killed a devilish figure called Cholera, who was living near the spring and plaguing the inhabitants. This comparatively recent myth — presumably explaining deliverance from the disease — is a good example of the fertility of the Greek mind, and its literalness.) Tithorea is in an even more spectacular position than Davlia, since the village lies beneath a huge cliff towering over a deep ravine which runs back into the heart of Parnassos. Firs reach high up the cliff, and a solitary tower stands amongst them; below in the village itself are the remains of another tower, and some walling from the 4th C. Greek city. You reach the famous cave, once used by the klepht Odysseus Androutsos, by walking along the side of the ravine from the top of the village, and continuing some way beyond an oak grove near a spring: the cave is high up on the right. It's a grandly romantic setting for a story of bravery and treachery, for in 1825 during the War of Independence Androutsos, at one time a hero of resistance against the Turks, was captured (and later killed) after fighting against his own countrymen.

The Schist Road

The new road from Davlia joins the direct Levadia-Delphi route, near the main (second) turning for Distomo (3 kms), in a valley enclosed by mountains. The Davlia road emerges from the north into the valley at 'the cross-roads of Megas', so called after one Johannes Megas, a local police officer who lost his life in 1856 after surrounding a band of brigands on the rocky hillock nearby; they had just robbed the Jerusalem Monastery. The 'cross-roads' is at the base of the Zimeno, a deep cleft between Parnassos and Mt Kirphis (and thus easily identified from the main road on the other side of the valley), and here the ancient track from Delphi met those from Davlia and Thebes. This was the great Schist Road, and it was hereabouts that Oedipus was said to have killed his father Laius as they encountered each other travelling in opposite directions. Pausanias speaks of seeing Laius' tomb in the middle of the 'cross-roads', and he was probably only referring to the hillock itself, now (inevitably) topped by a Christian monument in memory of Megas. (I have often walked around this area, and I believe it is a mistake to place this legendary encounter in the defile to the north, near the first turning to Distomo, as many people do.)

It is necessary to drive through Distomo on the way to the Byzantine monastery of Osios Loukas. Distomo which has the memory of a particularly awful massacre of its inhabitants during the German occupation is now an unattractive small town dependent on the local bauxite industry. The reddish earth so noticeable in this area contains bauxite from which aluminium is made, and on the coast at Aspra Spitia is one of the biggest bauxite factories in Europe, near the uninspiring village of Andikyra.

Osios Loukas   The monastery of OSIOS LOUKAS is 8 kms to the east of Distomo, on the side of a hill which looks over the valley towards Helikon. It is said that monks take all the best sites for their monasteries: that is certainly true here. On the terrace of the monastery a huge plane-tree gives shade as you sit and look at the rich earth and listen to the echo of the bells from the flocks in the valley below.

Beyond the handsome tower is a courtyard with monastic buildings lining two sides, while the refectory occupies another, and two churches together the fourth side. The churches are built adjacently, in such a way that a passage runs from the monastic buildings through the loggia of the church on the left to the gallery of the north transept in the larger church. A good idea of the relationship between these two buildings can be gained by walking around to the back of them, under the buttresses on the south of the larger church (and past the entrance to its crypt), so you can see the external facades of the apses. The smaller church is that of the Theotokos or Mother of God; the larger is the church of St Luke.

Its history   St Luke of Stiris (the village between the monastery and Distomo) was a local hermit who died in about 950. His disciples built a church over his tomb, which may possibly be identified with the crypt. Ten years later a monastery was founded here by the Byzantine emperor, Romanos II, and the church of the Theotokos may date from then. In the early 11th C. the larger church of St Luke was built, complete with its mosaics; its crypt has 11th C. frescoes.

The church of   It is the church of St Luke which has earned for the
St Luke   monastery its fame as one of the most important Byzantine buildings in Greece. The rough external walls of stone and brick conceal a startling richness inside: the church, which is in the conventional cross-in-square form

with a narthex, at one time had all its flat surfaces covered with marble of different colours while all the curved surfaces were decorated with mosaics against a gold background. A lot of the marble still survives and a good many of the mosaics, though they are gone from the central dome where they have been replaced by paintings. The light is subdued and the corners between the arms of the cross remain dark owing to the windows being partly filled with sculptured marble, but that only increases the mystery.

The narthex   The mosaics in the narthex are the most easily seen. Of these the *washing of the Apostles' feet* and the *Resurrection* are particularly fine, and they well illustrate the combination of grave majesty and lifelike expressions and gestures characteristic of the mosaics as a whole. In the first, as Christ washes their feet, the Apostles share an uncertainty, even diffidence, expressive of their lack of understanding and the general frailty of mankind compared to the certainty of Christ or God. Christ's quiet confidence in that mosaic becomes in the Resurrection a strident triumph expressed by the cloak flowing behind the figure as His strong left arm firmly holds the limp hand of Adam who is being pulled, again uncertainly, to his salvation: here the contrast is at its greatest between the autocratic Byzantine God and the paltry human being.

The nave   In the nave, the squinches supporting the dome have fine mosaics of the *Nativity, Presentation* and *Baptism.* The hands of the Virgin Mary in the Nativity seem almost to caress the cradle as the Child looks wide-eyed at the animals. A graver *Mother and Child*, of conventional form, is to be seen in the apse.

The mosaics, while they follow a strict decorative system and sufficiently emphasise the various important Biblical events, are dominated by portraits of saints of every description. St Luke himself amongst an important group of mosaics in the north transept is represented as a stern ascetic: the strength of the dark figure comes partly from the contrast with the smallness of his hands, but the mosaic is characteristic of the spirituality of the portraits as a whole.

Mosaic of St Luke

It is necessary to realise that both the saints and the scenes from the Bible depicted on the walls are not of consequence to the Orthodox as pieces of art history but are there like ikons to instruct us in the Orthodox faith. John of Damascus said, "if a pagan asks you to show him your faith, take him into church and place him before the ikons". The saints themselves are examples of faith for the rest of us, and form a backcloth which is both historical and contemporary since the saints are with us, watching us, as indeed is Christ from the dome and elsewhere. Their ikons, like those of Christ and the Virgin Mary or Panagia, are symbols, idealised symbols of ideal figures, and form a route by which we can more easily approach the subjects of the images. In the church of St Luke there are four beautiful 16th C. ikons on the marble ikonostasis. As the bus or taxi drives away from the monastery, the colourful cardboard ikons in front of the driver perhaps have slightly more significance.

From the Distomo cross-roads the road climbs up the side of Mt Kirphis past low animal shelters. On the rocks on the left I once saw 27 Egyptian Vultures — the birds which, more often than eagles, haunt the cliffs above Delphi. Beyond the 'Khan of Zimeno', at the point where the ravine of the Pleistos opens out to the left, travellers formerly had the choice of descending into the valley, where a path led up again to Delphi, or of ascending to Arachova: Gell, for example, in the early 19th C. preferred the first route, and it is probable that the same choice existed in the time of the oracle at Delphi. The road now passes through Arachova, while the valley of the Pleistos is disfigured by the aqueduct carrying water to Athens from the Mornos dam project.

Arachova   The town of ARACHOVA (38 kms from Levadia) hangs on the side of the mountain, 3090 ft high. Even in the summer it is cool, particularly in the evenings (and hence the object of much local praise) and in winter the road is sometimes blocked with snow. Many of the fine-looking inhabitants are shepherds who in summer graze their flocks on Parnassos but in the hard winters are forced to quarter their animals away, in the plain of Kephissos or as far afield as Athens. They produce the best cheese in the area.

Apart from cheese Arachova has two other well-known products: they make an unresinated 'black' wine which is free of the chemicals often added to Greek wines, and is usually very good; and from the plentiful wool they hand-weave colourful rugs or blankets, good examples of which can be found amongst the other bric-a-brac in the tourist shops. But there are other simpler pleasures in Arachova, like sitting in the small plateia by the fountain and listening to the rumble of men's voices under the Judas trees, or walking into the small streets away from the road, past stone houses where rugs hang over iron balconies and chopped wood is neatly piled beside elegant arched door-ways, and where the red roofs hide secret gardens.

A long flight of steps leads from the plateia up to the

church of St George: on St George's Day at Eastertime the old men race each other up the steps to the church — one year two of them found it so easy they even stopped midway and performed a dance before resuming. At the top, above the fountains behind the church, is a small restaurant which, if you're lucky, will give you some of the food they've cooked for themselves, and it is delicious.

On leaving Arachova you see a road to the right signposted to the ski club. When it reaches the top of the ridge the road passes over a large plateau, called Livadi, which in late spring is carpeted with wild flowers; at its far end, you can turn off the road (which otherwise continues to the old Phocian towns of Lilaia and Amphiklia), to the left to reach the Corycian Cave (see below), or to the right to drive up to the ski club. The club is about 2½ hours' walk from the **Climbing** main summit of Parnassos, Liakoura (8061 ft); the summer **Parnassos** is the only practical time to attempt it. Above the club near the ski lift there are red markers to show you the way, but it is better to take a guide because only with a guide can you travel in the very early hours and thus reach the summit at dawn and obtain the fabled view over much of Greece, before it recedes in the mist. A guide can be found in Arachova, and you then stay the night at the refuge not far from the ski club. If however you insist on doing it by yourself, take plenty of warm clothes and, if you intend to sleep out, a warm sleeping bag and enough food — it gets very cold indeed at night.

Delphi DELPHI is situated 10 kms from Arachova, below a huge crack in the wall of Parnassos. Vultures and eagles wheel around the crags of the cliffs above, a pattern of terraced olive-green land slopes sharply away to the gorge of the Pleistos below. Rugged, savage, lonely Delphi where the shrine of Apollo camouflages the earlier appeasement of the Earth Goddess. Here there is no chance of disappointment: this is one of the most magnificent sites in Greece. I've been here with the mist swirling up the valley and over the monuments, I have seen the sanctuary warmed by the sunrise and in the white light of a full moon; even in the rain it is magical.

As the road descends from Arachova, around a corner you see first the museum and then the sanctuary itself, identified by the columns in brownish-pink tufa of the Temple of Apollo, which lies at the bottom of the more western of the two Phraedriades, the Shining Rocks. The modern town of Delphi is around the next corner, beyond the museum. Another dramatic approach is to walk up through the olive trees from Kirrha, the old port of Delphi, along the banks of the Pleistos stream and under the rock which holds the modern town of Delphi: you then look up at the sanctuary as many a visitor did in the past and realise how ideal is its position not only in relation to the cliffs above but in its height above the valley — it's at the meeting point between the two. (This walk takes about 3 hours.)

Both of these approaches draw you towards the sanctuary, but it is from the sanctuary that the true magnificence of Delphi's position is appreciated for it faces out not only over the olive-filled valley but across the gorge to the blank walls of Mt Kirphis. The sanctuary, within the bowl formed by the twin cliffs above, relates also to the hills opposite, so that the whole forms a huge amphitheatre.

It is a very beautiful place, but no enumeration of the physical characteristics of Delphi can ever completely describe its beauty, because this lies as much in a mystery or atmosphere beyond the power of words. The place is numinous — it has a presence and it feels very old. Perhaps centuries of worship have caused that: more likely Delphi always possessed this feeling, and was thus an obvious place **The oracle** for an oracle. Certain it is that the first oracle was that of Ge or Earth, the chthonic goddess worshipped by the pre-Hellenes in the second millenium BC. Delphi was well suited to be considered the centre of the Earth in view of its natural position, and the springs and fumes which came from its rocks. Above the sanctuary, the twin cliffs of the Phraedriades echo the two (invisible) peaks of Parnassos, and possibly recalled the breasts of the Earth Mother. More concretely, Delphi was and still is in an earthquake region, and the worship of the Earth Goddess here was probably an attempt to mitigate these forces: Poseidon, the 'Earth-shaker', was also associated with the cult at this early stage. The early oracle known as Pytho was situated at a cave or fissure in the ground, guarded by the serpent Python: the goddesses' priestess, the Pythia, was the oracle's mouthpiece and delivered prophesies after breathing vapours from the fissure.

Mythological origins Later, Apollo took over the oracular shrine of Mother Earth after killing the Python. According to Robert Graves, certain northern Hellenes invaded central Greece and the Peloponnese where they were opposed by the pre-Hellenic worshippers of the Earth Goddess, but they captured her chief oracular shrines: at Delphi they killed the sacred oracular snake, and to placate local opinion regular funeral games were instituted in honour of the dead hero Python, and the priestess was retained in office. In some legendary accounts Apollo had to obtain purification from the river

122

Pineios in the Vale of Tempe, and from there brought back the bay-tree, the leaves of which were chewed by the priestess before giving the prophesies. The god's coming to Delphi is also associated with Crete: in one version he came ashore in the form of a dolphin, hence Delphoi. In any event Apollo, a male Hellenic god, displaced the Earth Goddess before the end of the Mycenaean period.

Its history   The oracle's subsequent history was bedevilled by natural disasters, periodic warfare between Greek rivals for its control (the so-called Sacred Wars), and foreign intervention and plundering. The calm, serene sanctuary was not always so: after all, it contained immensely rich offerings to the god. At the beginning of the 6th C. BC the Amphictyonic League — a 'united nations' of Greek tribes and states, of which Delphi was the centre — declared war on neighbouring Krisa because it was taxing the oracle's visitors who landed at the port of Kirrha: both Krisa and Kirrha were destroyed, and their territories — the plain below Delphi — confiscated and dedicated to the god. No cultivation was allowed there, and it is extraordinary to think that during the ancient period one's eyes could not have feasted on the sight of the silvery olive-trees stretching down to the bay of Itea.

The 6th C. became a period of prosperity, amidst comparative calm: the Pythian games were properly organised, and were now held once every four years in late summer: several treasuries were added which held rich offerings from various cities. Gifts were received from the kings of Lydia and Egypt. In 548 BC the temple built by Trophonios was burnt down, and a new temple built, munificently faced with Parian marble by the Alkmaeonid family from Athens. Following the Persian Wars at the beginning of the 5th C. — when the oracle's reputation for impartiality suffered owing to its favourable attitude towards the invaders (made unnecessary in fact when divine intervention or human hands sent large rocks crashing down on Xerxes' approaching force, destroying both the force and the Temple of Athena in the process) — Delphi lost further prestige as it became involved in the rivalries between the Greek city-states. The Athenians, who after Marathon had dedicated a treasury with spoils from the battle, in the Second Sacred War in the mid 5th C. attempted to place the control of Delphi in the hands of its allies the Phocians, but the Delphians aided by Sparta managed to retain their autonomy.

In 373 BC the temple was destroyed by earthquake, and it is the new temple built later in the 4th C. that we see partly restored today. The first large-scale pillage of the sanctuary treasures occurred in about 356 BC when the Phocians, who had been fined for cultivating the Krisaean plain, seized the sanctuary and then used some of the treasures — chiefly the gold — to finance the war which developed: the Phocian general Philomelos built a fortification on the spur west of the stadium which can still be seen. Philip of Macedon intervened and destroyed the Phocian cities, and the Macedonians took the place of the Phocians on the Amphictyonic Council: the Phocians were then fined a large amount, which was used towards the rebuilding of the temple. Delphi was now central to the entire fortunes of Greece: in 339 the city of Amphissa was accused of cultivating the sacred plain and in the Fourth Sacred War the appeal by the council to Philip resulted in his large-scale invasion of Greece, the battle of Chaironeia and the effective loss of autonomy of the Greek city-states, including Delphi itself, to the power of the Macedonians.

Following the Macedonians Delphi was subject first to the Aetolians and then the Romans. In 86 BC Sulla plundered the sanctuary, and later Nero took away some 500 statues, but Pausanias found the sanctuary still rich and substantially intact in the 2nd C. AD. It was the Christian emperors Constantine and Theodosios who dealt the finishing blows to the sanctuary and oracle: Constantine took many of the treasures to Constantinople, and Theodosios abolished the oracle towards the end of the 4th C. AD. The priestess had uttered her last oracle to the Emperor Julian:

> Tell ye the King: the carven hall is fallen in decay;
> Apollo hath no chapel left, no prophesying bay,
> No talking spring. The stream is dry that has so
> much to say.

By the 19th C. there was little visible except the stadium, and the village of Kastri occupied the site. Since 1892 French archaeologists have revealed the sanctuary and theatre, but they have not lessened the mystery and the secrets remain: where for example was the oracular chasm? What caused the Pythia's trance? Where lay the power of Delphi in its great days? No sign of any cave or chasm has been found beneath the temple, and no vapours which might induce a trance (chewing bay leaves doesn't do so). As to the influence of Delphi, its prophecies were often vague, or even misleading; Oedipus was told he would murder his father and marry his mother. After deciding not to return to Corinth, the home of his imagined parents, he unknowingly killed his real father Laius only a few miles away. The historical figure Croesus, King of Lydia, was told that his projected expedition would destroy a great empire, which turned out to be his own. Although in many instances the prophesies must have amounted to practical advice both in large affairs of state and in more personal matters like a possible marriage, Delphi's influence cannot have lain chiefly through the mouth of its oracle. Rather through its position at the centre of the Amphictyonic League and through its network of informants in the Greek cities, which were necessary to give the oracle any degree of credibility in its oracular responses, we can imagine it the centre of political and commercial dealings of every kind. The treasuries and offerings of the cities are rather the expression of their prosperity, and political or military fortunes, than of religious zeal. But all this is not to deny its sacred nature, especially for the ordinary worshippers.

Pausanias is the best guide to the site as a whole, and many of the objects have only been identified through his help. This guide will be more selective.

The Marmaria   The Marmaria are to the left of the road as you arrive, a group of buildings significantly placed at the approach to the sanctuary of Apollo and so called because their marbles were later quarried. There are the ruins of 5 buildings side by side forming a sanctuary of Athena. The first building (from the east, or Arachova) was the *Temple of Athena Pronaia* — Pronaia meaning fore-temple (to the larger Temple of Apollo). This temple was destroyed by the falling rocks in 480 as the Persians approached: the rocks now lying about the ruins came from a similar accident in 1905. Next to the temple were two treasuries and the round building further again to the west is the famous *Tholos*, a rotunda of the early 4th C. BC: 3 of its Doric columns from the peristyle have been re-erected, the two metopes being copies of originals in the museum. Finally there are the foundations of the *new Temple of Athena* built in the 4th C. to replace the older one.

The gymnasium   If you walk out of the western end of the Marmaria the path leads to the area of the gymnasium. The existing remains are from the 4th C., as rebuilt by the Romans. On the upper level were two *tracks* for training purposes, one covered, one open, and both the length of a Pythian stade, 583 ft. Below was the *palaestra*, a square building for the wrestlers, and a cold *bath* with a round pool.

The Castalian Spring   The Castalian spring is at the point where the two Phraedriades form an angle or cleft between them. Here has been found the base of a statue dedicated to the Earth, and here it was said the Python lived and Apollo brought back the bay-tree from Tempe. It is possible that this was indeed the site of the original oracle itself, but its subsequent function was as the place where all the visitors to Delphi purified themselves in the pure waters of the Castalia. The water was collected in a large basin from a trough-like reservoir behind, above which was once an elaborate facade: steps enabled visitors to wash in the basin.

The Sanctuary

The sanctuary is reached by a path, bordered by bay and oleander shrubs; unfortunately, it is now fenced — and the entrance from the road is the only official way in, since the other entrance near the stadium, reached from above the town, seems permanently closed.

The ancient town spread up the hillside to the sanctuary, and it is not difficult to imagine visitors being persuaded to buy small offerings as they passed through the streets and arrived at the *paved square* immediately outside the walled enclosure. The village of Kastri or Delphi was moved in the 1890s by the French to its present position further west, but the rows of expensive shops are in a good tradition.

The sanctuary is contained within 4 great *walls* dating from the 6th C. (the north and west), the 5th C. (the south) and the 4th C. (the east). Inside we have to imagine it was crammed with countless offerings of every description, literally thousands of statues and scores of treasuries. There were tripods and weapons dedicated to the God. There were statues of gods, men and beasts — some of gold, others gilt, yet others bronze or a mixture of each. Statues of marble and clay were brightly painted, as were the friezes and decorations on the buildings. Rising above the cluttered terraces was the large Temple of Apollo, resplendent white but with coloured sculptures and gold armour below its red-tiled roof. The total effect would have seemed extraordinary to our eyes.

The way through the sanctuary is by the 'Sacred Way'. Immediately you pass inside the wall you see the bases of various statues, and the near ones provide a good example of the rivalries of the city-states and the spirit in which their dedications were often made. On the left is a long base for 16 statues, an *offering of the Athenians* erected some years after the battle of Marathon of 490 BC; directly opposite is a large rectangular or recessed structure, once containing 37 bronze statues of gods and generals, an *offering of the Spartans* made after their victory over the Athenians at Aigospotami 80 years later. However, immediately in front of the Spartan monument was placed the *offering of the Arcadians*, 9 bronze statues to commemorate their recent successes against the Spartans. Moreover

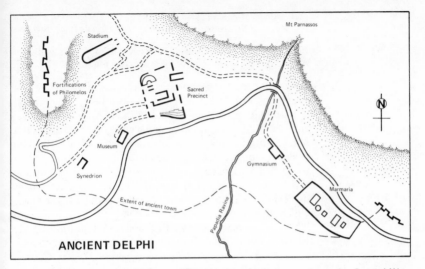

ANCIENT DELPHI

next door to the Spartan monument along the Sacred Way is a semi-circular exedra known as the *monument of the Kings of Argos,* put up to commemorate the foundation of Messene under the Theban Epaminondas in about 370 BC — another slight to the Spartans.

Further up the path on the left were two treasuries, first the Sikyonian and then the Siphnian. The *Sikyonian Treasury* was built about the beginning of the 5th C. with material from previous buildings: from one of these survive some metopes now in the museum. The *Siphnian Treasury* built in about 525 BC had two caryatids at its west entrance, parts of which are in the museum, and a frieze of Parian marble also in the museum. Turning the corner on the path you see in front the reconstructed *Treasury of the Athenians* — inscriptions on the walls enabled the reconstruction to be made. This elegant little building of Parian marble was built from the spoils of Marathon, trophies from which were displayed on the triangular terrace. Parts of the frieze of metopes are in the museum, those on the building being copies. The inscriptions on the walls include decrees in honour of Athenians, lists of Athenians sent in official capacities to the Pythian festival, a hymn to Apollo with musical notations, and on the supporting wall at the back of the Treasury records of the liberation of slaves. After the humiliation of the Athenian expedition to Sicily in 415 BC, it seems the Syracusans could not resist putting up a treasury almost opposite.

Ascending the Sacred Way and past the *Council House* of the Delphians, where day to day administration of the sanctuary would have been looked after, you arrive at a circular area or *Threshing Floor;* here at the Pythian festival the story of the killing of the Python by Apollo was re-enacted. North of this, under the *south retaining wall of the temple* (of fine polygonal masonry of the 6th C. BC and covered with decrees of a much later date granting freedom to particular slaves), is the *Stoa of the Athenians:* on the top step is an inscription which reads, "The Athenians dedicated the colonnade and the arms and the figure-heads which they took from their enemies". It is unclear from which naval victories the Athenians took the ships' figure-heads, possibly from those both over the Persians (notably at Salamis) and over her later Greek rivals.

To the left of the stoa is a rock which formed the base of the *Naxian column* supporting a large sphinx of about 560 BC, now in the museum. Further to the left it seems was the old *sanctuary of the Earth* near a spring: between this and the Sacred Way can be seen a large rock with a fissure, known as the *rock of the sibyl,* since it may have been here that the early priestess or sibyl chanted the oracles.

The path now passes in front of the temple: on the right were several offerings, amongst which is a circular base which supported the common Greek *monument of Plataea,* a gold tripod and basin set on three large bronze serpents, dedicated from the spoils of the battle of 479 BC. The bodies of the serpents even without their heads were over 17 ft high, and on them was engraved the list of the Greek cities who had taken part in the battle, to whatever slight extent. The Phocians took the gold parts of the monument in the Third Sacred War in the mid 4th C.: the emperor Constantine took the bronze serpents, which were later used as fountains and can still be seen without their heads and tails in Istanbul. It is possible too that the gilt horses now outside St Mark's Cathedral in Venice were originally taken by Constantine from the *Chariot of the Sun,* the base of which is behind the Plataean monument.

At the top of the Sacred Way, where it turns left to the temple terrace, is the base of the *monument of Gelon,* the tyrant of Syracuse: he and his brothers erected 4 tripods and Victories of gold, weighing in all some 1300 or more pounds, to commemorate their victory over the Carthaginians at Himera in 481 BC. To the left was the

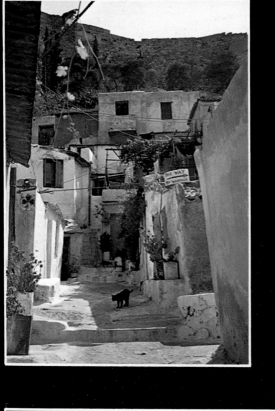

A fishing boat in an island harbour, and a no less colourful butcher at the Athens meat market.

The Theatre

Acanthus column, now in the museum: behind was the *Thessalian monument* erected in honour of the tyrant Daochos, several statues from which are in the museum.

Outside the temple is a terrace with a large restored *altar* erected by the inhabitants of Chios. On this terrace, to judge from Pausanias, were a great number of statues, many of them of Apollo. The remains of the *Temple of Apollo* are of the 4th C. and clearly it was designed to dominate the sanctuary: the bare tufa of the columns re-erected by the excavators is misleading, as originally they were covered with a lime and marble stucco. The columns are of the Doric order, and the temple had 6 columns at the front and rear, and a single row of columns along the sides. Inside, in the pronaos were the famous inscriptions "Know Yourself" and "Nothing in Excess", maxims which the god Apollo himself only learnt late in life after a tempestuous and violent youth. The pronaos also held a statue of Homer. Within the cella there was an altar of Poseidon, plus statues of the Fates and of Apollo and Zeus, and the hearth of Apollo where a fire was kept perpetually burning. Pausanias also speaks of a gold Apollo in the innermost part of the temple, or adytum. Under here was the oracle, where the priestess sat on a tripod over a chasm, breathing its vapour and munching bay leaves, before delivering a babble of words which usually had to be translated by a priest into intelligible (although often ambiguous) verse for the waiting enquirer. Nearby seems to have been the Omphalos, the circular 'navel of the Earth', which some took to mark the grave of the Python or of Dionysos. An omphalos found in the area of the temple is in the museum, but the mystery of the oracular chasm remains.

The pediments on the outside of the temple (completely gone) included the figures of both Apollo and Dionysos with his Thyiad women (or Maenads). Why Dionysos? This is another of the surprises at Delphi: apart from Apollo, the god of the intellect, they worshipped Dionysos, the god of the senses and of wine. For the winter months, Apollo was absent and his oracle was silent; in his place reigned Dionysos. Plutarch, who was himself a priest here, says that Delphi belonged as much to Dionysos as to Apollo. Behind the cool facades were deeper passions which sometimes ran free in the orgiastic rites on Parnassos, itself sacred to Dionysos and his Maenads.

Above the temple, in the northwest corner of the enclosure

is the Theatre. Nearby was a statue of Dionysos, and the god also had a small sanctuary directly to the east of the theatre. (Further to the east still was the *Cnidian Club*, a meeting place built in about 450 BC and decorated by the painter Polygnotos with scenes of the capture of Troy and the Underworld — none surviving.) Dionysos was closely connected with the ancient theatre: at the festivals in praise of the wine god, the songs and dances slowly developed into the recognisable forms of drama of the 5th C. The theatre at Delphi dates from the 4th C. and contains 35 tiers of seats which could hold about 5000 people. One wishes its unique position was used more often for ancient tragedy: what better setting for Sophocles' *Oedipus Tyrannus?*

The Pythian Festival consisted initially of music competitions and hymns in honour of Apollo, held in the theatre, and athletic competitions in the stadium: later, performances of drama were added, and chariot-racing in the Krisaean plain. The prizes were merely crowns of bay.

The Stadium   The Stadium is a short climb through the pines above the theatre. (Between the theatre and stadium is the Kerna spring; this fed the Kassotis fountain somewhere to the east of the theatre, from the waters of which the priestess also drank before prophesying.) It is on a high piece of ground which was artificially levelled in the 5th C.: you can see the supporting wall on the south side. The stone seats, probably built at the expense of the benefactor Herodos Atticus, could contain 7000 spectators. Half-way along the seats on the north side can be seen the place for the officials. Lines are also visible at the start and finish of the Pythian stade (583 ft). At the eastern end are remains of a Roman triumphal arch.

From the stadium you can see across to the uplands on Kirphis: the dark sides of the hill look uninviting enough, but there is a spectacular zigzag path up its side to the village of Desfina hidden from view. A good place to picnic is above the stadium in the pines, or best of all on the fortress of Philomelos to the west (it's outside the fence and so requires a little enterprise although it can also be reached from the town): from there, you can look in every direction from Kirphis to the peaks of Mt Giona, and sometimes see Egyptian Vultures wheeling below.

The museum   The museum has many good exhibits, which are all well labelled. The following therefore includes only some of the more important items. (As the museum at Delphi is the one major museum in Greece in which the rooms are not numbered, a plan with rooms numbered in relation to the

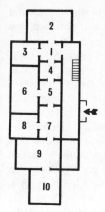

text is here provided.) On the *landing*, the Omphalos. *Room 1* includes an exquisite bronze figurine of a young man c650 BC. *Room 2:* here there is most of the frieze of the Siphnian Treasury, the best preserved being the north side (battle of gods and giants) and east side (gods watching the Trojans fight the Greeks): the sculpture is surprisingly naturalistic for the date (c525 BC) — especially the fallen figures. Also in this room is a graceful Caryatid from the Treasury, and the Naxian sphinx. *Room 3* has the famous statues of Kleobis and Biton, two large kouroi of the early 6th C., very strong figures and illustrative of the monumental style briefly borrowed from Egypt. There are also 5 metopes from the Sikyonian treasury c560 BC, the best of which contains Kastor and Pollux and Idas bringing home cattle stolen in Arcadia. *Room 4:* metopes from the Athenian treasury, of uncertain date but probably after 490: they show the exploits of Herakles and Theseus, and the battle of the Amazons — there is now far more movement if you compare, for example, Herakles and the Arcadian stag with the earlier Sikyonian or even Siphnian sculptures. *Rooms 5 and 6* have statues from the pediments of the old Temple of Apollo (destroyed in 548). *Room 9* has 4th C. sculpture: there is the Acanthus column (which once supported a tripod) with 3 women, probably Thyiads, dancing around it; of the 5 statues from the Thessalian monument the most notable is that of the Olympic victor Agias, one of Daochos' ancestors.

Room 10 has the Charioteer which would probably be less admired if it were not one of the very few surviving 5th C. bronzes. The figure has been crowned and commemorates a victory at the Pythian games: the self-confidence and steady gaze from the beautiful onyx eyes seem to say "I won, but it really wasn't that important". Through all the human statuary runs one unifying theme, a brave assertion of Man's importance, from Kleobis and Biton to the Charioteer — there may be gods, but Man is still expressed confidently as an end in himself. *Room 11:* miscellaneous items include a fine, effeminate Antinous (the emperor Hadrian's boyfriend) and objects from the Corycian Cave, such as the offerings of small clay Pans, one of which is surrounded by Thyiads.

In the town of Delphi itself there are several adequate restaurants which overlook the valley of the Pleistos and give wistful views of the sea on a hot day.

The Corycian Cave Expeditions from Delphi include the Corycian Cave and Mt Kirphis and Desfina. The Corycian Cave takes about 3 hours to reach, so take food. Get to the fortress of Philomelos from the town by following signs for the stadium and ascending the hill to the left of the (closed) entrance, and you then take the winding track up the cliff. After an hour you reach the top of the Phraedriades — near here those whom the Delphians judged guilty of sacrilege, like poor Aesop, were thrown over the edge. You turn to the north along a fold in the land to some watering-troughs (1½ hours), and then turn east, when it is easiest to follow the dirt road which skirts the valley. The cave is high up on the side of the leftward hill at the valley mouth: this hill is about half a mile beyond a new chapel beside the road, and takes about an hour to reach from the troughs. You then trust there is a cave up there and scramble up the hill, following goat tracks, when you are amazed to see first the low dark mouth of the cave and then a road which the Greeks have thought to bulldoze right up to it — this goes down the other side of the hill, joining the Arachova road, and would take much longer from Delphi.

The large cave was sacred to Pan and the Nymphs, as inscriptions testify: Pan was an old shepherd-god from whom Apollo learnt the art of prophesy, but he was also a consort of the Maenads, who celebrated the Dionysian orgies in the plain below. The high, dripping cave with its large stalagmites and stalactites and greenish light is impressive. As impressive are the bare slopes of Parnassos across the plateau of Livadi. Descending the road, then across Livadi and down to Arachova takes 3 hours.

Mt Kirphis Mt Kirphis and Desfina by the zigzag path on the hill opposite Delphi also takes about 3 hours. You get down to the Pleistos by descending the terraces to the left of the town of Delphi, and then turn towards the sea, underneath the cliffs on the right which hold the town. About one hour from Delphi, beyond a large bluff on the left, you trace the path from Chriso to Desfina, and you shortly get on to the zigzag, which takes only about an hour to the top: Delphi looks very small. It is a further hour across the red earth (and in June wild delphiniums) to Desfina, a poor but picturesque village: much of the population works at the factory at Aspra Spitia. The plateia has one or two tavernas. There is usually a bus down to Itea at about four o'clock in the afternoon (check first).

Chriso The road down to the Krisaean plain bypasses the village of Chriso, anciently Krisa: the only ancient remains are traces of an enclosed wall of the Mycenaean period near the chapel of Agios Georgios. The village has a plateia with fountains and plane-trees and several tavernas nearby, and makes a good stop. When the road hits the plain, it divides, straight on to Amfissa (20 kms from Delphi) or left to Itea (16 kms).

Amfissa   Amfissa is at the head of the Krisaean plain, an old Locrian city destroyed by Philip of Macedon, and now a substantial market town. The Franks here built a castle on the walls of the ancient acropolis above the town; it is pleasant to walk up to it.

Itea and Kirrha   Itea is an expanding town which now embraces at its eastern end the village of Kirrha, once the port of Delphi. You pass through Kirrha to the campsite further round on the coast or to go up the giddy ascent to Desfina: at Kirrha is a small restaurant near the Pleistos stream with a terrace which overlooks the bay, and the large oil tankers latterly laid up there. Apart from the cafes on the sea-front the best feature of Itea is its demotic song of the same name. The ferry to Aigion has stopped, although one to Brindisi is planned, and the harbour is chiefly used by cruise ships for Delphi.

From Itea a new road runs along the north coast of the Corinthian Gulf to Navpaktos (70 kms) and the Andirrion-Rion ferry to the Peloponnese. This stretch of coast is very beautiful, apart from the impact of the road itself, and has several small villages and bays where you can swim: on clear days there are dramatic views across the water to the Peloponnese. After you pass some large-scale bauxite **Galaxidi** operations the first village is Galaxidi, 17 kms from Itea, which sits on a small promontory with an attractive harbour. In the 19th C. it became an important ship-building and ship-owning community — the small museum in the town hall has pictures of old sailing vessels and of the busy port: now many of its handsome houses are empty, and idly reflect the bright light from their gaily painted doors and windows. The 4th C. walls of the old Hellenic city (probably Oeanthia) are visible in places, and the large church of St Nicolas has a fine early 19th C. wooden screen, but the chief pleasure is to sit at one of the several kafeneions or tavernas on the harbour and look past the pine forest, across the bay to Delphi and Parnassos. From this point the mountain appears exactly like a reclining woman. (And if Parnassos looms large in this chapter, it is probably because for 6 months I lived in a house in Galaxidi which looked directly at it.)

On the hills behind Galaxidi, about an hour's walk away, is the small monastic church of St Saviour. It is in a wonderful position, looking down over almond trees at the village, which itself in the Middle Ages and before was often forced to take refuge on the hills, owing to the frequent raids by pirates and other adventurers on this coast.

Navpaktos

Navpaktos, formerly Lepanto, about an hour's drive from Itea along the coast, is a beautiful small town, with a 15th C. Venetian castle, the walls of which run down to the sea and form a very picturesque harbour: you can walk through a gateway onto the beach, and the Peloponnese seems so close you could swim to it. Navpaktos, an old Locrian city, long had importance being at the mouth of the Corinthian Gulf. The Athenians kept it under control, through a colony of Messenians, for half a century until the end of the war with the Peloponnesians. The town often changed hands between Venetians and Turks, and in the famous sea battle of Lepanto in 1571 the Christian fleet of the Holy League destroyed a large Turkish fleet — although in the end the Turks outlasted the Venetians, and ended their squalid, oppressive rule in proud idleness inside the walls.

Andirrion to Rion ferry

Andirrion is 10 kms to the west: the ferries to Rion are frequent, each quarter to half-an-hour in the day, slightly less often at night, and relatively cheap.

EUBOEA AND THE NORTHERN SPORADES

Aulis

From Thebes a road goes northeast across wooded hills towards Chalcis, the capital of Euboea. Before crossing the narrow channel between the mainland and the island, you can turn right along a bad road, past the cement works, to the ruins of ancient Aulis, which has the remains of the Temple of Artemis (10 kms). Here it is said Iphigeneia was sacrificed to the goddess by her father Agamemnon, the leader of the Greek expedition against Troy which was held up at Aulis by adverse winds. The sacrifice was used as a pretext by Klytemnestra for killing Agamemnon on his return years later.

Euboea

The enticing island of EUBOEA (Evvia) is about 170 kms long, lying roughly parallel with Boeotia and Attica, and there are ferries to the island from several places on the mainland, including Rafina and Skala Oropou in Attica and Arkitsa in Phthiotis (north of Boeotia). Second in size only to Crete, Euboea is heavily wooded and wonderfully green, with mountains rising to nearly 6000 ft but also several fertile plains. Roads are few and often poor, and the east coast, where the mountains drop suddenly into the sea, is particularly undeveloped. The island is only just beginning to attract visitors, and the west coast near Eretria is being developed for tourism.

History of the island

Anciently, the two main cities were Chalcis and Eretria on the west coast, both being on the important north-south trade route through the Evripos channel and both prolific founders of colonies elsewhere. Athens took Chalcis in 506 BC and divided its land amongst settlers. After the Persian Wars, during which Eretria was destroyed by the Persians as punishment for assisting the Ionian revolt, Athens established control over the whole island to ensure her corn supply. In the Middle Ages Euboea was fought over by the Byzantines, Franks and Venetians, and nowhere in Greece is there such a concentration of medieval towers and fortresses to be seen. The Venetians, who lost the island to the Turks in 1470, regarded Negropont, as they called it, as one of their most prized possessions.

Chalcis

The Evripos is the dangerous, fast-flowing channel of only about 40 metres across between the island and the mainland. Inexplicably it changes direction six or more times a day, and it is said that Aristotle was so baffled by this that he drowned himself in its waters. A modern retractable bridge crosses to CHALCIS (Halkis), an unattractive, large industrial town. The name probably derives from the Greek word meaning bronze (chalkos), for the manufacture of which Chalcis was famous; its name was then given to the Chalcidici (Halkidiki) in northern Greece through the number of colonies sent there by the mother city. The former Venetian walls have been demolished, but there is one unique monument in the older part of town, namely the church of Agia Paraskevi, near the plateia. This is a basilica which the Venetians converted into a Gothic cathedral with pointed arches. In this quarter there is also a disused mosque, and a Turkish fountain, while across the channel you can see the Turkish fortress of Karababa.

Museum The museum in Leoforos Venizelou has several interesting pieces of Classical statuary, in particular the group of Theseus carrying off Antiope, from the west pediment of the Temple of Apollo at Eretria.

North Euboea The north of the island has particularly fine scenery, and a good journey to make is between Chalcis and Loutra Aidipsou (153 kms). The road first climbs over the ridge between Mt Kandilion and (on the right) Mt Dirphys; the slow winding descent from 2000 ft presents a grand panorama across forests and ravines to the sea and the Sporades beyond. Below, in a broad and beautiful valley is Prokopion,

Akmetaga also known as Akmetaga, at the centre of a large estate formerly in the possession of a Turkish pasha and now run as a model farm by a British family, the Noel-Bakers. The village contains a chapel with the relics of St John the Russian, brought from Turkey by refugees in 1923; the story of the battles with Chalcis over the saint's body is amusingly told by Osbert Lancaster. Proceeding, you will

Limni see a fork left to the picturesque fishing village of Limni, with good swimming off a sandy beach nearby.

Artemision At the northern tip of Euboea is Cape Artemision, reached by a track shortly before Agriovotanon. Here there are the ruins of a temple of Artemis, but more famous are the straits below, where the Greek and Persian fleets fought inconclusively before the battle of Thermopylae. To the west of the modern town of Istaia, which looks over the plain in the north of the island, is Orei, the site of ancient Histaia. It has a Venetian fortress on Hellenic foundations. At the end of the road is Loutra Aidipsou, an important spa, used by ancients and moderns alike.

Eretria From Chalcis across the exuberantly fertile Lelantine Plain dotted with medieval towers lies ERETRIA where surprisingly there are extensive ancient remains, whereas Chalcis has none. For although Eretria made some recovery after destruction by the Persians, it was destroyed again during the Mithridatic Wars (87 BC) and not rebuilt. Above the modern town are the remains of a 4th C. palace, a theatre and, higher up, an acropolis with Hellenic towers from where there is a magnificent view all around: the shores of Attica to the left, Pentelikon and Parnes in front, Kithairon a little to the right and further right still Parnassos. In front, near and below lies the Lelantine Plain, latticed with vineyards. In the middle of the town are the foundations of the Temple of Apollo (c510 BC). The city produced some good pottery, examples of which are in the local museum at the northwest of the town, but most of the finds are in the Archaeological Museum in Athens. The modern town has become a popular seaside resort.

South Euboea East of Eretria there is also a beach at Amarinthos, and at 57 kms from Chalcis the road divides, going left to Kimi on the east coast (a further 36 kms) and right to Karystos Kimi on the south coast (a further 69 kms). Kimi, a cheerful town embraced by vineyards and orchards, stands on an 860-foot ridge overlooking the sea and the island of Skyros. It is reached by an attractive route through a valley mutely guarded by Frankish towers and across hills covered with olive trees. Its port, 4 kms distant, is the only harbour along the mountain-walled east coast of the island.

Off the road to Karystos is a marshy lake, on the east Dystos side of which are the ruins of ancient Dystos. It is reached in about half an hour by a path south from Krieza. Within the walls the ground plans of houses of the 5th C. BC can be made out. Part of the acropolis was made into a Venetian fortress. There is another Venetian castle at Stira, further on the road to Karystos, while Nea Stira is a coastal Karystos resort. Karystos, an attractive town and resort, also has a Venetian fortress of reddish stone on the site of an ancient acropolis. The Hellenic city was famous for a white and green marble (cipollino) popular at Rome, which is still visible in the old quarries nearby.

To the north and east of Euboea are the nine islands of The Northern the NORTHERN SPORADES, though only the four largest Sporades — Skyros, Skiathos, Skopelos and Alonissos — are dealt with here. Skyros, the most southerly, is usually reached from Kimi, on Euboea; the others are reached either from Volos or, if coming direct from Athens, via Agios Konstantinos in Phthiotis, north of Boeotia. The islands are varied and attractive, with picturesque villages of the Cycladic type.

The largest of the islands is SKYROS, rugged and mountainous. Its southern face is barren and forbidding, and the southerly port of Tris Boukes is often swept by

137

gusts of wind down from the mountains. The only interest here is the grave, set in a peaceful olive grove, of Rupert Brooke who died on Skyros in 1915. The boat arrives at Linaria, further up the southwest coast, and it is usual immediately to take the bus the 12 kms across to the capital, Skyros, on the green and fertile northeast side of the island. Here, beneath a dramatically abrupt rock crowned by a medieval citadel, the streets are narrow and winding, the white cubic houses topped by flat black roofs. An invitation to someone's house should be eagerly accepted; the interiors are famous for their Byzantine-style carved furniture and tapestries. Also you should visit the museum, housed in the town hall, for its collection of medieval church furniture. There is a beach nearby — the island has several good beaches.

Skyros was anciently a dependency of Athens. Kimon found here the giant bones he imagined were those of Theseus and carried them back to Athens to be housed in the Theseion. In legend, Thetis sent young Achilles here disguised as a maiden to keep him out of the Trojan War, but Odysseus lured him away and he died by Paris' arrow.

The gentle slopes of SKIATHOS are green and wooded, its landscape sharing the softness of Pelion on the nearby mainland. For those who do not miss sharp Cycladic outline, it is the most beautiful of the Northern Sporades. A community of English have built villas here, and the island is becoming increasingly popular with tourists. Skiathos' only town (of the same name) drapes attractively over two low hills above the harbour on the southeast coast, and a few kilometres westwards is Koukounaries, the Aegean's finest beach, sandy and fringed with pines, though with the building of a Xenia, less tranquil than it once was. Three hours' walk to the north is the deserted medieval town of Kastro, perched upon a rocky outcrop, abandoned early in the last century when piracy was finally eradicated. There is a derelict Church of Christ (with frescoes) and the remains of two monasteries — that of the Annunciation has a fine Byzantine church.

SKOPELOS, like Skiathos, is green and even more intensely cultivated, though it is also more rugged, its landscape and architecture having more character. There are vineyards and groves of olive and fruit trees, and it is most enjoyable to come in August when plums, the island's speciality, are being home-dried in slow ovens, and removed now and again for tasting. Pottery and weaving also flourish. Skopelos town, towards the northeast of the island,

Skyros

Theseus and Achilles

Skiathos

Koukounaries beach

Skopelos

rises like an amphitheatre round its bay, abundant in chapels and houses deliciously washed in white or blue, ochre or red, the eaves and ridges of their blue slate roofs picked out in strokes of white, boldly emphasising their irregular geometry. But the town is exposed to the intermittent blasts of the summer meltemi, and Glossa, on the northwest coast, is the first — and in strong winds the only — port of call.

A walk up from this pleasant hamlet into the especially lush hills on this side of the island is rewarding for its views across to Skiathos and distant Euboea.

In 1538, having performed the same service for Aegina the year before, Barbarossa paused at Skopelos to slaughter the entire population.

Alonissos

Westwards lies ALONISSOS, a hilly and wooded idyll only sparsely populated and hardly frequented. On the summit of the southwest peak of the island, nearly 1000 ft above its harbour, is the attractive unspoilt village of Alonissos. The only other settlement is the small fishing village of Votsi, just to the east. There are many sandy beaches and the clear waters are excellent for underwater fishing.

CENTRAL GREECE

Across the centre of Greece there is a great mountain barrier, which stretches from the Euboean Gulf in the east to Levkas on the western coast. The two modern highways which go northwards to Epiros and Thessaly skirt these mountains to left and right, and there is only one road through the middle, where the roads from Amfissa and Levadia join together and traverse the Bralos pass, between Mt Oeti and Kallidromon. This road, after a steep descent, emerges onto the Maliac plain slightly to the east of the gorge of the river Asopos; anciently, the city of Trachis (later called Herakleia — it was the last home of Herakles before his death on Mt Oeti) guarded a track over these mountains to the cities of Doris, and ruins of the acropolis of Trachis have been identified on the top of high cliffs at the mouth of the gorge. But the track guarded by Trachis was not suitable for a large force of men: as the Roman historian Livy tells us, the only military road which afforded the means of transit to an army was by the **Thermopylae** seashore through the pass of THERMOPYLAE, "when it meets with no impediment from an opponent".

In 480 BC when the Persians invaded Greece in enormous numbers, the Greeks sent a force of some 7000 men under the Spartan general Leonidas to defend the pass. At that time Thermopylae was a narrow defile of about 6 kms long between the steep wooded slopes of Kallidromon and the sea; the pass was only a few paces wide at either end, although it widened somewhat in the middle, near the hot springs. Thermopylae, which means 'hot gates', still has these mineral waters and is a spa with a big hotel visible on the landward side of the National Highway; this road roughly follows the line of the ancient track, although it tends to the north of it. But 'the gates' have gone, no longer is there a pass between mountains and sea, because mineral deposits from the springs, and the silt carried down by the river Spercheios, have created a large expanse of land on the seaward side. As Robert Liddell observes, Thermopylae originally would have looked more like Kammena Vourla, a pleasant seaside resort (also a spa), further to the east. Moreover, the ugly monument of Leonidas, erected in 1955, would have found itself in the sea.

It was almost opposite this monument that the Greeks under Leonidas restored an old wall across the pass, the 'wall of the Phocians', and for several days, advancing in front of it into the wider part of the pass, fought off Xerxes' army of over a quarter of a million men based at

Trachis. Xerxes might have been forced to abandon his expedition at this point, had not a Greek, Ephialtes, shown a Persian force the way through Kallidromon to take the Greeks in the rear: the path, still traceable, comes out about 1½ kms to the east of the monument. Leonidas had stationed 1000 Phocians to guard the path, but they ran away: hearing of the Persian move, he then sent away all his force except 300 Spartans, 700 Thespians and 400 Thebans. Surrounded on both sides, Leonidas' men retired first to the wall, then to a small hillock nearby, at which point the Thebans deserted, and almost all the remaining Greeks were killed. On the hillock, which is across the road from the monument, there is a new plaque with the old, poignant inscription:

'O stranger, go and tell the Lacedaimonians, we lie here obedient to their commands.'

Why did the Spartans, and the Thespians, stay behind? Perhaps it was just obedience, perhaps a gesture had to be made, as at Borodino. In any event, the Persians swept on and only at Plataea a year later were they finally defeated on land.

There was an odd sequel. Brennus leading the Gauls in 279 BC turned the Greek position at Thermopylae in the same way. When he later arrived at Delphi, like Xerxes' force his army was also panicked by rocks crashing down from Parnassos.

The area of the Maliac plain has other historical associations. At the Alamana bridge over the Spercheios a small Greek force under Diakos heroically fought a Turkish army in **Lamia** 1821. Across the plain at Lamia, now the capital of the nome of Phthiotis, the Athenians, after Alexander the Great's death in 323, almost put an end to Macedonian dominion when they blockaded the Macedonian general, Antipater, in the town. However, the seige was lifted, and the Greeks were later defeated at the battle of Krannon in Thessaly. In the Middle Ages the town belonged first to the Frankish dukes of Athens (like Thebes) and then to the Catalan Duchy of Neo-Patras — on the hill above the town are the ruins of the Frankish and Catalan castle built on the ancient acropolis, from which there is a fine view of Oeti and the valley of the Spercheios. West of Lamia along the valley, beyond the spa of Ipati, is the **Ipati** charming village of Ipati (24 kms); this is the site of the ruined castle of Neo-Patras, possessed in turn by the Franks, the Greek Angeli of Epirus, the Catalans (their second capital) and the Turks (the seat of a pasha). Much further up the valley, and below Mt Timfristos is Karpenis a small country town (78 kms from Lamia); from there it is 109 kms by a spectacular road to Agrinion, which is on the route to Epirus.

Lamia's former importance owed a lot to its position commanding the Furka pass into central Thessaly over Mt Othrys; the road went (and still goes) via Thaumakoi (now Domokos), so called because of the wonder − *thauma* − caused by the sudden view of the apparently unending plain of Thessaly. Once over the pass into the plain, the road divides after 53 kms, left to Karditsa (91 kms from Lamia), Trikala (118 kms) and Kalambaka-Meteora (141 kms) and right to Farsala (67 kms) and Larissa (113 kms). Alternatively, the National Highway, which goes round Othrys to the east and passes a little to the west of Volos (111 kms from Lamia) then continues to Larissa (146 kms) and, after the Vale of Tempe, along the east coast to Thessaloniki.

Volos The town of VOLOS is situated at the base of Mt Pelion, which then extends to the southeast and hooks round to form the Pagasitikos Gulf, so that the town stands at the head of a large enclosed bay. The capital of the nome of Magnesia and an important outlet for Thessalian produce, Volos is a prosperous town with several good hotels and restaurants, but with little charm: it was badly damaged by earthquake in the 1950s, and is largely rebuilt, although the old district of Ano Volos remains above the town. There is an attractive fishing harbour at the western end of the long quay. On the large square behind, a bazaar is held in early August, of the kind that travels around central Greece in the summer selling everything from clothes and rugs to frying pans and walking-sticks − and, of course, souvlakia; villagers come from miles around for their one big shopping expedition of the year. My landlady from Tsangarada spent several thousand drachmas on this occasion, probably more than usual because she thought the Turks were coming.

The museum, which is at the other end of town, about 2 kms from the centre, is quite exceptional, and illustrates the long occupation of the area around Volos. A visit to the museum should be made before going to any of the sites of Iolkos, Sesklo, Dimini and Pagasae-Demetrias which are rather specialist tastes.

The museum The unique collection of painted stelai of the Hellenistic period, found at Demetrias, is the principal attraction, more perhaps for their survival in their present state than for their subject matter − several are clearly copies of the same theme, probably from the same workshop, although others have the poignancy of the best relief

142

stelai (of which there are also examples in the museum, notably from Phalana and Pherae) and their faded earthy colours have a delightful, soft effect. There is a very well laid out room of exhibits from Sesklo — fine Neolithic pottery with striking abstract patterns, well worked stone daggers and knives with bone handles, and household goods including pottery sieves. There are also Neolithic objects from Dimini, and Mycenaean finds from Iolkos. At the other end of the museum are two rooms, showing Thessalian graves and grave goods over the ancient period: finest of all is the gold jewellery of the 4th and 3rd C. BC which alone justifies a visit to the museum.

The ancient sites   Sesklo is, like Dimini, to the south of the road to Larissa. Both these sites are Neolithic, Dimini dating back to the 4th millenium BC and Sesklo is even earlier, indeed one of the earliest sites found in Greece. (Buses go to both places from Volos and it is possible to walk between the two in
Sesklo   about 1½ hours.) To reach Sesklo: turn off the Larissa road across the railway after 12 kms, continue towards the village, and just before it turn left for the site (1 km further on). The site (fenced but with an attendant about) is on a hillock, which backs onto a small ravine issuing out of higher hills, and has something of a Mycenae on a far smaller scale; there are low walls, the ruins of a large palace,
Iolkos   and small pieces of pottery littered everywhere. Iolkos, the home of Jason and the leading city of Thessaly in the Mycenaean period, was situated within present day Volos; a mound (Agioi Theodori) showing traces of two Mycenaean palaces has been found on the northwest side of the town, between the railway and a dry river-bed, on the right of the Larissa road (just before it branches left to Lamia).
Pegasae-   The site of Pagasae-Demetrias spreads on either side of
Demetrias   the Lamia road, beginning 4 kms south of Volos. (There is a bus stop nearby, or you can walk to it in about 45 minutes.) By tradition it was at Pagasae, the port of Iolkos, that Jason's ship the Argo was built which brought back the Golden Fleece from Colchis with the help of Medea; later it was the port of Pherae (modern Velestinon) in the 5th and 4th C. BC. When Demetrias was founded adjacently in the early 3rd C. it depopulated Iolkos (long since shrunk in importance anyway) and succeeded Pagasae. The ruins extend over a wide area, the principal remains being the walls of Demetrias, best preserved on the west of the road.

Pelion   PELION is the name not only of the mountain, but of the whole peninsula area which forms one of the strangest regions of Greece. It has few Classical or historical associations, although it was the legendary home of the Centaur

Chiron, who here taught Jason and Achilles. It is remarkable rather for its climate and vegetation, and the different style of its villages and churches. The climate is comparatively cool in summer and often damp, and in winter there are large snow falls: consequently, the vegetation is exceptionally rich from the plentiful water, particularly on the east coast where the beech-woods and sweet chestnuts, and the oaks, planes and walnut trees reach down to the olives near sea level. Most of the villages are high up on the leafy slopes, with distant views of the sea. The attractive houses, usually of whitewashed stone under slate roofs, lie spread over the valleys on the east coast, amongst fruit trees and gardens of hydrangeas and chrysanthemums; only the small plateias with a church and perhaps one or two shops and a kafeneion attract any concentration of buildings. The churches too are different in Pelion: built in the style of the old aisled basilicas they have a refreshing, almost Renaissance look in contrast to the conventional Byzantine cross-in-square, frozen in tradition. Their interiors are usually uncluttered except for elaborate candelabras and heavy screens, while outside the distinctive feature is a cloister of wood or stone running along part of the building. The churches spread low over the ground, rather than reach up, as if pressed by the too-close sky.

Pelion is an ideal area for exploration, for one day or several days, and it's become a popular summer resort for Greeks and foreigners alike. Coming from the bare rocks of central Greece I found the lushness an extraordinary shock, overwhelmingly beautiful at first: but after two weeks I confess it became too much, too green, and the dank houses (particularly my dank house) began to seem part of the living, rotting process around them — so I left.

There are plenty of hotels and rooms in the area, particularly at Portaria, Tsangarada, Zagora, and Agios Ioannis. Buses serve all the larger villages from Volos. For a short expedition (although longer than it looks on the map, as the roads are narrow and winding, like Devon lanes) you can drive in a circle round the central part of Pelion, via Portaria and the Chania pass over Pelion itself (with marvellous views over the gulf), Kissos, Tsangarada, Milies and Kala Nera. There is swimming on the east coast at Chorevto (below Zagora), Agios Ioannis (below Kissos) and Milopotamos (below Tsangarada), and at several places on the west coast. Walking is a little difficult, at least in central Pelion: I found I was either forced on to the road or through almost impenetrable woods, for example between Milies and Tsangarada.

There are some 30 villages on the slopes of Pelion: the

Swimming

144

following three may serve as examples for the others.
Makrinitsa Makrinitsa (from Volos 16 kms) is a beautiful little village reached by turning left at Portaria: it hangs on the southern slopes of Pelion, a greener and smaller Arachova. The plateia looks directly over Volos and the gulf (you can see particularly well the area of Pagasae-Demetrias) and, apart from the standard plane tree, has a sculptured fountain (maybe it will be decorated with a watermelon cooling under its water) and a small church, with a stone-pillared cloister along two sides, and a sculptured exterior to the apse. Above the plateia, inside a courtyard reached by a stone track past handsome white houses is the large 18th C. church of the Panagia (it was formerly a monastery): a wooden cloister runs around three sides of the building.

Tsangarada Tsangarada (55 kms) is typical of the Pelion villages on the east coast, being spread out over a long distance, mostly off the road. Stone tracks run beside banks of rigani between the four plateias, which form separate local centres within the village. The principal plateia of Agia Paraskevi (near the post office) has some attractive old buildings, a monstrous plane tree with the church bell hanging from it — unfortunately the church itself is modern and ugly — and a good taverna. From here it is a ½ hour walk to the next plateia to the south, that of the Holy Taxiarchs, which is exquisite, with a whitewashed church, cloistered on north and south, a shop and kafeneion: this plateia is only a short step from the road (where it curves, by a restaurant) and yet is hidden from sight. (Between these two plateias a road descends in 8 kms to Milopotamos which has two tavernas and some excellent swimming.) Further on, actually on the road, is the church of Agios Ioannis, rather similar to the Panagia in Makronitsa: outside there is a wooden cloister on three sides; inside it has elegant aisles behind high arches, and local people told me that the wooden slats above the windows were used to store arms, under both the Turks and the Germans.

Milies Milies (27 kms) is in the middle of the peninsula. At one time a railway ran from Volos through the olives, but no more: it must have been one of the prettiest stretches of line in Greece. The principal plateia, some way above the desolate area around the old railway station, has several cafes, a cloistered church and the library of Agios Athanasios — at one time the village was a centre of
Walking Hellenic culture under the Turks. It is possible to walk from here, southeast, to the chapel of Agia Triada (one hour) and then south to the modest remains of the ancient town of Korope. But if you really want to get to grips with the countryside you can walk up through the village, then past

the planes and the water and the patches of fruit trees, into the woods on top of the hills, then go northeast through the chestnut groves to a small village on the road near Tsangarada: it took me 4½ hours, but in the past there was a good path between the villages and it would have taken half that time. All over Greece the new roads are ruining the old paths, by their disuse. One encounter I had that day was with an old man with a bad eye, who was strapping firewood onto his mule; he was using just his arms, as years ago some dynamite had blown off his hands. *"Ti na kanome"* — "What can one do", he said with a sad smile.

Larissa After bypassing Volos, the National Highway on its way north crosses the eastern side of Thessaly via Larissa (58 kms from Volos), an important town and capital of the province of Thessaly. It has little to show for its long history. From the Turkish occupation of almost 500 years up to 1881, there remains in the centre of the city near the market a mosque with a minaret, which now contains the Archaeological Museum with a large collection of Palaeolithic and Neolithic objects found in Thessaly, amongst other exhibits. Otherwise you can sit in the large central square under the orange trees and sip an ouzo or eat some halva (a sweet made of honey and sesame), for both of which products Larissa is well known, or stroll across the Pineios river to the park (on the right of the Kozani road) where there are some remains of a large temple. Twenty-four kms south west of Larissa is Krannon, near the site of the battle in 323 BC when the Macedonians re-established control over the Greeks: earlier it was an important city, and remains have been found of a temple of Asklepios and also two 5th C. beehive tombs.

Vale of Tempe At the northeast corner of the plain of Thessaly the Pineios finds an outlet to the sea through the Vale of Tempe, between the slopes of Lower Olympos to the north and those of cone-shaped Ossa on the south. The valley, along which the Pineios flows past plane trees and willows, is a narrow defile about 10 kms long, under high cliffs. Anciently it contained a sanctuary of Apollo, who was said to have purified himself in the waters of the Pineios after killing the Python at Delphi; later at intervals a procession of young men came from Delphi to gather the bay which still grows here. Tempe was also one of the main routes into Greece, and at first sight a good position for defence: in 480 the Greeks took up position here until Xerxes found a way round to the north via Gonnos, and then the Greek force retired to Thermopylae. Whatever beauty and tranquillity Tempe formerly possessed have been destroyed by the modern road and the railway which both go through its middle.

The road emerges onto the coastal strip to the east of Olympos, and after several depressing-looking camping and swimming places passes on the right of the road at 52 kms from Larissa, the castle of Platamon built by the Crusaders in the early 13th C. It is worth visiting, as it is well preserved and has good views towards Olympos and the coastal area to the north, known anciently as Pieria. At 58 kms there is a turning left for Leptokaria and a poor road through Olympos to Elasson via Karia and Kriovrisi, beyond which a road to the right leads up to the Army Ski Centre. This is one way to approach the ascent of OLYMPOS, but Litochoron, a small town on the east slopes of the mountain, is the usual starting point for climbing up to the legendary home of the gods. The mountain has 7 peaks of 9000 ft or over, the highest of which is Mytikas, 9570 ft: it is, like Parnassos, only practical to climb it in the summer owing to the presence of snow for most of the year. From Litochoron it is about 10 hours to the summit, and a night should be spent at Refuge A at 6890 ft, 2½ hours from the summit (take food). There are red markers to Mytikas from the town, but it is advisable to engage a guide: information, etc., from the Greek Alpine Club in Litochoron. The summit can also be reached by driving via Elasson (southwest of Olympos and 61 kms from Larissa), Elevtherochorio, Kallithea and Olympiada, and then taking the military road on the left up to the Army Ski Centre (the approach to this from the east has been described above); nearby is Refuge B, and from there Refuge A can be reached, but get good directions or preferably a guide first — it can be a dangerous mountain.

The National Highway continues past Katerini, a market town (85 kms from Larissa), from which there are good views of Olympos to the south; it then passes between the village of Kitros and the site of ancient Pydna on the coast (this was a Macedonian city, near which in 168 BC the Romans inflicted a decisive defeat on the Macedonians), and crosses the wide Aliakmon river and finally a large area of reclaimed land to Thessaloniki (153 kms).

More interesting than the coastal route to Thessaloniki is the inland route via Trikala and Kalambaka-Meteora. (The obvious solution is to do one route going north, and another on the way south, if you can). Trikala is 63 kms from Larissa by a good road across the plain. If you come from the direction of Lamia, at 53 kms there is the fork right to Farsala, to the west of which at the battle of

Crusader castle

Climbing Mt Olympos

The coastal route north

The plain of Thessaly

147

Pharsalus in 48 BC Caesar defeated Pompey and so won control of the whole Roman world. You take the Karditsa road to the left; the huge wall of the Pindos mountains draws closer on the west as you drive past agricultural villages rich in cows and tractors beyond the dreams of most Greek farmers. Sometimes, near the villages, you see groups of the distinctive circular tents of the gypsies. Karditsa itself is an uninteresting market town — apart from the storks' nests, which are on almost every roof in late spring. 41 kms to its south in the Pindos foothills is the pleasant spa of Smokovo.

Trikala   Trikala, 27 kms further on across the river Pineios, has more interest. As ancient Trikka it had the oldest sanctuary in Greece of Asklepios, the god of medicine, and attracted many visitors: from the pastures around the city came the best of the famous Thessalian horses. Now the capital of its nome, it is a pleasant town making the most of its position on either side of the river Lethaios: in the town centre, two plateias face each other across the river, while in the northwest of the town is a Byzantine fort, below which is the former Turkish bazaar with old houses and many churches amongst the narrow streets. Like Karditsa, Trikala is the winter quarters of a good many Vlachs who come down from the summer pastures in the Pindos. Southwest of Trikala there is an attractive way into

Pili   the mountains: you take the road to Pigi, and then Pili (19 kms), a village at the entry of a defile which carries water down from the Pindos and was formerly a route through to Arta. At 1½ kms above the village in a beautiful position by the side of the stream is the Porta Panagia, a basilical church founded in 1283 by the Greek rulers of Neo-Patras: it has some 13th C. mosaics and early 15th C. frescoes. Further upstream is a narrow 16th C. bridge built by St Bessarion, the abbot of Dousiko, a monastery which he founded visible to the north of Pili. It is possible to drive on up to the mountain village of Petrouli and beyond.

Kalambaka   Kalambaka, 23 kms from Trikala, is the usual place to stay when seeing the Meteora, as it lies below one of the largest of the blue-grey rocks, which rise dramatically and inexplicably from the plain: as at Delphi, Egyptian Vultures fly overhead, and the small town seems dwarfed by the massive pedestals "gathering like silent troops of mammoth halted in meditation on the tundra's edge" (Patrick Leigh Fermor). Across the wide, sandy bed of the Pineios is the facade of the Pindos mountains. Kalambaka itself is a modern town and not particularly attractive: it was burnt by the Germans in 1943. If you wish to spend a night nearby, Trikala might be preferable, but Kalambaka does retain undamaged the extraordinary, former cathedral church of the Koimisis: you find it towards the top of the town, not far from the station. The existing church, an aisled basilica, was founded in the mid-12th C., but it incorporates features and materials from several earlier buildings: in its middle, is an ambo, a canopied pulpit made from marble, said to be unique in present day Byzantine churches; in the apse behind the ciborium, an elaborate canopied altar, is a three-stepped synthronon, where the priests used to stand. According to the nice caretaker, who is probably as reliable as anyone else, these features belonged to a previous church of the 7th C. or earlier: the mosaics visible under the floor near the screen belonged to the earliest church built about the 5th C. Whatever the exact history, the continuity of worship is obvious: the church was already very old when most of the frescoes were done in the 16th C. The pillars in fact derive from a pagan temple, and you can see Ionic capitals on the two nearest the door; outside, on the south wall there are clear traces of Classical or Hellenistic masonry, with one piece of ancient statuary actually built into the wall — a man or god with a child.

| The Meteora | The METEORA are the monasteries built on the huge rocks behind Kalambaka, so called because they are 'suspended in mid air'. The rocks and monasteries form an extraordinary congregation, which are deeply impressive at any time, whether in the rain when the rocks menace you with their blackened walls, or in the sunshine when they gleam like metal and the red-roofed monasteries look peacefully over the green valleys. |

The Meteora

The METEORA are the monasteries built on the huge rocks behind Kalambaka, so called because they are 'suspended in mid air'. The rocks and monasteries form an extraordinary congregation, which are deeply impressive at any time, whether in the rain when the rocks menace you with their blackened walls, or in the sunshine when they gleam like metal and the red-roofed monasteries look peacefully over the green valleys.

History of the monasteries

The precise history of the monasteries is not entirely clear. At first hermits and ascetics came to live in the caves amongst the rocks, and by the late 13th or early 14th C., and possibly before, a group of hermits had their centre at the skete of Doupiani. Then during the 14th C. the hermitages began to be developed as monasteries on top of the rocks, where they would be immune to the troubled times beneath them. The largest monastery on the largest rock, the Great Meteoron, was founded by St Athanasios in the mid 14th C.: this monastery and the others were totally inaccessible until recently — except by way of retractable ladder or rope and windlass. How then did Athanasios (and others like him) get up there in the first place? The story goes that *he* at any rate got there on the back of an eagle — and they might be right.

At one time there were over 20 monastic communities on these precipitous rocks. They continued to flourish even under the Turks — as often happens with the church, under oppression the monasteries were both a refuge and a symbol — and their decline has only been in the last century or so. At the end of the 19th C. the Bishop of Trikala was given control over the monasteries, and in the 1920s he ordered steps to be cut up to them. Their properties have since been confiscated or looted, and they have become almost emptied of monks. The 4 major remaining monasteries of Great Meteoron, Barlaam, Agia Triada and Agios Stephanos are with the exception of the last (which is a nunnery) little more than museums.

The Meteora are reached by a road to the west of Kalambaka, which goes past the village of Kastraki into a valley between the elephantine rocks. It is about 21 kms by road to visit the furthest monasteries and to return, so a car or tour is necessary (no local buses) unless you slog it out on foot, either on the road or by the shorter paths. If you are pressed for time, I would suggest visits to Agios Nikolaos, the Great Meteoron and either Agia Triada or Agios Stephanos.

After 2½ kms on the left is the chapel of Doupiani, probably built on the foundations of the first communal church of the then hermitages: the skete of Doupiani was on the rock above. Shortly after, again on the left, is the
Agios Nikolaos monastery of Agios Nikolaos, founded in the 14th C. and recently restored. Although it is almost an anti-climax to see the small building perched amongst other far higher rocks, it is worth the climb: tucked away in the attractive monastic buildings is a tiny church with magnificent frescoes by the Cretan Theophanes (1527), which for once are easy to see owing to the church's scale. Further on the right is the monastery of Roussanou, founded in about 1380 and now it seems being restored.

After 6 kms the road forks left to Barlaam and the Great Meteoron, and right to Agia Triada and Agios Stephanos. If you go left, after ½ km a road on the left goes to the
Barlaam monastery of Barlaam, founded in the early 16th C. by two members of a Ioannina family on the site of an earlier hermitage. It is reached by an iron bridge across a great cleft, and then by steps in the rock. The Church of All Saints, with a narthex, has frescoes painted in the mid 16th C. by Frangos Kastellanos of Thebes, who like Theophanes also worked on Athonite churches: the frescoes, now restored, are somewhat fussy compared to those at the Great Meteoron. The refectory houses a museum for the monastery's treasures.
The Great The Great Meteoron is, as it always was, the most
Meteoron important of the monasteries. Founded by the athletic

Athanasios in the 14th C. it enjoyed the protection and support of the Serbian rulers of Thessaly, one of whom under the name of Ioasaph lived here as a monk. It is approached across a bridge, and through a tunnel cut in the rock, under the old tower which retains the original wooden windlass (now aided by an electric motor): a retractable ladder still hangs against the wall.

This monastery, like Barlaam, has much the same form as the monasteries on Athos: Athanasios had in fact first become a monk on the Holy Mountain. The monastic buildings surround the Katholicon, the main church, giving a courtyard effect. The Church of the Transfiguration built in the mid 16th C. but retaining the 14th C. apse of Ioasaph's church, is very like the Katholicon of an Athonite monastery: it is a domed, cross-in-square church with a square narthex, apsidal ends to the transepts which are lined with wooden stalls, and every inch covered with fine frescoes; there is a carved, gilded ikonostasis (as at Barlaam), and overall the interior has something of the warm, golden light of an Athonite church. Outside, in the cloistered gallery to the north hang the 'simantra', huge wooden beams the shape of a waisted ice cream stick which a monk would beat with a mallet, in groups of three sharp notes commemorating the Trinity, to bring his fellows to worship.

The monastery's refectory, a barrel-vaulted room of the 16th C. has the monastic treasures, which are comparable to those on display to the average visitor on Athos. It has early illuminated manuscripts, 14th C. crysobuls, and many 16th C. ikons; there are old vestments and intricately carved wooden crosses. A good 18th C. engraving shows all the monasteries at that time — and the Great Meteoron towering over them all.

Nearby is a cloister with the monks' cells, and an ossuary, if you like skulls.

You can escape the crowds (which are a problem) by walking for half an hour to the north of the Meteoron to the ruined 14th C. monastery of Hipapanti: there is a church in a cave, with frescoes.

Agia Triada   Agia Triada (Holy Trinity) is 2½ kms in the other direction from the junction. It is across a deep ravine from the road and the rock must have been one of the most difficult to ascend: there are now steps. The monastery's foundation and its church are ascribed to the 15th C., and there is a later chapel of St John the Baptist hewn out of the rock. It has attractive monastic buildings, with arches and columns, under a solitary cypress tree.

Agios Stephanos   Shortly after is Agios Stephanos, founded in the 14th C.

This is the one monastery which can just be seen from Kalambaka, and from it you get a good view over the town and the Pineios to the Pindos wall: it is also the easiest to reach, across a small bridge. The building is now a thriving nunnery, and their feminine touch is evident in the neat balconied courtyard. The only charge you pay is for visiting the modest treasures in the refectory, as if a reminder that everything else is definitely not a museum. The late 18th C. Church of Agios Charalambos without any frescoes is strangely bare, except for its carved screen; a silver reliquary contains the saint's head. The earlier church of St Stephen is apparently closed at present: its 14th C. frescoes were damaged by German gunfire in the last war. The monastery was also looted by the Italians. In the civil war the Greek Communists committed several atrocities here, apart from desecrating a portrait of the founder. Until those years, this monastery, and the others, had remained inviolate on their great rocks.

NORTHERN GREECE AND THE ISLANDS OF THE NORTH AEGEAN

The Katara pass to Metsovo

Leaving Kalambaka, after 10 kms there is a fork in the road: you turn left onto a spectacular road (which requires some care from the driver) over the Katara pass (5600 ft) to reach Metsovo (67 kms), an attractive Vlach town, and eventually Ioannina (126 kms). The right fork leads north via Grevena (70 kms); 28 kms north of Grevena beyond the Aliakmon river, which here has carved out from the red stone limbs of land like mini Meteora, the road again divides, going right to Kozani and ultimately Edessa (173 kms from Grevena) and left to Kastoria (93 kms).

Kastoria and the lakes

Kastoria is pleasantly situated on a lake: it has old wooden houses and countless churches, which are almost all of basilical form and many are frescoed. This is the Lake District of Greece: northwest of Kastoria are the two Prespa Lakes, the larger of which lies between the three countries of Albania, Yugoslavia and Greece. Both lakes are important ornithological areas (permit needed). The road north of Kastoria goes within a few kilometres of the Lakes, then turns east via Florina to join the road from Kozani. Then the road to Edessa (which is 139 kms from Kastoria) passes through beautiful, rolling country between the mountains on the Yugoslav border, and the misty lakes below Mt Vermion.

Edessa

Edessa, the capital of the nome of Pella, is situated on a plateau above the plain which stretches to Thessaloniki in the east, and beyond the border with Yugoslavia to the north. With its abundant streams, which fall in great waterfalls over the cliffs below the town, and its commanding position looking over the fields of Macedon, Edessa was chosen by the Macedonian kings as their capital (Aigai): even after the capital was transferred to Pella at the end of the 5th C. BC Edessa remained the spiritual home of the Macedonian monarchs and their burial place — until Alexander's death in Asia. It was here that Philip of Macedon was assassinated when attending the games in honour of his daughter's wedding. Under the Romans, the town was again of importance, being on the Via Egnatia which ran across the province of Macedonia, between Brindisi and Byzantium (Istanbul). It should be a romantic place (perhaps Mary Renault's *Fire from Heaven* is too vivid) but it isn't: the falls are channelled below a tourist development comprising shops and a restaurant, and the town itself is ugly and modern. (But see page 154 for the startling new discovery at Vergina.)

The road descends into the fruit trees, and follows the old Via Egnatia eastwards, past the site of Pella to Thessaloniki (95 kms). But first, some 14 kms from Edessa is a right turn for Verria: taking that road, you will see not far before the turning to Naoussa (a town with an exaggerated reputation for its red wine) a small road on the left, across the railway, to a large temple tomb, the Tomb of Levkadia. This is one of several similar 3rd C. Macedonian tombs in the area (another is the Tomb of Vergina, near the Palace of Palatitsa, southeast of Verria): its facade, part Doric order, part Ionic, has well-preserved paintings. The distinction of Verria is the number of small churches built behind houses to deceive the Turks: some have frescoes. You need a guide, as they deceive tourists as well. (Late in 1977 Professor Manolis Andronikos announced the discovery at Vergina of the tomb of Philip II. If his claim is supported by the evidence of further excavations it would mean that Vergina, and not Edessa as has long been supposed, was the Macedonian capital known as Aigai.)

Temple tombs

Pella

The main excavated area of PELLA lies just to the left of the road some 40 kms from Thessaloniki in the middle of a dull, empty expanse. Formerly there was marshy lake to the south, navigable from the sea, and the city lay between the lake and its acropolis, which was on a hill to the west of the present village of Palea Pella, north of the main road. The few buildings excavated so far were probably somewhere in the city centre. As the eventual capital of the Macedonian kings, Pella was thus a large, important city. The court of King Archelaos (413-399) attracted painters and writers — Euripides for example died here — but the later kings, in particular Philip and Alexander, sought to assert their Hellenism more by leadership and conquest than by the civilised cultivation of the arts. With one exception, Macedon's major legacy remains the memory of the militarist ambitions and exploits of Alexander the Great, whose birthplace it was. Following Alexander's death, the whole Greek world was subjected to the rivalries of the successor kings. Finally in 168 BC, Pella and Macedonia fell to the Romans, after the battle of Pydna.

The mosaics

The one exception is the group of mosaics found amongst the three excavated buildings. The building to the east, the foundations of which have been completely exposed, was a large important structure, perhaps a government office, built in about 300 BC and containing several open courtyards with porticoes: it was surrounded on three sides by streets complete with sewers and waterpipes. In the rooms on the west were found the best of the mosaics now in the new museum across the road, including the famous Lion Hunt, and the mosaic of Dionysos riding a panther. Other mosaics still remain *in situ*.

These pavement mosaics are very different from the later religious examples which were primarily used in decorating walls: they are made from pebbles and not from cubes of stone and glass paste; parts of the pictures are also outlined with strips of metal. Partly as a result of the differences in technique they are more fluid, less stiff than most of the religious mosaics — note the movement in the hunting scenes and the grace in the Dionysos, two qualities largely absent in the Byzantine mosaics. They are worth going out of your way to see. In the attractively laid out museum, amongst other exhibits is a romantic head of Alexander, and a fine round table inlaid with ivory.

Thessaloniki

THESSALONIKI (often called Salonika), situated on the lower slopes of Mt Chortiatis at the head of the Thermaic Gulf and historically at the cross-roads of international trade, has long been an important centre of commerce. Now the second largest city in the country and the seat of the Ministry of Northern Greece, it spreads far beyond the confines of the old Byzantine city walls. The walls still dominate the upper part of the town and define, even where they are missing, the central area of the modern city, which rises in layers from the sea front esplanade to the old Turkish quarter huddled under the remaining ramparts. You can walk across this central area inside half-an-hour, and unlike Athens there is a reasonable *modus vivendi* between traffic and pedestrians. In fact, Thessaloniki has several good points over Athens: the atmosphere is metropolitan without being that of a bazaar (despite the long occupation of the Turks who only left in 1912) and there is some degree of style in the planning of the modern city, albeit the result of the disastrous fire in 1917 which destroyed part of the town. Without having a supreme monument such as Athens possesses in the Acropolis, Thessaloniki has a number of exceptional Byzantine churches, many of them with important mosaics, although the feast is less full than one is sometimes led to expect. The churches reflect the long history of the city as an important Byzantine centre.

Its History

Although founded in the 4th C. BC, Thessaloniki only achieved real importance after 146 BC when it became the capital of the Roman province of Macedonia. It was of increasing importance under the later Roman Empire, as the balance shifted to the east, and it became the second city of the Byzantine Empire. It managed to withstand the constant attacks by Goths and Slavs, but was sacked by the Saracens in 904 and the Normans of Sicily in 1185. After the Fourth Crusade, Thessaloniki became the capital of a Latin kingdom for a few years until taken by the Greek rulers of Epirus, but it soon reverted, in 1246, to the Byzantine Empire of Nicaea. Despite the destructive rivalries of different religious factions within the city in the mid 14th C., and temporary occupation by the Turks in 1387 and 1394, Thessaloniki did not finally fall to the Ottoman Empire until 1430. Under the Turks the city was comparatively prosperous, particularly after the influx of a large number of Jewish refugees from Spain at the end of the 15th C. There developed a very mixed population of Greeks, Slavs, Albanians, Vlachs and Armenians — apart from the Jews, and of course the Turks. In 1912 the Greeks retook the city, and in 1923 under the exchange of populations the majority of the Turks were replaced by Greeks from Asia Minor. In the last war the city lost almost the entire Jewish population of over 60,000 people.

Layout   Owing to the grid-like layout of the streets, Thessaloniki is quite an easy town to get about in. The sea front is called *Leoforos Vasileos Konstantinou:* several streets run parallel with it to the north, *Megalou Alexandrou* (Tsimiski), *Ermou, Egnatias, Filippou* and *Agiou Dimitriou.* In the middle of the sea front, an avenue leads at right angles from the *Plateia Aristotelous* to a huge, rather empty area in the city centre called *Plateia Dikastirion,* in the upper part of which was recently found the old Roman Forum when they were about to build new law courts. Beyond Agiou Dimitriou, the streets of *Olympiados* and *Athinas,* meeting at the *Church of Profitis Ilias* (1) in the form of a crescent, contain the old *Turkish quarter.*

Plateia Aristotelous (2), facing the sea front, is a good place to sit and have an expensive cup of coffee before looking around: it's close to the banks and travel agents, and to the British, American and other consulates (to which a visit is necessary for those wanting to go to Mount Athos). Walking eastwards (strictly southeastwards, as the city is not quite on a north-south axis, but I shall describe it as if it were, with the sea to the south) you pass the *Museum of Popular Art* (3) which has traditional local costumes, etc. At the farther end is the *White Tower* (4), built in about 1430 at the southeastern angle of the walls. From its top, you get a good view of the whole city: the walls enclosing the upper area are obvious to the north; the new city extends chiefly to the right (to the east). The boundary between old and new is roughly formed by the

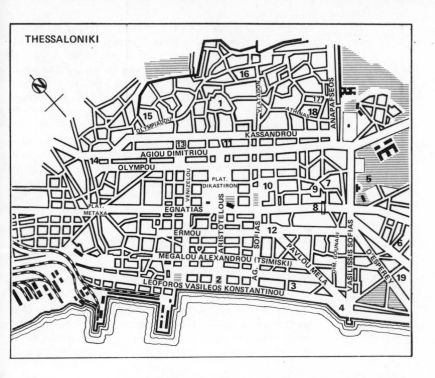

THESSALONIKI

University (5), the *International Fair* (6) and the gardens below the White Tower, on the far side of which is the Archaeological Museum. One of the city's landmarks is *Agios Georgios* (7), identified by its tall minaret.

Walking up Dimitriou Gounari towards Agios Georgios, you first encounter at the end of Egnatias the *Arch of Galerius* (8): this was a triumphal arch built by the Emperor Galerius in about AD 300 to commemorate his victories over the Persians, and has relief sculptures showing how he won them. Originally there was another arch to the east, and a dome rested on the four central pillars covering the cross-roads. The Arch was central to a large development: in the southern part was the palace and the hippodrome (where in 390 the Christian convert Theodosios forgot himself to the extent of having 7000 or more citizens massacred in revenge for the lynching of his governor); to the north was the Rotunda, reached by a porticoed avenue. This building was probably designed as Galerius' mausoleum, but was never used as such and was converted into a Christian church at about the end of the 4th C. AD, becoming known

Agios Georgios

as *Agios Georgios* (7). The Turks converted it into a mosque, like most of the churches in Thessaloniki, and added the minaret. Now it is a museum. In the dome and recesses it contains very fine mosaics against a background of gold, dating from its conversion to a church. The most interesting are the panels in the dome, of 8 saints in prayer portrayed in front of huge architectural facades, exemplifying a sort of baroque Hellenism not found elsewhere. The mosaics higher in the dome are fragmentary, and in parts restored by painting. Those in the recesses are of birds and flowers. To the left of the apse is a mosaic panel of St Andrew, while the apse has fragmentary 10th C. frescoes.

Very near Agios Georgios, to the southwest, is the church of *Agios Pandeleimonos* (9), dating from the 12th or 13th C. From here a street leads westwards, in the direction of the central Plateia Dikastirion, to the church (10) of *Agia Paraskevi* (or Panagia Acheiropoietos — so named after an ikon miraculously painted without hands). This is a basilica of the first half of the 5th C., with a narthex, a nave and two aisles; the columns within the arcades have fine capitals and inside the arches are elegant mosaic decorations of fruit, flowers and birds, together with various pictorial symbols like the Cross and the Book of Scriptures. The building is magnificently simple compared to the domes and decorations of the later churches.

From Agia Paraskevi, the famous churches of Agios Dimitrios and Agia Sophia lie in opposite directions: Agios Dimitrios to the north, on the other side of Agiou Dimitriou, and Agia Sophia to the south in an attractive garden at the end of Ermou.

Agios Dimitrios   *Agios Dimitrios* (11) is the earlier of the two, dating from the 5th C. St Demetrius was martyred in the reign of Galerius (303), and in the early 4th C. a church was built on the site of his martyrdom: this was superseded by the basilica in the 5th C., which was then partially rebuilt in the 7th C. after a fire. The church has been very largely reconstructed again, after being badly damaged in the fire of 1917.

Agios Dimitrios, the largest church in Greece, is a double-aisled basilica with slightly projecting transepts giving a cruciform effect. Some of the pillars inside have very fine early capitals, but the church's main distinction is the remaining mosaics: in the corner to the left of the west door is a 5th C. mosaic of St Demetrius, with angels hovering over him in a cloudy sky, but the most important mosaics are those on the piers of the choir. The right pier has three mosaics, including a 7th C. mosaic of St Demetrius with an official and a bishop, who are described as the founders of the church, and were perhaps those responsible for the building of the basilica in the 5th C. and the rebuilding in the 7th C., respectively. The subjects are treated more severely than in Agios Georgios, and Osbert Lancaster calls this "the greatest remaining masterpiece of the pictorial art of the pre-ikonoclastic era in Greece". I prefer the mosaic on the left pier, also from the 7th C., showing the saint with the two children of the donor of the mosaic, which was in effect a votive offering: the smaller child who shyly presses against the saint's white cloak is very appealing.

Agia Sophia The church (12) of *Agia Sophia* (or Divine Wisdom) which was probably built in the 8th C. represents the transition between an aisled basilica and a domed cross-in-square; the narthex is a feature common to both forms. The capitals of 'windblown acanthus' leaves are probably from an earlier building. The church was badly damaged by fire in 1890, when it was a mosque, and rather tastelessly restored. The mosaics mark the resumption of mosaic decoration after the ikonoclastic period (726-843): in the dome is a superb Ascension of Christ, with the Pantokrator (Almighty) and angels, below which are the Virgin Mary and 12 apostles. The inscription is the Greek original of 'ye men of Galilee, why stand ye gazing up into heaven'. In the apse is an enthroned Virgin and Child: you also see traces of a large cross, which was all that the ikonoclasts allowed in the way of representational art. The mosaics as a whole if a 'little uncouth' have an exciting directness in expression and composition.

The Plateia Dikastirion (to the northwest) has at the bottom right corner a 15th C. Turkish bath-house (still in use) and, opposite, the Panagia Chalkeon founded in 1028, a classic Greek cross-in-square church with a narthex: there are frescoes, mostly of the 11th C., in the dome, the apse and the narthex. Below the plateia is the market-area and south of this, across Ermou and Vasileos Irakliou, is a small square in the middle of which is another old Turkish bath-house now converted into a market: there is a taverna with tables on the pavement, where you can eat cheap, adequate food and look at the flower shops. The next street down, Megalou Alexandrou, is the main shopping area. This crosses Eleftheriou Venizelou, which then goes up, northwards, past a large Turkish building built in the 15th C., now a cinema but formerly a mosque, and continues across Olympou into a square in front of the Dioikitirion (13): here are the offices of the Ministry of Northern Greece — another place to visit if you wish to go to Athos (see the last section of this guide for details).

If you follow Olympou westwards you come to a beautiful church in an old tumbledown square. This is *Agioi*

Agioi Apostoloi

Apostoloi (14), the Church of the Holy Apostles, built at the beginning of the 14th C. and a good example of the artistic renaissance under the Palaeologue emperors. The cross-in-square church has two additional aisles to north and south, a narthex and exo-narthex: outside, the 5 domes and elaborate brickwork, particularly at the east end, give a very rich effect while inside there are fine 14th C. mosaics, chiefly in the vaults under the drum.

The old quarter

The old quarter is now squeezed into the northern corner of the town: the small streets with their timber-framed houses and colourful gardens are a legacy from the Turks, and even if insanitary and inconvenient they are hardly inferior to the concrete tenements, the instant modern slums which crowd them out. The tiny streets are almost impossible to navigate by map or description: it's best just to wander and see where you arrive. Here are some possible starting points and objectives.

About a third of the way along Olympiados (from the west) is a street leading north to *Agia Ekaterini* (15), a little church rather similar to that of the Apostles, although slightly earlier (late 13th C.); it has contemporary frescoes. *Profitis Ilias* (1) at the junction between Olympiados and Athinas, dates from the 14th C. and was originally a monastic church; it has had to be heavily restored inside, but does retain rather a grand narthex. From Profitis Ilias you should be able to reach the small church of *Osios David* (16), by taking a left turn off Athinas, up Odos Vlatadon, and then the second on the left, and continuing northwards; but the church is difficult to find as it is tucked away in its own courtyard, and you may have to ask. Here we go back into time, to the 5th C. The church's unusual shape is because it has lost the nave and so only the top part of the Syrian cross remains. You enter by the south door and to the right, in the apse, is a remarkable 5th C. mosaic showing Christ appearing in a vision to two prophets, Ezekiel (on the left) and Habbakuk, who both look a little uncertain. Once again the figures are static, archaic.

Byzantine walls

Not far above Osios David are the *Byzantine walls* which date from the 14th C. AD although rebuilt or added to in places. The best preserved portion is that which also forms the south wall of the acropolis — it has several large towers, the one in the northeastern angle being contemporary with

the White Tower. Within the acropolis is a fortress, now a prison, the central tower of which was built by the Turks in 1431. If you follow the line of the eastern ramparts back down, you should find yourself in Apostolou Pavlou: to its west reached by a parallel street is the charming 14th C. church of *Agios Nikolaos* (17) with contemporary frescoes;

Ataturk's house almost at the bottom of Apostolou Pavlou is the house (18) where Mustapha Kemal — Ataturk — (1881-1938), first president of Turkey, was born.

Archaeological Museum The large *Archaeological Museum* (19) at the east end of town, has a good presentation of exhibits which are generally not perhaps of the first importance. There is a large room of finds from Macedonia, from the Neolithic to the Iron Age period, including pottery of the Sesklo style. The collection also includes the superb 4th C. and Hellenistic grave goods found at Derveni and Neapolis respectively.

Panorama From Thessaloniki you can drive part way up Mt Chortiatis to the small village of Panorama (9 kms) for a view of the area south, or go southwards to one of the **Beaches** seaside resorts on the Thermaic Gulf, such as Agia Triada (23 kms) and Nea Michaniona (30 kms), the second of which has long shallow beaches to the east, and one or two good fish restaurants in the centre.

The Chalcidici East of Thessaloniki is the CHALCIDICI (Halkidiki), a lump of land terminating in three peninsulas, like a jellyfish trailing thin tentacles through the sea. Its name derives from the colonies anciently sent to the area by Chalcis in Euboea, but it attracted many other colonies as well. Chalcidici appears also to have been inhabited at the earliest moments of human existence. At the Petralona Cave, 15 **Earliest** kms beyond Nea Kallikrateia, a 400,000-year-old skeleton **European man** of a youth was found embedded in a stalagmite in 1976, as well as cooked animal remains at a level corresponding to a period of between 700,000 and 1,100,000 years ago — implying the earliest man-made fire in Europe.

The middle of Chalcidici is mostly wooded hills, but a fertile coastal strip runs above the three peninsulas, which are called (from the west) Kassandra, Sithonia and Athos.

Of these, Kassandra and Sithonia with their many sandy beaches are being rapidly developed for tourism, and roads have now been built along virtually the entire coastline of both peninsulas. Kassandra, which is the most fertile of the three and therefore attracted many ancient colonies, has been developed in particular on the east coast, notably at Kallithea (100 kms from Thessaloniki) and near Paliouri (132 kms). At the neck of the peninsula is Nea Potidaia which marks the site of the important ancient city of Potidaea, a Corinthian colony, later destroyed by Philip of Macedon; rebuilt by Kassander, it became the most important town in Macedonia, but was finally destroyed by the Huns. There are no very obvious remains of either Potidaea, or of the city of Olynthos, 15 kms to the northeast. Olynthos, of importance in the 5th and 4th C. BC, was also destroyed by Philip (to the dismay of the Athenian orator Demosthenes who had encouraged its opposition to the Macedonians) but was never built: its excavation taught much about the ground-plan of a Greek city — chiefly, square houses laid out in streets crossing at right angles — but there is little left to see.

You reach Sithonia most easily via Poligyros, a picturesque small town (69 kms from Thessaloniki) in the interior of the Chalcidici; it is the capital of the nome, and has an archaeological museum of finds from the area. Sithonia, the middle peninsula, is also midway in terms of appearance, more hilly than Kassandra and less wooded than Athos. At present it is comparatively unspoilt, but there is a grandiose new development on the west coast near Marmoras (130 kms), called Porto Carras, after the shipowner who has built it. On the opposite coast is Sarti (148 kms), a pleasant village built for Greek refugees from Asia Minor, after the exchange of populations in 1922. The single-storeyed houses, plastered with flowers, stand on the edge of the wide beach, and from here you have a wonderful view across the sand to the pale slopes of Mt Athos emerging from the haze.

The road through the middle of the Chalcidici via Arnaia passes near the birthplace of Aristotle at ancient Stageira, and then goes down the coast to the fishing town of Ierisos (129 kms), the site of ancient Akanthos. Beyond Nea Roda, you cross over a shallow ditch which marks the site of Xerxes' canal. This was dug in 480 BC to avoid the fate of a previous Persian fleet lost going round Athos in 491. The road ends at Ouranopolis (143 kms), another village built by refugees in 1922, and now a popular summer resort. Its small harbour serves the Holy Mountain of Athos, which stretches away to the southeast, and you often see the black habits of monks and (in greater numbers) the rucksacks of visitors, who are travelling to or from the mountain. Near the harbour there is a large tower on the sea-edge, built in the 13th C. by the Emperor Andronikos II as an offering to the monastery of Vatopedi: in this tower "on the doorstep of the Holy Mountain" lived a Scotsman, Sydney Loch, the author of a book on Athos which perhaps best conveys the atmosphere of this extraordinary place.

Athos   ATHOS is certainly one of the most beautiful places in Greece. A long central ridge runs the length of the peninsula to reach up to the bare shoulders of Mt Athos, which rises to 6670 ft before falling steeply into the sea. Except for the stark sides of Athos itself the entire peninsula is heavily wooded, and dripping with water. It is as if the old legend of the Giants piling Pelion on Ossa to reach Olympos has been changed, and Ossa piled on Pelion to reach a different God.

Mule paths thread through the trees and the scrub. "It is on the rocky tracks, worked into paths by the hoofs of mule generations, that the note of this wild land sounds even more loudly than in the monasteries" (Loch). Little has changed since the first hermits arrived. As the path continues through the thickets, "there increases a hope that round this approaching bend, or behind the rise ahead, a mystery will be revealed such as the early saints were allowed as medicine in their spiritual sicknesses". No mystery is revealed to the humble modern visitor: the path leads on, past the crosses planted at the roadside, up shimmering slopes and down into shady gulleys where fountains pour cold streams of water; it passes decayed buildings of stone and slate hiding anonymously behind the trees, and finally arrives almost unexpectedly at the tall walls of a monastery, where for up to a thousand years Man has worshipped the Creator of this earthly paradise. It is said that the Virgin Mary declared the mountain hers, when she stopped here on the way to visit Lazarus in Cyprus. Her garden has since been jealously guarded.

Athos' History   The history of the monastic settlements begins with the advent of hermits in about the mid 9th C. AD, roughly 100 years before the foundation of the first monastery. St Peter the Athonite was perhaps the earliest to arrive, after his ship had miraculously stopped still off the coast of Athos: he lived in a cave for 50 years. St Euthymios served his training in asceticism by moving about on his hands and knees eating grass for 40 days, and then living in a cave for 3 years, before he founded the first lavra or community of hermits on Athos. The first monastery, the Great Lavra, was founded by St Athanasios the Athonite in 963, and endowed by the Emperor Nikephoros Phocas. Before the saint's death, other monasteries had been founded, which like Lavra enjoyed independence from everyone except the emperor. By 1046 the Great Lavra had some 700 monks, and together with the other established monasteries controlled the general assembly of the monastic community at Karies. The monasteries were thus able to control or absorb the hermitages around them. The prohibition on any animals of the female sex was put to the test towards the end of the 11th C. after 300 Vlach families (who looked after the monastic flocks) had settled on Athos. Their eventual expulsion was only at the cost of the interference of the Patriarch of Constantinople, which has continued to a greater or lesser extent ever since.

At the beginning of the 13th C. there were scores of monasteries on Athos. But they suffered greatly from being plundered by the Latins after the Fourth Crusade, and then by the Catalans about 100 years later. Only 25 monasteries survived into the 14th C. Towards the end of the century, a move began towards a more lax form of regimen, which in the following centuries led to many monasteries abandoning the coenobitic form (see below). In 1430 Athos prudently capitulated to the Turks after Thessaloniki had fallen, and secured both freedom from plunder and almost total independence. In the 16th C. several monasteries were rebuilt, and this was also the period of the decoration of many of the churches with frescoes of the Cretan School. In the last quarter of that century the number of ruling monasteries was fixed at 20, as it remains today.

In 1821 the monks rose against the Turks but the Turks invaded, and imposed a heavy indemnity. From 6000 monks the numbers dropped to 1000, before reviving in the later 19th C. The mountain then suffered an invasion of a different kind, from Russian monks, which helped to restore flagging numbers, but also threatened to overrun Athos: by 1912, at the end of Turkish rule, the Russians had one monastery (Panteleimon) and many grandiose lesser establishments (like the sketes of St Andrew and Profitis Ilias) and formed a majority of the monks. The Russian Revolution of 1917 removed this threat, by drying up the sources of manpower and finance. Under the 1927 constitution, agreed between the Greek state and the Athonite community, Athos is now part of the Greek state but has administrative autonomy in the form of a Holy Assembly, which has a representative from each of the 20 ruling monasteries; a committee of four representatives, the

Epistasia, is the executive body. The Patriarchate exercises ecclesiastical jurisdiction. The Greekness of Athos is secured by the provision that all foreign monks become Greek subjects on entry. The representative of the Greek state on Athos is a governor at Karies who has a small police force.

Entry
formalities

Entry formalities

The procedure for entering Athos is suitably Byzantine, and transport is also not without its difficulties. Details will be found in the last section of this guide.

It is impossible in this guide to describe all the monasteries and other items of interest on Athos. What follows are some general remarks about the monasteries, and a short itinerary involving a few of them, by way of example only. (In planning an itinerary you should not be too ambitious. First, time is limited, and it is better to see a few monasteries in a leisurely way, than rush about seeing as many as possible. Secondly, you may find that a few days visit at a time is enough: after 6 days of a possible 8-day visit, I happily fled the paradise, back to 'the world'.)

Life on Athos

Each monastery has a different character, a different history and usually its own stories of a miraculous ikon. Some monasteries are grand like Lavra, others are more modest while still possessing important features — Dochiariou, for example, is thought to have the finest church on Athos. Some are thriving like Philotheou, many like Panteleimon continue to dwindle in numbers. Some like Stavronikita are stricter than others. At present 12 of the monasteries are coenobitic, where there is strict obedience to the abbot, property is divided and meals are eaten in common in the 'trapeza' or refectory: in the other idiorrythmic monasteries (which include the three largest, Lavra, Iviron and Vatopedi) there is no property in common, and each monk provides his own food and clothing, etc., from his own resources. All the monasteries are now Greek, except for the Russian Panteleimon, the Bulgarian Zographou and the Serbian Chilandari, and all except Vatopedi keep the old Julian calendar, 13 days behind the rest of us, and Byzantine hours which commence at sunset and so vary every day.

Every monk, who generally goes through the same 3-year novitiate, should spend at least 8 hours a day in prayer — much of it in the small hours. In the coenobia, on 4 days a week two meals are eaten, one after Litourgia or Mass in the morning and one in the late afternoon after Vespers (about 6pm in summer), while on fast days (Monday, Wednesday and Friday) only one meal is eaten — without olive oil, eggs, butter and cheese. Meat is never eaten in the coenobia, although fish sometimes is. In the idiorrythmic monasteries they don't fast on Mondays, and they eat meat. In addition there are special fasting periods before various feast days — in the case of Easter, 7 weeks. If you go at the time of a major fast (for example in August, before the Feast of the Assumption on the 15th, which is celebrated on the 28th by our calendar) and you cannot stand beans, it might be wise to take something else with you.

Whatever else they are, the monasteries are incomparable Byzantine monuments. Most of them have exquisite churches, usually painted a dull red, cruciform with several cupolas. Inside, where there is generally a double narthex flanked by side chapels, they are completely covered with frescoes on a traditional plan. Their treasuries include important relics, such as fragments of the True Cross (Lavra), the Belt of the Virgin Mary (Vatopedi), the left hand of Mary Magdalen, which are usually enclosed in cases studded with precious stones. There are old crysobuls, gold chalices, colourful vestments and patriarchal crowns. The libraries possess beautifully illuminated early manuscripts, notably 'evangelions' or gospels often encased in elaborate covers. The monastic buildings themselves, somewhat like a small walled town around the central church or 'Katholicon', are always intriguing in their variety, even if there is a certain drabness in the empty corridors, the black gowns and the builders' rubble. Some indeed of the monasteries seem dead, but there are many monks whose gentleness and spirituality are transparent on their pale, sleepless faces.

In fact the monasteries are only part of the picture. At present there is a population of between one and two thousand monks and laymen living permanently on Athos. About one half lives in the monasteries, the others are spread between Karies and the smaller monastic establishments, the sketes and kellia dotted about the peninsula. The sketes, like the kellia, are dependent on one of the 20 monasteries and with the exception of the large Russian sketes are monastic villages formed round a central church, for example the skete of St Anne's. The kellion or cell is a single building with a chapel inhabited by a small number of monks. There are also the hermits who carry on the tradition of St Peter the Athonite, living at the southern end of Athos, particularly on the cliffs at Karoulia. For everyone, money remains a problem: the monasteries have been dispossessed of their properties outside Athos, and much of their income now derives from the exploitation of the timber around them. The smaller communities often concentrate on ikon-painting and wood-carving. They nearly all grow their own food. There is a firm belief that somehow the Panagia will provide.

Karies

Karies, high on the central ridge, is full of block-like buildings amongst the trees, which look at best little used. Its central church, the 10th C. Protaton, has important frescoes from the Macedonian School, most probably by Manuel Panselinos (early 14th C.). Near Karies (to the north) is the amazing skete of St Andrew, a vast Russian foundation of onion-shaped domes built with imperial help about 100 years ago and now completely abandoned: there is one monk there, the Caretaker Father Athanasios, who also keeps a bookshop in Karies; he entertained me with a banana liqueur, as we sat in a large room on faded settees, under the proud countenance of a portrait of Czar Nicholas.

You can stay at one of the inns in Karies or go a short way through hazel trees to the attractive monastery of Koutloumousiou to the southeast. About 2 hours further

Philotheou

on is Philotheou, which recently reverted to being a coenobitic monastery, and which has almost doubled the number of monks in the last few years: it now has over 60, many of them young. Situated amongst woods, it has the air of careful cultivation outside and good repair inside. If your experience were like mine, this would provide a perfect introduction to monastic visiting: the loukoumi (Turkish delight) and coffee welcoming the visitor as you show your 'diamonitirion', a wander around the courtyard, monks rushing to arrive at church after the beating of the simantra; following the service, a short visit to the church, and the embarrassed view of the relics being paraded for the Greek pilgrims, then supper of beansoup, some last talk with fellow guests on the terrace outside the monastery and finally after the gates have been closed at sunset, a hard dormitory bed and a night of little sleep.

From Philotheou it is about 6 hours walk to Lavra, past the attractive monastery of Karakallou, then along the coast. It must be one of the best walks in Greece, with clouds of butterflies and lots of hoopoes, and Athos itself looming

The Great Lavra

closer through the trees. The Great Lavra, which stands on a slope overlooking its harbour, is approached through a vaulted entrance: inside the crenallated walls every kind of building spills over into the courtyard, "towers and storehouses, church and chapels, refectory, library, treasury, and guesthouse, fountains, shrines, trees, flowerbeds and endless rows of cells" (Sherrard). Built in the 10th C., alone of the monasteries it has not been damaged by fire. In the centre of the courtyard is the refectory, which has very fine frescoes of the Cretan School (16th C.). Opposite its entrance is the church built by St Athanasios, who died after falling from the roof while building its dome. Between these buildings are two huge cypress trees, said to have been planted by Athanasios and his bursar Euthymios (who also founded Dochiariou): nearby is a beautiful 17th C. phiale, a canopied basin used for blessing the holy water. The Katholicon was completed in the early 11th C., and is painted a dull red colour. The elaborate cruciform structure with three cupolas retains some of the features of a domed basilica, for example the arcades. An unattractive exonarthex, built in 1814 like a conservatory, leads through painted wood doors into the narthex. On entering the church you see two chapels to left and right, that of the 40 martyrs which contains the Tomb of Athanasios, and the chapel of St Nicolas which has 16th C. frescoes by Frangos Kastellanos. The main part of the church is covered with 16th C. frescoes by the Cretan Theophanes, but dark and difficult to see. In the nave there are portraits of the monastery's benefactors, the Emperors Nikephoros Phocas and his successor (and murderer) John I Tzimisces. The marble screen holds ikons heavily sheeted with silver, and elsewhere in the church there is a miraculous ikon of Christ which is said to have exuded blood when wounded by a Turkish bullet. The apsidal ends of the transept are covered with a frieze of Persian tiles, and nearby are fine ivory lecterns. The interior is thus immensely rich, but the chief impact is made by the soft, honey colour of the many objects of bronze and gold, the brazen doors and the huge chandeliers and the ceiling decorations which reflect the light until the whole area seems to vibrate with warmth.

The Treasures possessed by the monastery include a silver-gilt reliquary encrusted with jewels and containing a fragment of the True Cross, and the famous Bible, its cover of equal richness, both given to the monastery by Nikephoros Phocas. In the handsome library building, beyond the church, there are also many beautifully painted Evangelions, amongst numerous other early manuscripts.

It is another long walk by a difficult path round the extremity of Athos, through the desolate area inhabited by the hermits, to the skete of St Anne's. More comfortable will probably be an early morning boat ride to Iviron, as dawn dims the stars.

Iviron   The impressive walls of Iviron, founded in 979, rise up to balconies above a pasture near the sea. Inside it has a neglected air, and there is little charm amongst the confusion of buildings. The Katholicon, dating from the 11th C., is similar to that of Lavra. The monastery possesses the miraculous 9th C. ikon of the Panagia Portaitissa — Our Lady of the Gate. The story is that the ikon, having been committed to the sea at Nicaea to escape destruction by the ikonoclasts, sailed over the waves for 70 years until one day the monks at Iviron saw a pillar of fire rising from the sea: a voice from the ikon insisted that it would only come ashore if Gabriel, a hermit, came to fetch it. Gabriel was found, and eventually walked over the water to collect the ikon. The monks placed it in the Katholicon, but three times it moved back to the gate. The Virgin then appeared to Gabriel, and told him the ikon should be placed in a new chapel near the gate, where she could protect the monastery. There it still is, weighed down with sheets of gold and votive offerings. I saw the ikon move back to the main church on the day before the great feast of the Assumption: the monks preceded it, singing, the ikon was carried with some difficulty by several large men, and crowds of pilgrims milled around, while the bells rang a series of hair-tingling notes. Later there began an all-night service, and I listened to Gregorian chants in the candlelit interior. Almost a fortnight before, on the same occasion, I had seen the dancers revolving in four concentric circles around the small plateia at Sarti.

From Ouranopolis you can reach the main road east from Thessaloniki to Kavala via the pleasant sea side resorts of Olympias and Stavros, on the northeast coast of the Chalcidici. This main road follows the Via Egnatia and at 104 kms from Thessaloniki crosses the river Strymon, guarded by a Hellenistic Lion: on the other side of the
Amphipolis Strymon are the ruins of the ancient town of Amphipolis, near the modern village (off the Serres road). This was an Athenian colony wealthy from the gold mines on Mt Pangaion, which surrendered to the Spartans early in the Peloponnesian War. It was taken by the Macedonians in 358, and became again of importance under the Romans largely owing to its position on the Via Egnatia which here turned north to go round Pangaion. The city was built on a hill above the Strymon by which it was protected on 3 sides. There is little worth seeing on the site, but the remains have been discovered of 4 Christian basilicas with fine mosaics and, nearby, before the village, some Macedonian tombs and a Hellenistic cemetery (with finds in the Kavala museum).

The modern road passes south of Pangaion through a beautiful valley; and after Elevtheroupolis you cross a ridge with a fine view across to Thasos and beyond, before descending to Kavala (165 kms from Thessaloniki).

Kavala KAVALA is in a beautiful position, spreading over the hills which reach down to the harbour. Anciently, as Neapolis, it was the port of Philippi: now its harbour is used chiefly for the export of Macedonian tobacco, and it has become the second largest city in Macedonia and is the capital of its nome. Its chief interest lies in the area of the Turkish quarter, within the Byzantine walls, on the promontory to the east of the harbour. The town remained under the Turks until 1912, although this was not the last of its foreign occupants — it has since also suffered from the Bulgarians. A 16th C. aqueduct is clearly visible to the north of the ruined Byzantine citadel. On the west of the promontory is an almshouse (identified by its many towers) built by Mehmet Ali (1769-1849), later pasha of Egypt, who was born at Kavala. His house is to be found on the

The museum south side of the promontory. The town's museum is on the west side of the harbour, and includes gold jewellery of the Hellenistic period and other finds from Amphipolis, also terracotta figures and other items of the 6th and 5th C. BC from the sanctuary of Parthenos (excavated to the north of the almshouse).

Philippi The ancient city of Philippi, 14 kms north of Kavala, lies on either side of the road to Drama. The modern road closely follows the old Via Egnatia at this point. The city was founded in the 4th C. by Philip of Macedon, but gained in importance under the Romans. In the famous battle in the plain of Philippi, in 42 BC, Brutus and Cassius the republican assassins of Julius Caesar were defeated by Anthony and Octavian (later the Emperor Augustus): both committed suicide. After the battle, Octavian settled many of his veteran soldiers at Philippi. St Paul came here in AD 49, and was imprisoned. Later, the city became an important centre of Christianity, and only declined after the arrival of the Franks. Apart from the 10th C. Byzantine

defences, mostly built on Macedonian foundations, like the acropolis with its three towers, the ruins are mostly Roman or early Christian.

To the left of the road, along the line of the Via Egnatia, is the Forum, which seems to date from the 2nd C. AD in its present plan: it possessed porticoes on 3 sides, and flanking temples to east and west. Beyond the Forum is perhaps the most interesting of the remains at Philippi, an early Christian basilica known as the 'Direkler'. It was built in the 6th C. AD but never completed, because the east end collapsed under the weight of a brick dome. It was thus an early attempt which failed to impose a dome on a basilical plan. (It was also to have had a cruciform appearance from the two apsidal buildings to north and south). Parts of the dome are still visible on the ground. The tall pillars, a little forlorn, have capitals of the acanthus-leaf type. The only part of the church used as such was the narthex, converted in the 10th C. To the west of the basilica are the remains of a palaestra, most of which was removed when the church was built, and to the south, a large public lavatory, very well preserved.

To the east of the Forum are the remains of an octagonal church, approached by a portico from the road. Across the road, on a terrace, is another large basilica in ruins, dating from the end of the 5th C. AD. It was approached by steps, and then through a porticoed atrium. To the right of the steps a passage leads to a 'crypt' of the Roman period, which it is said was St Paul's prison. To the northeast is the theatre, reached from the road: nearby is a **Drama festival** tourist pavilion for the Ancient Drama Festival held here in August.

The theatre dates from the 4th C. BC but was later remodelled by the Romans for gladiatorial shows, etc., and the bas-reliefs of Nemesis, Mars and Victory (on the left of the stage) are of this later period. Above the theatre, in the direction of the acropolis are numerous votive reliefs cut on the rocks, mostly dedicated to Bendis, a Thracian hunting goddess.

There is a new museum west of the basilicas.

Thasos THASOS, the most widely appealing of the northern Aegean islands, lies close off Kavala. A new 90-kilometre road encircling the island gives easy access to its wonderful variety, especially the grand scenery of its southern coast, and makes it worthwhile bringing your car. Forests cover the slopes of the central mass, Mt Ipsarion, and in many places descend to the sea edge. There are several good beaches, and numerous villages (with ample accommoda-

171

tion) spread around the coast.

Limen   The capital is Thasos or Limen, a village of 2000 people whose houses, lying amongst the ruins of the ancient city, are somewhat overshadowed by this ancient rampart of Hellenism facing the barbarians of Thrace and the North. Gold mines, marble and good wine made ancient Thasos prosperous, and the construction of 3 safe harbours at this junction of trade between East and West, and between Greece and the Black Sea, caused Thasos to flourish over hundreds of years.

Ancient Thasos   The extensive remains of ancient Thasos include all the principal features of an ancient Greek city. In the centre is the Agora. This was developed into its present plan over several centuries, much of it under the Romans, notably the porticoes (except that on the northwest, built in the 3rd C. BC). The centre of the agora contained statues, altars, a sanctuary of Zeus and nearby a sacrificial hearth. On the northeast side, next to an intruding Christian basilica, are the ruins of ancient shops; behind the southeast portico there are houses facing onto an ancient street.

Stretching across the middle of the city were various sanctuaries: they included those of Dionysos (to the east) and Herakles (to the west), who were the city's guardians. The remains of the 4th C. theatre are to be found against the city's east wall. It is the city walls that are of most interest. They descended from the acropolis and enclosed both the city and the naval harbour. The first circuit of about 494 BC had a unique feature, the gates being decorated with relief sculpture; these reliefs are still visible in places and lend charming detail to your walks about the ruins. The remaining walls however mainly date from rebuilding towards the end of the 5th C. BC.

Walking eastwards from the modern quay you pass first the site of the ancient naval port, now occupied by a few caiques, and then encounter a stretch of marble wall remaining from the earliest circuit. It has two gates, both decorated with reliefs — the first, the better of the two, shows the goddess Artemis in a chariot.

Nearby is the sanctuary of Poseidon, in front of which remains a large altar to Hera. From here you can proceed directly south to the acropolis, which was built on the furthest east of three hilltops. The existing citadel dates from the 14th and 15th C. AD, but there is on the outside wall an ancient relief of a funeral feast. The middle hill, to the southwest, has the foundations of a 5th C. temple of Athena, while on the north of a third hill is a sanctuary of Pan with a Hellenistic relief. Following the line of the walls, beyond a tower, you see a rock carved with two eyes, to ward off evil (like on modern caiques). Near the southern angle, you pass the 'Gate of Parmemon' (from a block nearby which says "Parmemon made me"), and further on you reach the Gate of Silenus, slightly to the left of the road to the village of Panagia. This was a postern gate, and retains a very large relief of a naked Silenus holding a cup. Two towers away is the Gate of Herakles and Dionysos (identified from inscriptions, the reliefs having gone) and another two towers on is the Gate of Zeus and Hera, with reliefs.

The museum The interesting museum includes many Archaic pieces, and some good Roman imperial portraits.

Beaches Two kms east of Thasos is a good beach at Makri Ammos, with tavernas; you reach this off the Panagia road, or by motor boat. Panagia (9 kms) and Potamia beyond are both attractive villages, away from the sea, though below them are idyllic beaches. On the south of the island, again inland, is the village of Theologos, which was the medieval capital — nearby are the ruins of a castle.

The islands of Samothraki (Samothrace) and Lemnos are both part of the Eastern Sporades, but as Samothraki can only be reached by boat from Alexandroupolis, a pleasant town in eastern Thrace near the Turkish border, and Lemnos is most easily reached from Kavala (though also from Lesvos), they are included here.

Samothraki SAMOTHRAKI rises magnificently from the sea, as much a mountain as an island, rugged and lonely. From the 5250-foot peak of Mt Saos, Poseidon surveyed the battlefield of Troy: Mt Ida distant beyond the Trojan plain returns the gaze; the coast of Thrace and Macedonia, the Chalcidici peninsula and Mt Athos are included in the grand panorama. The ascent of Saos (also known as Phengari) is made in about 5 hours from the village of Chora (Samothraki) on a crag in a fold of the hills overlooking the harbour.

The Sanctuary of the Great Gods The visitor is more often content to visit the Sanctuary of the Great Gods in a peaceful valley between the lower flanks of the mountain and ancient Palaiopolis on the northern coast. When the Greeks came to colonise the island in the 8th C. they found a Thracian Mystery cult and grafted their Olympian gods onto the far older chthonic deities worshipped here. The local mother goddess Axieros became Demeter; the phallic fertility god Kadmilos became Hermes; the twin demons Dardanos and Aetion became the Dioskouroi (sons of Zeus); and the divinities of Nature and rebirth, Axiokersos and Axiokersa, were identified with

Hades and Persephone. Hekate, Aphrodite, Kadmos and Harmonia were later introduced. From the 6th C. onwards the cult drew pilgrims from all round the Aegean, including Herodotos and Philip of Macedon, father of Alexander, who first met his wife Olympias here.

The Arsinoeion

The oldest part of the sanctuary is a Thracian rock altar from c1000 BC enclosed within the much later (c285 BC) Rotunda of Queen Arsinoe at the north end of the site (all the temples and buildings throughout the sanctuary are clearly labelled). Arsinoe was a Macedonian who married her brother Ptolemy II Philadelphos and ruled Egypt with him as Arsinoe II. With a diameter of 65 ft, this was the largest round building in ancient Greece, its cylindrical wall of Thasos marble elegantly crowned by a circular row of pilasters supporting a Doric entablature (a reconstruction is in the museum). It was here that the public sacrifices of the cult were performed before representatives of the Greek cities. The adjacent Anaktoron was a hall of initiation into the Mysteries, the Sacristy built onto its south end probably the place where initiates were enrolled.

The Anaktoron

The Temenos and Hieron

The Temenos, an enclosed courtyard, was perhaps the scene of holy feasting; to its south is the Hieron, a long Doric structure used for the higher initiation ceremonies. Both date from the 4th C. BC, but the Hieron was extensively restored in the 3rd C. BC, and in 1956, 5 columns of the pronaos were re-erected, lending an imposing appearance to the ruins. Beyond the scant traces of the theatre is the Nike Fountain, its centrepiece once the famous Winged Nike of Samothrace, removed to the Louvre in 1863.

Winged Victory

The museum

The well-arranged museum improves understanding of the site: in Hall A, sections of each building have been reconstructed. Sculpture, pottery and grave goods from the site and the ancient city are collected in the other halls.

Beaches

The Thracian sea is often rough and stormy, swept by the prevailing north winds — the climate on the island can be refreshingly bracing in the summer, in contrast to Thasos which is often humid, but then swimming, especially off the stony beach of Palaiopolis, is not good. Instead, and when the weather looks fine, you should take a small boat round the south side of the island to the beautiful and deserted beach of Ammos. There is no accommodation here; if you stay overnight it will be on the beach.

Lemnos

LEMNOS is nearly bisected by inlets at the north and south, its isthmus barely more than 3 kms across. The east half of the island is sparsely cultivated plain; the west is rugged and hilly with a fine beach at Mirina (Kastron), the

Mirina

island capital and port of call for boats plying between Kavala and Piraeus. Built under a rocky promontory surmounted by Turkish walls, a Genoese castle, and on its slopes the outlines of a prehistoric Pelasgian city, Mirina commands a superb view across to Athos, which, it is said, casts its shadow upon Lemnos twice each year.

Moudros

Poliochni

From Mirina a road runs east across the isthmus to Moudros, which overlooks the almost landlocked southern inlet (base for the disasterous British attack on the Dardenelles in 1915); further, near the village of Kiminia, is Poliochni where 4 cities have been found layered upon one another, the oldest going back to the 4th millenium BC, older than the most ancient remains at Troy and centre of the most advanced Neolithic civilisation in the Aegean. The walls, with gates and towers, of the third oldest of these cities (c2000 BC) stand 16 ft high in places.

It was on Lemnos that Hephaistos fell when he was thrown from Olympos by his father Zeus. Hephaistos particularly, but also his wife Aphrodite, were the subjects of Lemnian cults. When Aphrodite committed adultery with Ares, the Lemnian women neglected her worship. In revenge, Aphrodite caused the men of Lemnos to neglect their women who in turn murdered every last one of them. Aphrodite, known for her savage aspect, must have been pleased and did not allow the women to suffer the consequences of their pique for long: Jason and his Argonauts chanced to put in here, and indeed found themselves putting in here for the next two years, until a future generation of Lemnians was assured.

NORTHWEST GREECE

Adriatic
ferries
The shortest passage between the south Italian ports (Bari,
Brindisi and Otranto) and the mainland of Greece lands you
at Igoumenitsa, not far from the Albanian frontier. The
ferry will almost certainly have called in at Corfu first, and
after Igoumenitsa most lines sail down the coast to Patras,
linked to Athens by the fast National Highway. But
Igoumenitsa Igoumenitsa, an insignificant village promoted to international transit point by the Adriatic ferry service, is the
place where anyone less in a hurry should begin their
adventure on Greek soil.

After the torpor of southern Italy, there is an alertness,
a strength in the faces of the people here; after the
domesticity of the Italian countryside and the lushness of
Corfu, there is the hard, uncompromising and virile landscape. The road winds up from the bay and into the
mountainous interior, wild and desolate, where silence
hangs in the valleys like a crystal waiting to be shattered
by the haunting music of sheep-bells and shepherds' pipes.
It was this primitive and remote part of Greece that
awakened a response in the 21-year old Byron; here that he
felt the need and summoned the discipline to embark on his
first major work:

> Childe Harold pass'd o'er many a mount sublime,
> Through lands scarce noticed in historic tales.

Geography
and roads
Northwest Greece is cut off from the rest of the country
by the great Pindos range running down from the Balkans
to the Gulf of Corinth. So formidable a barrier are these
mountains that they are traversed by only one major road,
from Ioannina to Trikala over the 5600 ft Katara pass. And
travel within the region is only really easy along the north-
south valleys and gorges (the road from Ioannina all the
way down to Messolongi is excellent), or along the new
'coast' road from Igoumenitsa to Parga and Preveza.

The three provinces of the northwest are Epirus, Aitolia
and Akarnania: geography denied them central roles in the
"historic tales" of Classical times, though Pyrrhus and
Antony passed dramatically across this side of the stage;
and Byron's own visits, first (in 1809) to Ioannina, capital
of the at once genial and monstrous Ali Pasha, later (in
1824) to Messolongi where he died in the cause of Greek
freedom, puts this far side of Greece forever at the centre
of Romantic lore.

From Igoumenitsa
to Ioannina
The 104 km road from Igoumenitsa to Ioannina replaces
as the principal east-west route between Rome and
Thessaloniki and Constantinople the ancient Via Egnatia

which ran further north from coastal Dyrrhachium (Durazzo) in what is now not very transit-minded Albania. Greek army positions are evident along these mountainous folds of the Iron Curtain. It was in Epirus in November, 1940, that Greece humiliated Mussolini by driving back into Albania the invading Italian army and inflicting on the Axis its first land defeat.

'Monastic Zitza'
At Klimatia, 81 kms east of Igoumenitsa, there is a turning north leading, in 5 kms, to Zitza, a small, picturesque town of paved streets and sturdy stone houses — legacies of prosperity under the Turks — with a now deserted monastery at which Byron stayed during his first visit to the country. The view is magnificent, and on the outer wall of the monastery are two lines of tribute from *Childe Harold:*

> Monastic Zitza! from thy shady brow,
> Thou small, but favoured spot of holy ground!

The Vikos Gorge
There is a more awesome sight, the Vikos Gorge near Monodendri, 50 kms north of Ioannina off the road towards Konitsa. Narrow, deep and dark, with the diminutive 15th C. monastery of Agia Paraskevi perched on a rocky outcrop, there is the sound below, like distant thunder, of the boiling river fed by melting snow. Shepherds bring their flocks up to these high reaches of the Zagora mountains in summer, where the air intoxicates, the grass and trees grow springtime green, and the water gushes cold as ice from the living rock.

The crossroads above Ioannina
The mountain road from Igoumenitsa debouches onto an upland plain where it joins the roads from Konitsa to the north and Metsova, Kalambaka and the Meteora to the east. Metsova (58 kms) stands nearly astride the high Katara pass over the Pindos, the five great rivers of the mountain range having their sources within a few kilometres around. The houses are built of stone and exposed beams; the townspeople — many of them Vlachs, speaking a Latin dialect similar to Rumanian — still daily dress in their traditional dark blue costume, and are renowned for their attractive woollen rugs and embroidered textiles. A museum displays the handicrafts of the region. Kalambaka is only another 67 kms, but the entire journey from Ioannina involves arduous and seemingly endless mountain driving (rewarded though by superb views when crossing the pass) for which half a day should be allowed.

Metsova

Ioannina
From this crossroads on the upland plain you look down upon a long valley, well-cultivated with grain and tobacco, IOANNINA standing upon and behind a promontory projecting into Lake Pambotis opposite the bare and

precipitous grey slopes of Mt Mitsikeli on the flank of the Pindos range. In summer when the mountains are bleakest, the virid fields and blue-green surface of the lake shimmer like a mirage. It can be oppressively humid then, and in winter bitter cold.

But as you descend through the busy streets of this provincial capital of Epirus, there is disappointment that so much of it is modern and ordinary, that so little atmosphere lingers from its lurid past. Appearing in books and on maps variously as Jannina, Yannina or Ioannina, its name is said by some to derive from the 6th C. Byzantine emperor Justinian, by others from an early monastery of St John the Baptist, though these claims of pedigree are without evidence and both name and founding remain buried in obscurity, though not antiquity: the existence of Ioannina can be documented only from the 11th C., and it's been a mongrel tale since then. After the sack by the Fourth Crusade of Constantinople in 1204, Ioannina filled with refugees and grew in importance, tempting Serb invasion a century and a half later: their leader Stefan Dusan proclaimed himself Emperor of Serbia and Greece here in 1346; and one of his successors, Thomas of Ioannina, "possessed of the most unnatural and enormous vices", was fond of quartering and then chopping into pieces prominent clergymen, then turning their flesh on a spit. Ioannina perhaps gratefully surrendered to the army of Sultan Murad II in 1431, from that time until 1913 remaining part of the Ottoman Empire.

Approaching the town from above, there had been a glimpse of minarets, a touch of the Orient still, rising from the frourion or Byzantine fortress built upon the promontory. Here by the lakeside there is a thick sweet fragrance, perhaps of mountain herbs borne across Pambotis by sluggish currents of air. The fortress walls, restored by Ali Pasha in 1815, are extensive and encircled on their lakeward side by the pleasantly tree-shaded Leoforos Kosta Karamanlis, the townspeople promenading here on Sundays, or picnicking or boating; and there is a small seasonal fairground nearby. A cave in the cliffside traditionally marks the spot where Bishop Skylosophos, leader of a Greek uprising in 1611, was caught and skinned alive by the Turks. On the landward side, the walls were protected by a now filled-in moat.

It is here by the lake, down by the walls, that Ioannina is still haunted by its Moslem past. Ali Pasha, born in Albania in 1741, was a brilliant, ruthless and vindictive adventurer who deployed his talents on behalf of the Sultan against the Austrians and was rewarded with the pashalik of

Its history

The frourion

"Since the days
of our prophet
the crescent
ne'er saw/A chief
ever glorious
like Ali Pasha"
— Childe Harold

Trikala in 1788. But ability combined with ambition and treachery: in the same year Ali seized Ioannina and made it his headquarters, from then on allying himself with Napoleon or the British, or following whatever other policy that would augment his possessions and bolster his increasing independence from the Porte. Ioannina prospered for a time, became renowned for the filigree work of its silversmiths, and enjoyed a flowering of Greek culture; this, and his nose-thumbing at the Turks, have made Ali something of a Greek hero, though any regard he had for his Greek subjects was at best opportunist and transient. Peter Sheldon writes of "Ali's massacre of the entire male population of Gardiki, over 700 men and boys, while the women had their clothes cut off below the waist, and thus indecently exposed were driven up the mountains to die from cold. This was Ali's long-delayed revenge for his mother's violation by a rather large number of Gardikiots".

Byron's encounter with Ali

Ali was at the height of his power when Byron came to see him at Ioannina, and discovering that he was away to the north, in Tepelene, pursued the encounter over the mountains into Albania: "He told me to consider him as a father", wrote the bisexual Byron to his mother, " . . . indeed he treated me like a child, sending me almonds & sugared sherbet, fruit & sweetmeats 20 times a day. . . . His Highness is 60 years old, very fat & not tall, but with a fine face, light blue eyes & a white beard. . . . He has the appearance of any thing but his real character, for he is a remorseless tyrant, guilty of the most horrible cruelties, very brave & so good a general, that they call him the Mahometan Buonaparte. . . . He has been a mighty warrior, but is as barbarous as he is successful, roasting rebels &c. &c.".

The Cami of Aslan Pasha

Old Turkish houses crumble sadly within the fortress walls. Headstones stand broken or lie fallen in the long grass of the Moslem graveyard at the steps of the Cami of Aslan Pasha, an early 17th C. mosque, moss- and lichen-covered like a tree stump. From the northwest corner of the frourion, the Cami pleasantly overlooks the lake more like a gazebo built for whiling away a hot summer's evening, though the dome and soaring minaret (now closed to the public), and the recesses in its vestibule where the faithful once left their shoes before entering, remind you of its once religious purpose — it has been preserved against the creeping rot to which Greeks normally abandon anything of Turkish provenance because it has been pressed into service as the Municipal Museum. Its rustic interior contains a fine collection of Epirot costumes, including brightly coloured village weaves, the black dresses and leggings of Sarakatsani

Epirot costumes

nomad women, and the elegant streetwear of Greek merchants' wives from Ioannina's heyday. There is also a portrait of Ali, the 'Lion of Ioannina' himself, purring in the arms of his mistress, Kyra Vasiliki.

The murder of Kyra Phrosyne

But one beautiful woman, Kyra Phrosyne, was to fall victim to the Lion's claws. The wife of a rich Greek merchant, she would sleep with Ali's son while her husband was away. One night Ali invited her to his own lair but she declined the pleasure. Outraged, he raped her and then had her and 17 of her companions sewn up in sacks and tipped into the lake where it laps below the Aslan Pasha mosque.

The inner citadel

At the southeast corner of the frourion is Its-Kale, a citadel within the citadel, now a Greek army confine (the public only sometimes admitted), with the graceful but decrepit Fetichie Cami (Victory Mosque), Ali's restored palace where Byron sojourned, and Ali's tomb.

Ali's execution

Ali had practised a lifetime of treachery yet was surprised by treachery at the end. Determined to crush this most dangerous of rebels before suppressing (as he hoped) the Greek uprising that had begun in 1821, the Sultan sent an army of 50,000 against Ioannina. By January, 1822, it was besieging Ali in his citadel. The Sultan's general accepted Ali's offer to talk terms at a meeting to be held on the island in the lake, but when Ali arrived he found a firing squad waiting for him instead. Bullet marks in the floor of the 16th C. monastery of Pantaleimon mark the spot where Ali fell. His head was displayed about the provinces he had once ruled and was finally exposed outside the Seraglio at Constantinople.

The island in the lake

The leafy, reed-encircled island with its numerous monasteries can be reached by boats departing at least hourly from the town; the chief pleasure is to wander amidst the trees and flowers, whether purposefully visiting monasteries or not, and then enjoying a simple meal at the taverna here.

Silversmiths and stalactites

Returning to the town, Odos Averof runs uphill from the landward wall of the frourion and is lined with silversmiths, all that remains of Ioannina's once flourishing bazaar. At the top of the street is a museum exhibiting archaeological finds of the region. At the north end of the lake, 4 kms from town by Perama, are caverns bristling with stalactites and stalagmites. Guides will lead you through nearly a kilometre of electrically lit galleries.

An increasingly rare delight in Greece is to visit a grandly situated archaeological site and to find hardly anyone there. An opportunity for that lies 22 kms distant from Ioannina, following first the Arta road. After 8 kms, take the turning on your right marked 'Dodoni'. The road makes a sharply winding ascent with magnificent views of the Pindos along the eastern sky and of Lake Pambotis below, an astonishing, seemingly misplaced jigsaw piece of blue locked into the valley's pattern of greens. Then the crest of the ridge is reached and you descend into the isolation of DODONA, the oldest oracle in Greece. Robert Graves says that patrilineal invaders replaced Dodona's Earth Goddess with Zeus, but both men and women continued to deliver oracles, listening "to the cooing of doves, or to the rustling of oak-leaves, or to the clanking of brazen vessels suspended from the branches".

The oracle of Zeus at Dodona

There is accommodation and a terraced restaurant nearby where I spent the better part of a September Sunday afternoon with my family but not another soul in sight; we had earlier shared the oracle with only one or two brief visitors. In August, the theatre is used for the annual drama festival; it was first built in the time of Pyrrhus (297-272 BC), but at the time of Augustus the Romans, typically, replaced the lowest rows of seats with a protective wall so that it could be used as an arena. The cavea is recessed into the acropolis hill and is supported by retaining walls 70 ft high and towers on either side.

The theatre

Climbing above the highest rows of the theatre, you find a gate leading into the acropolis, its walls as much as 15 ft thick though now reduced to no more than 10 ft in height. From here a path descends to the sanctuary (which can be reached directly from the front of the theatre); the foundations of several buildings are evident and clearly labelled — the Temenos of Zeus Naios being the complex ruin that grew up round the site of the oracle. At first, going back to 1000 BC or more, there would have been only the sacred oak-tree itself. There are no oaks here now, and the sanctuary ruins are not impressive. But there is the rustling still of other trees, and puffy flocks of sheep wandering across the landscape, causing a constant clanking of their deep-toned bells.

The acropolis

The sanctuary

What is marvellous, from the sanctuary or from the theatre, is the length of cultivated valley running off into the distance, a verdant river between grey slopes perenially dressed for the change of season in firs and stubbly bush. "Wintry Dodona", Homer called it in his epics, and it is as though the hush of snow, like the rustling of the oak-leaves, might come at any time. From the upper rows of the theatre, the landscape must have overwhelmed any daylight drama on the stage. The cavea stands as audience to the whisperings of the sacred valley.

The Louros Gorge

Rejoining the Arta road (Ioannina to Arta: 78 kms), a causeway carries you over marshy bottom land; the road then rises to over 2000 ft and descends again into the beautiful Louros Gorge where it runs deep between the dark and densely tufted mountain walls, the river skittering fresh and cold over its smooth-worn bed of rocks, shaded by plane trees. Road and river pace one another nearly the whole distance to Arta. The valley broadens and is cultivated with bamboo, then narrows again, more ragged now, caves and spectacular stone arches at its heights. All too soon, for it is one of the most agreeable drives in Greece, you are out upon the Ambracian plain, a sea of orange groves. The Louros follows its own course towards the southwest while the road continues the last 8 kms southeastwards to where Arta sits encoiled within a great bend of the Arachthos which has run down through the Pindos from Metsova.

The 'coastal' route through Epirus

Instead of heading for Ioannina and the alpine scenery of the interior, an alternative route through Epirus is to leave Igoumenitsa by the road which brushes the coast from time to time, passing first through the village of Plastaria (12 kms), with a good beach, then continuing inland to Morfion (38 kms) where the road divides. The leftmost turning continues on to Preveza or Arta; the rightmost turning leads you down a spur road to the sea at Parga (51 kms from Igoumenitsa).

Parga

PARGA is a delightfully picturesque town and now that it is easily accessible is becoming a popular coastal resort. The old whitewashed houses, two and three storeys tall under gently sloping roofs of red tile, ascend amidst olive and orange trees from two coves either side of a rocky headland, Norman battlements at its crest. Parga came under Venetian protection at the beginning of the 15th C. (accounting for the Lion of St Mark on the keep of the Norman fortress), passed in and out of French hands during the Napoleonic wars (from 1800 to 1807 even enjoying independent statehood under Russia's aegis), and in 1814 was taken by the British who promptly sold it for a song to Ali Pasha. The Pargiotes decamped with the ashes of their ancestors rather than live under Ali's rule and were replaced by Moslems who remained here until the exchange of populations between Greece and Turkey in 1924.

Steps and winding streets spill down to the tiny eastern cove, the waterfront lively here with numerous cafes looking out upon the rocks and islets close by, sailing boats gliding past. The larger western cove has a long sandy beach, a part of it taken over by the Club Méditerranée. A few tourist hotels are going up along an open bay to the east of Parga, but development is still modest.

Back at Morfion and continuing along the Preveza road, it is about 15 kms to the Acheron river. Immediately beforehand there is a turning right to the village of Mesopotamo. On a rocky hill overlooking the confluence of the Acheron and Kokitos is the Necromanteion of Ephyra, sanctuary of Porsephone and Hades and entrance to the underworld, where pilgrims came to communicate with the souls of their dead. Circe's description of the place to Odysseus is given by Homer: when the North Wind "has brought you across the River of Ocean, you will come to a wild coast and to Persephone's Grove, where the tall poplars grow and the willows that so quickly shed their seeds. Beach your boat there by Ocean's swirling stream and march on into Hades' Kingdom of Decay. There the River of Flaming Fire and the River of Lamentation, which is a branch of the Waters of Styx, unite round a pinnacle of rock to pour their thundering streams into Acheron".

The oracle of the dead

The Necromanteion is a labyrinth of corridors and windowless rooms descending underground and dating from Hellenistic times, though the site is far older. The pilgrim would have been conducted on a disorientating tour within, then possibly given hallucinatory drugs before witnessing a spectacle involving mechanical trickery to produce the desired effect of a spiritual visitation.

On the main road again and about 25 kms further south, there is a turning left to the village of Zalonga, in the heart of Suliot country. The Suliots were a tribe of rugged mountain people, fierce resisters against Moslem encroachment. Ali Pasha cornered the greater number of Suliots at the monastery here — the few who fought their way across country to Parga settled on Corfu, returning to the mainland again in 1824 as Byron's bodyguard. When the monastery was overrun, 60 Suliot women and their children escaped to the summit of the cliffs above and as Ali's soldiers relentlessly approached began to sing the old Suliot songs, dancing with their children in their arms ever closer to the edge, then one by one throwing themselves down the precipice in suicidal defiance.

The monastery of Zalonga

From here to Preveza it is 17 kms. At 10 kms is Nikopolis from where you can head northeastwards round the Ambracian Gulf to Arta.

City of Victory

NIKOPOLIS was founded by Octavian, the future Augustus, to commemorate his victory over Antony and Cleopatra off

Aktion (Actium in Latin) in the preceding year, 31 BC. The Ambracian Gulf narrows to a strait, barely a kilometre across, where it meets the sea: the ruins of Nikopolis and the modern town of Preveza are on the north side of the strait; at its south side is a sandy headland bearing the slight remains of the Temple of Apollo Aktios. Here Antony and Cleopatra camped with their 120,000 infantry and 12,000 cavalry they had massed for their invasion of Italy.

But in spring, Octavian's daring admiral, Marcus Agrippa, had captured Antony's vital supply station at Methoni in the Peloponnese, and in summer had succeeded in blockading Antony and Cleopatra's combined fleet within the Ambracian Gulf. Antony's greatness was as a land commander; in Agrippa he was now facing perhaps the only Roman who ever understood naval strategy. As the blockade wore on throughout the hot month of August, time too turned against Antony: his men became restless, some (including Ahenobarbus) deserted to Octavian's side, while so many rowers died of fever that when finally battle was joined Antony could man only 230 ships to Octavian's 400.

The battle of Actium

Antony considered abandoning the fleet and striking across Greece with his army where twice before, at Philippi and Farsala, the fate of Rome had been decided. But abandoning the fleet meant abandoning Cleopatra's major contribution to his cause, and abandoning Cleopatra could mean losing Egypt and all its wealth. Antony instead decided to try and break through the blockade and return to Egypt with Cleopatra, leaving instructions for his army to cross Greece under his generals in preparation for a Macedonian campaign under Antony's direction the following spring.

What in fact happened was distorted by Roman propagandists to show Antony, supposedly feckless and unRoman, deserting his fleet and his army to be with his treacherous Oriental queen. Far from intending to flee, Cleopatra and Antony were carrying out their plan to break through the Roman blockade. True, most of their fleet was captured or destroyed, but as one naval historian has written, "to save even 60 ships out of 230 was a creditable achievement for a man embayed on a lee shore and vastly outnumbered". The real disaster struck when Antony's army began marching towards Macedonia but was intercepted by Octavian's emissaries who offered them favourable terms, including the Roman soldier's traditional plot of land in Italy, if they would surrender. It was not that Antony lost the world in that one battle, nor that he lost it for a woman, but that over the course of a combined land and sea campaign, Octavian prudently avoided engagement by land, while Antony was checked and checked again by

Agrippa at sea. It was morale that finally deserted Antony's waiting, onlooking army that September day — Antony only discovering the awful truth when it followed him to Egypt.

Settlement of Nikopolis

By the forced transfer of populations from towns over much of Aitolia and Akarnania, and adding veterans from the wars, Octavian settled his Roman city amidst a foreign land. The Vandals and Huns sacked it in the 5th and 6th C. Justinian rebuilt it, reducing the compass of its walls. Nikopolis fell once and for all to the Bulgars in 1040, and remains today abandoned, lonely and overgrown.

Roman and Byzantine walls

The southern sector of the site is encircled by the extensive though badly ruined Augustan walls; along their western stretch ran an aqueduct bringing water to the city from the Louros. Better preserved is the smaller circuit of Byzantine walls built by Justinian and broached by the great West Gate; within these is a museum — there is a Roman portrait of Marcus Agrippa. A small odeion lies outside the Byzantine gate, within the Augustan walls.

Early Christian churches

Within the Byzantine citadel are the ruins of three early Christian basilicas; a fourth lies outside the walls. The huge church of Bishop Alkyson, with five aisles and a threefold transept, lies at the centre of the Byzantine citadel. To find the other churches may require the services of the phylax: the church of St Doumetios possesses fine mosaics representing the Universe — earth, sea and air alive with beings; Basilica D, beyond the walls, contains a well-preserved peacock-design mosaic. Nikopolis was a hotbed of Christianity: peripatetic Paul wintered here in AD 64, and the 2nd C. Pope Eleutherios was born here.

The stadium

In the northern sector of the site there is a long depression, its outline picked out by the shrub that overgrows it. It is the stadium, rounded at both ends in the Roman way, and seeming like some sunken hulk — indeed the locals call it 'the ship'. This was the site of the Actian Games. At its

The theatre and the site of Octavian's tent

eastern end is a theatre, built into a hillside in Greek fashion. A road running between theatre and stadium and up the hill past the village of Smyrtoula brings you to the remains of the commemorative monument erected by Octavian on the site where his tent had been pitched preceding the victory.

Preveza

Preveza is 8 kms south, a town without interest, though nicely situated with the gulf on one side, the Ioanian (and some good beaches) on the other. The strait marked the border between Turkey and Greece from 1881 to 1912; a car ferry makes the brief crossing every half hour.

Whether coming from Preveza or Nikopolis through the fragrant orange groves north of the Ambracian Gulf, or down the mountain road from Ioannina, you approach Arta from the northwest. Just before the modern road carries you over the Arachthos, there is a turning on the left signposted 'Old Arta Bridge', it perhaps sticking in Greek throats to identify it more precisely as a Turkish packhorse bridge, well paved with stone and gracefully arched across the river which loops about the town. There is an unmistakable Oriental artistry in the pleasingly irregular span placed against the backdrop of mountains behind. Constructed in the 17th C., the story goes that its completion had long been thwarted by the vagaries of the river until a bird revealed to the master builder that his wife would have to be immured in the foundations supporting its central span. This the builder did and the arches were joined, whereupon he committed suicide. The theme is found in many ballads sung about beautiful bridges throughout the Balkans.

The Turkish bridge across the Arachthos

Arta

ARTA, or Ambracia as it was first known, was founded by Corinth around 625 BC. In the 3rd C. BC, Pyrrhus, that king of Epirus who complained that his victories against the Romans were so costly they would ruin him, made Ambracia his capital. A century later the Romans did triumph and razed the city; whatever had been built up again was depopulated by Octavian when he founded Nikopolis. When Pausanias passed this way, he found nothing standing; and despite recent excavations, there is little of that period for the layman to appreciate today.

But apart from its friendly atmosphere and river-beribboned situation (it is the ample presence of water that makes so much of the northwest delightful), Arta does offer the visitor several curiosities from its second period of greatness under the Byzantine despotate of the Angeli who established themselves here after the seizure of Constantinople by the Franks in 1204. The 13th C. frourion with its crenellated walls in part constructed of reused Classical blocks once enclosed the despot's palace and now provides a romantic river-view setting for the Xenia Hotel. The houses and little streets in this northeast salient of the town are full of character.

Byzantine Arta

The frourion

To the southwest, off Odos Pirrou, is the 14th C. church of Agios Vasilios, its well-preserved exterior showing off the intricate and colourful brick and tile design for which this area is noted. In the same direction is the 13th C. church and convent of Agia Theodora, similarly though less extensively decorated outside, lightened by numerous brickwork arches, and marvellously patterned within the

Agios Vasilios

Agia Theodora

Panagia Paragoritissa domed narthex. On a rise behind the Plateia Skoufas is the high rectangular former metropolitan church of Panagia Paragoritissa (Virgin Mary the Consoler), looking something like an Italianate Texas School Book Depository — in fact 13th C. Byzantine with a strong admixture of romanesque from the Angevin court on the nearby island of Kefallinia. There are six domes; within the gloomy interior the central dome can be seen to be supported by an extraordinary system of pillars, one atop the other, supporting projecting pendatives upon which the cupola seems uncertainly to rest. Original mosaics of Pantokrator and prophets tremble from on high.

The corniche After passing through more orange groves across the Arta plain, the Ambracian Gulf is reached. There are beautiful and varied views, especially at evening, along the corniche that has been cut into the mountain ridge defining the eastern shores of the gulf, the 'Thermopylae of western Greece'. And there is the time-collapsing sensation, looking across the water to its narrow opening upon the sea, that Actium is still being fought in the silent distance.

Amfilochia The road from Preveza via the strait joins with that from Arta at Amfilochia deep within a narrow inlet at the southeast corner of the gulf. Continuing southwards over rolling landscape and along the shore of two lakes, the road skirts the village of Stratos (halfway between Amfilochia and **Ruins of Stratos** Agrinion) on the left, sitting amidst the scanty ruins of the ancient capital of Arkanania. The broad Acheloos flows by below. Agrinion (84 kms from Arta) is bypassed and there **Agrinion** is no reason to object, though you can turn off here for one of the few roads across the Pindos, eventually reaching Lamia via Karpenision.

Thermon and Lake Trichonis Also from Agrinion you can follow the north shore of Lake Trichonis round to Thermon, the plateau sanctuary of the Aetolian League. The road is badly potholed, but the contrasting beauty of blue lake, snow-capped mountains and green fields dotted with agricultural villages is ample compensation. A 6th C. temple of Apollo is identified by a few column drums; nearby are the substantial remains of a prehistoric village. A museum displays Bronze Age, Mycenaean and Geometric finds. A better road leads back to the Agrinion-Messolongi highway around the south side of the lake via the village of Kato Makrinou; or from the village you can follow a poor mountain road — though with lovely views as it rises from the lake — direct to Navpaktos.

The Klissoura Gorge South of Agrinion, the main road soon slips between the towering sandstone sides of the Klissoura Gorge, eagles and hawks wheeling against the narrowed sky, until the walls fall away to reveal an olive-covered coastal plain, the medieval town of Aitolikon rising between an inner lagoon and the seaward Lagoon of Messolongi.

Defended by its shallow lagoon navigable only by flat-bottomed boats, its marshy ground, its walls and the cunning, courage and desperation of the fractious rabble within, Messolongi (Messolongion) had fought off two sieges, in 1822 and again in 1823. In January 1824, when Byron landed for the second time in Greece, it was still the headquarters, albeit only a toe-hold, of the Greek forces on the mainland. The 'forces' were merely the bands of quarelling brigand-captains who cared at least as much for their own welfare as for any national ideal; indeed, what nation there was barely existed beyond the imaginations of demoralised Greeks of western European education and a few broken Philhellenes: the Turks were reimposing their oppression on the chaos while Europe, after revolutions in France, Italy and Spain, and the long Napoleonic wars, was content to see the insurrection crushed.

Outside Greece, Byron was and remains the Romantic poet, the Satanic rebel, whose reputation rises and falls with the fashion and frustration of the times. In Greece, among these most infuriatingly inconsistent people, he has a constant value: national hero — because to Greece he came to fight and in Greece he died; and, curiously, because to Greece he came with fewer stars in his eyes than most travellers then or since. Byron detested hypocrisy in England; but for the factionalism and blatant larceny of the people for whose cause he was risking his life he showed patience. In his diary just before he died, he wrote: "After all, one should not despair, though all the foreigners that I have hitherto met with amongst the Greeks are going or gone back disgusted". And in one of his last letters from Messolongi: "Of the Greeks I shall say nothing, till I can say something better — except that I am not discouraged. . . . I shall stay out as long as I can — and do all I can for these Greeks — but I cannot exaggerate — they must expect only the truth from me both of and to them".

When he landed, Byron was greeted — more out of respect for the money he brought with him than for his literary reputation — with a 21-gun salute and made commander-in-chief of the Greek forces. His plan was to launch an attack on Navpaktos and to capture the fortresses at Rion and Andirrion, thereby establishing control over Greece's inland sea, the Gulf of Corinth. But in the miasmal airs of Messolongi he developed a fever and on 19 April he died. Messolongi, which then like today was a featureless, unhealthy and intrinsically uninteresting town, acquired a sudden world-wide fame, so that when finally it was taken by the Turks in 1826 its fall reverberated throughout Europe as though the infidel had sacked the second Jerusalem.

The main road from Agrinion (38 kms to the north) to Andirrion (41 kms to the south) bypasses Messolongi so that it requires a deliberate act of reverence, or at least curiosity, to see the few mementoes of the past. You enter through the 'Gate of the Sortie', so-named for the mass escape on the night of 22 April 1826 of 9000 of the towns-people after 12 months of siege by Turko-Egyptian forces. Betrayed to the enemy by a Bulgarian co-defender, 7200 of them were massacred on the slopes of nearby Mt Zygos, scene in mythology of the hunting of the Kalydonian boar. Those who remained within the walls blew up the powder magazines, and themselves and their enemies with them. The *Exodos* is solemnly commemorated each year. Beyond the gate, to the right, is the Heroon, the garden of heroes: on the left is a tumulus covering the bodies of unnamed defenders, to the right is the tomb of Botsaris who led the defence of Messolongi in 1823, and in the centre is a statue of Byron, beneath which is the poet's heart. At the central Plateia Botsari is the Museum of the Revolution containing Byron relics, while on Odos Levidou, at the bottom of Odos Trikoupis, is a memorial garden occupying the site of the house where Byron died, destroyed in the Second World War.

Mountains lie between Messolongi and Andirrion (ferry to Rion for the Patras-Athens highway) and you emerge on a corniche overlooking the Gulf of Patras, with fine views of Patras itself and of the mountains of the northern Peloponnese.

Venetian gate

The garden of heroes

Museum of the Revolution

THE IONIAN ISLANDS

The islands of the Ionian Sea run down the west coast of Greece like droplets. Green and lush throughout the year, forested with wildflowers in springtime, they are softer, even in the contour of their mellow landscapes, than the summer-dry, shimmering islands of the Aegean. In culture they are different too. Part of the Byzantine Empire, they fell prey to Frankish adventures from the 11th C., and with the Ottoman sack of Constantinople became outposts of

Western influence

Christendom and the West against the encroaching East. Until 1913, the Turks stood on the mainland only 3 kms opposite Corfu. Of the islands' Western conquerors, Venice remained longest, her rule here more benevolent and serene than in the Aegean. When Napoleon put an end to the Venetian Republic in 1797, the islands passed to the French, later to the Russians, and finally, in 1815, to the British until they were united with an independent Greece in 1864. In the gentility of the people, the prosperity of their well-tended land, in the architecture of castles, churches, country houses and town arcades, the influence of the West has left its still visible mark.

Corfu

CORFU (Kerkira) is the second largest, the most populous, and certainly the most popular island of the group. The Greek Tourist Organisation's brochure uses a feminine metaphor, "soft, mysterious, yielding", which turns out to be correct, though in summer she is nearly raped by tourists in town and along most of the beaches and you have to press well in from the port to enjoy her in any intimacy. The green hills are like the folds of a dress, their slopes brocaded with olive groves, tassles of cypresses decorate the valleys. Odysseus wandered amorously here, and before the war this was the home of Lawrence Durrell (he describes the island in *Prospero's Cell*) before he retreated to the exclusivity of Provence.

Corfu town

The town of Corfu is almost un-Greek in the elegance of its main streets and squares, though the scores of backstreets serve as open theatres of Greek life: nearly every radio on, all broadcasting the same song, everywhere people nodding, tapping or singing to it; the sunlight on pink and yellow walls, cooking and talking going on behind closed shutters, cats stalking each other down alleyways, children and chickens running about, washing hung high across the streets as in Naples, arches, church bells, flowers growing out of paint buckets and glimpses of the sea and Albania beyond.

Layout	Adriatic ferries berth at the new harbour just to the west of town; the Igoumenitsa ferries dock a bit closer in. The Neon Frourion (New Fortress) of the Venetians rises above both the new and the old harbour which is fronted by the tree-shaded Plateia Georgios B' where carriages drawn by straw-hatted horses may be hired. Passing through the Porta
Odos Nikiforou Theotoki	Spilia brings you to Odos Nikiforou Theotoki, the principal pedestrian way through the town since Venetian times, lined with shops, confectioners (try *kum-kwat*, the local speciality of crystalised miniature oranges) and tavernas.
The sea road	Alternatively, you can follow the sea road out of the plateia, tall stately houses on your right, fine views of the mountains of Epirus off to your left, until you round the headland at the point of the Archbishop's Palace (on the site of Capodistria's birthplace) and first gain a view of the moated Citadel. Kerkira derives from *Corcyra*, the ancient name for the island. Corfu is a Venetian corruption of the Byzantine *Korypho*, meaning breasts, another tribute to the feminine, this time referring to the twin peaks on which the Citadel is built. Running north to south between the town
The Esplanade	and the Citadel is the Esplanade, a great open space once the Venetian parade ground. At its north end is the Royal Palace which overlooks that half of the Esplanade which now serves as a cricket pitch; a bandstand and an Ionic rotunda erected in memory of Sir Thomas Maitland, first Lord High Commissioner, are set on the grassy south half. The Liston, an arcaded row of tall houses along the north half of the Esplanade, was designed by the French after Napoleon's rue de Rivoli: local teams play cricket on Sunday afternoons, sometimes against the crews of visiting British warships, and you can sit here at one of the numerous cafes, soaking up an ouzo, applauding the play along with everyone else in a most restrained English manner. At night you can dine here, lights in the trees above you, Odos Georgiou a wide promenade of evening strollers fresh out of church and dressed to kill. Odos Nikiforou Theotoki emerges nearby, and along with the sea road and the Esplanade, forms a triangle, convenient for reference, around the heart of Corfu town.
St Spirodon	The church of Agios Spirodon lies within the triangle, on a street that runs into the Esplanade and bears the name of this patron saint of Corfu. Plain outside, the 16th C. church is decked out High Renaissance inside and further graced by the presence of St Spirodon himself, standing tippy-toe in a gold-encrusted plankeen, face and feet visible through the glass cover, which is quite a goggle as he's been dead 1600 years. Born in Cyprus of humble origins, the Arian bishops

of that island feared his influence at the Ecumenical Council of Nicaea (AD 325) and so persuaded the governor to ban his passage on all ships off the island. But Spirodon took off his cloak and placed one half on the water, stood upon it, and attached the other half to his staff as a sail and pushed off to Nicaea, getting there *before* the Arian bishops who had left some days earlier. Clearly a man of formidable powers, when the Turks took Constantinople Spirodon's body was spirited away to Corfu where he has performed several posthumous miracles since. I was fortunate enough to be here during a celebration in Spirodon's honour. Spirodon buttons, bearing a picture of his corpse, were on sale everywhere, some of them even with close-ups of his brown and wrinkly raisin face. The church was packed, but I pushed in, only to find out too late that I was on a queue to kiss old Spirodon's feet. It is probably to most visitors' liking to hail the saint at a more formal distance: he is carried about town four times a year, on Palm Sunday, Easter Saturday, 11 August and the first Sunday in November.

The Royal Palace at the head of the Esplanade was built by the British for the Lord High Commissioners and then from 1864 to 1913 served as a residence for the kings of the Hellenes. Its state rooms have been restored but are not open to the public, though by visiting the library and museum within you can get some idea of the interior. The palace and the Maitland Rotunda give Corfu a Regency flavour reminiscent of an English spa town. The English lived well here, tempering their autocratic rule with an unusual degree of eccentricity. 'King Tom' Maitland, for example, became so exasperated with frequent bearers of petitions that to one he bared his behind in turn. Mon Repos, the vast summer villa of the commissioners a mere 2 kms south of the town, continues the Regency theme. It was built by Sir Frederick Adam, the second Lord High Commissioner, at the instigation of his Corfiot wife whose tastes were as extravagant as her moustache. When the British left, the Greek royal family would summer here, and here in 1921 Prince Philip, Duke of Edinburgh, was born. That "queer fish" Lord Guilford, as a colleague described him, established the Ionian Academy (now a school) at the bottom of the Esplanade to encourage a revival of Greek culture and promptly enacted his version of what that might be: "Lord Guilford goes about dressed up like Plato, with a gold band round his mad pate and flowing drapery of a purple hue".

Mon Repos is reached by following the pleasant promenade, backed with gardens, along the Bay of Garitsa (there is a beach beyond the point). Near its southern end, and a few streets landward, is the 12th C. Byzantine church of Saints Jason and Sosipater, disciples of St Paul. You are in fact within the precincts now of Palaiopolis, or ancient Corcyra, which occupied the peninsula between the Bay of Garitsa and the lagoon of Kalikiopoulo, though almost all of what there is to see is found within the Archaeological Museum near the sea front at the southern end of the Esplanade. Particularly striking is the Archaic pediment of the Temple of Artemis (c580 BC), filled with a gorgon and panthers.

Ancient Corcyra

The Archaeological Museum

It's easy to walk to Mon Repos, and enjoyable to cover the entire distance to Kanoni at the point of the peninsula (4.5 kms from town) on foot; but there are buses. Kanoni was the site of a French gun emplacement but is visited for its familiar though still wonderful view of the two miniature islands of Vlakerena and Pondikonisi (Mouse Island), the first barely large enough to float a church and solitary cypress, the second just managing a chapel surrounded by trees.

Kanoni and Mouse Island

At Gastouri, 8 kms south of Corfu town, is the pride and joy of the Empress Elisabeth of Austria and, later, of Kaiser Wilhelm — the ludicrous Achilleion. Open year-round, it was completed in 1892 in a jumble of juxtaposed mock-Classical styles including Pompeian rooms cluttered with fin-de-siècle Teutonic knicknackery and in the gardens nude gigolo statues passed off as Greek gods. In the evening the Achilleion is a casino, run by Baron von Richthoven — black tie, no Snoopies. A further 3.5 kms southwards on the coast is Benitses, the one real fishing village on Corfu, picturesque but smelly. The remains of a Roman villa lie in a nearby orange grove. There is a good shingle beach 7 kms further on.

The Achilleion

Benitses

Possibly the two best beaches on Corfu are Glifada and Agios Gordis, both on the opposite side of the island from Corfu town, but reached by separate routes. Glifada (14 kms), with its long lonely and golden sands backed by olive groves has now been assaulted by a huge new hotel and golf course; for some seclusion you should go to one of its sister beaches — Mirtiotissa and Ermones — just to the north. The rock pools at Ermones, some scholars have claimed, are those where Nausikaa came to wash her clothes when Odysseus swam ashore. Until recently the road was paved (and the bus went) only as far as Sinarades on the way to Agios Gordis (19 kms); from then on it was a 25-minute walk, first uphill, then sharply downhill to the long crescent

Beaches

Glifada

Agios Gordis

of sand lazing lovely and quiet between two headlands and hardly an edifice upon it. But now the road is paved, and who knows?

Paleokastritsa Paleokastritsa (24 kms) lies on the west coast between Agios Gordis to the north and Ermones to the south. It has been a popular tourist spot since Sir Frederick Adam built a road to it in 1828; already in 1862 Edward Lear, the limericking landscape painter, wrote that although its beauty seemed to make him "grow a year younger every hour" the pleasure could not last: "Accursed picnic parties with miserable scores of asses male and female are coming tomorrow, and peace flies — as I shall too". Well over a century on, the asses have multiplied.

After the shipwrecked Odysseus had washed and oiled himself and covered his nakedness with the cloak and tunic that had been given him, the Phaeacian princess **Odysseus** Nausikaa "gazed at him in admiration" and led him to her **among the** father's city, "surrounded by high battlements" with "an **Phaeacians** excellent harbour on each side . . . approached by a narrow causeway". The promontory of Kattro below the town of Lakones happens to fit this description, with the bay of Agios Spirodon to the right, the bay of Alipa to the left, and here too the islet of Vigla like the fast Phaeacian ship that took Odysseus home to Ithaka and was turned to stone by vengeful Poseidon upon its return. As yet archaeologists have found no suitable Mycenaean remains in the Paleokastritsa area to justify this identification beyond geographical similarity, but on the other hand the substance and details of the Homeric epics are now accepted as having a solid basis in fact, however much embroidered by poetic imagination, and the possibility that this was King Alkinous' capital cannot be dismissed.

The journey to Kassiopi (37 kms) runs you up the east coast of the island, as far as Tzavros (10 kms) covering the same route as you follow to Agios Gordis or Paleokastritsa.

Campsites	There are hotels, camps that are suburbias of tents, and a youth hostel around Gouvia Bay (8 kms), and then more campsites around Ipsos (16 kms) and Pirgi (18 kms) at either end of an inferior narrow beach. At Pirgi the road divides, the left fork leading to the 2972-foot Mt
Mt Pantokrator	Pantokrator, highest on the island, from the summit of which there are views clear down the length of Corfu and beyond as far as Lefkas, to Italy on the northwest horizon, and eastwards deep into Albania. The right fork continues to follow the coast, formed here by the bulk of Pantokrator pushing into the sea, and there is good swimming along the pebbly beach of Barbati Bay or in the coves just before Nisaki (22 kms). The loveliest part of the route is between Nisaki and Kouloura (30 kms) with prettily whitewashed
Kouloura	houses set amidst luxuriant vegetation and Kouloura itself with its romantic cove where caiques call daily from Corfu town, Nisaki and Kassiopi.

Beyond here the landscape grows harsh and Corfu has a Cycladic aspect in keeping with Roman rather than English

Kassiopi	lunacies: Durrell writes that at Kassiopi "the mad flabby Nero sang and danced horribly at the ancient altar to Zeus". By tradition the church stands on the site of the vanished temple and from here a path leads to the entrance of a 13th C. Angevin fortress, haunt of owls who hoot throughout the summer nights.

Paxos	It's 3 hours' sailing time from Corfu to PAXOS (Paxoi), the smallest of the main Ionian islands. Off its coast, so Plutarch wrote, the Egyptian captain Thamus heard the cry, "the great god Pan is dead", and carried the news to land where it was greeted with groans and laments.
Gaio	The chief town, or rather village, of this 3 by 8 km island is Gaio, an amphitheatre of surprisingly handsome pink and whitewashed houses around a tiny inlet on the east coast. Numerous paths meander through the peaceful olive groves that cover the island; a road runs north to the
Lakka	still smaller port of Lakka where there is a sandy beach. Better yet, a caique will take you south to the satellite
Antipaxos	island of Antipaxos where you can complement your picnic with the local sparkling red wine and enjoy a swim at Voutoumi Bay, a quiet beach of fine white sand on the east coast where the water is the clearest blue.

Lefkas	Thucydides reports that in 427 BC LEFKAS (referred to often in the accusative, Lefkada) was attached to the mainland, though centuries earlier Corinthian colonists had probably detached themselves by digging a canal which had silted up. Augustus built a new canal and the Venetians

maintained it, but Lefkas today still has an ambiguous quality: ruled sometimes from the sea as an island, sometimes from the land as a peninsula, the result is partly Ionian, partly western Greek — shimmering olives, sandy beaches and the finery of Venetian costumes against timber-framed houses, lagoon fishing as at Messolongi, and the melancholy of Epirot music.

Lefkas town is reached by chain ferry from Arkanania. Just on the mainland side of the crossing is Agia Mavra Castle, originally Frankish but given an Oriental caste by Turkish additions. A long sand-spit, the Yiro, encloses the Sea Lake at its north end — an excellent sand beach extends all along its seaward side and beyond to the Angevin chapel at Agios Ioannis — but the town is approached over a more direct causeway. Its houses have a ramshackle look, the upper storeys often of sheet metal or hardboard designed to place the least burden on ground floor timber and masonry walls sometimes shaken by earth tremors. The whole shebang is given a slapdash of paint, white or lime, blue or apricot, and after all manages a Greek dignity. The one main street, Odos Zakka, runs like an Oriental bazaar through the heart of town, capillaries of sandy alleyways off to either side.

A largely unpaved road encircles the high wild interior of the island, though a paved spur does penetrate the centre, taking you past Sfakiot villages settled by Cretan refugees in the 17th C. as far as Karia (15 kms), a hill-village overlooking the great sunken valley of Livadi. There are wonderful views of the Sea Lake and of the Arkananian ranges enroute.

The north and west coasts of Lefkas are barren, but along the east coast green valleys cultivated with orange and olive groves and dotted with attractive villages open out towards the mainland. Approaching the fjord-like Vliko Bay (21 kms) you can see offshore the island of Skorpios, owned by the late Aristotle Onassis. At southerly Cape Doukato where Childe Harold "saw the evening star above Leucadia's far-projecting rock of woe", a temple of Apollo stood upon the 200-ft high cliffs. In annual sacrifice to the god a criminal was thrown down into the sea, wings, feathers and live birds attached to him so that their flutterings might lighten his fall. Waiting boats carried survivors away to where the evil banished with them could do the Lefkadians no harm. Sappho took the leap as a cure for unrequited love. It proved fatally effective.

Immortalised in the *Odyssey*, the spur to life's adventure in Cavafy's poem ("Without Ithaka you would not have set

Agia Mavra Castle

Yiro beach

The town

Excursions from Lefkas town

To Karia

The east coast

'Sappho's Leap'

out . . . Poor though you find it, Ithaka has not cheated you."), you wonder if you should not continue to leave
Ithaka ITHAKA (Ithaki) to your imagination, or at least to your old age. Odysseus described it as "a rough land, a fit nurse for men", but Ithaka ruled a maritime empire; today its men try to eke a living from its stony soil and failing, they leave. But for the visitor there is no difficulty appreciating both the poetic and physical grandeur of this precipitous island lacerated by the sea.

From Patras and Kefallinia the boat beats along the wild and uninhabited eastern coast of Ithaka and rounds into the Gulf of Molos which almost separates the island into two halves. Empty mountains look down on you from all sides.
Vathi Then an unsuspected bay opens to port, Vathi sparkling
and the white cupped against its furthest end. Excursions about the
southern southern, less 'Homeric', half of the island may easily be
peninsula made from here: above Dexia Bay — where the Phaeacians left the sleeping Odysseus — is the cave of the Naiads where the returning hero supposedly hid his treasure; at the southeast of the island Arethusa's fountain is the spot — near a spring, a day's walk from the palace — that Eumaeus kept his swine. Piso Aetos on the west coast was claimed by Schliemann as the palace site, but dating to only 700 BC disproved the theory.
Stavros Stavros (18 kms) towards the north of the island is a more fruitful centre for Homeric sleuthing. Overlooking Polis Bay on the northwest coast, Stavros may stand on the
Odysseus' site of the Mycenaean town with Odysseus' palace 2 kms
palace north at Pelikata (some Mycenaean remains). The Cave of Tripods on the bay's north shore is the alternative to the Naiad cave near Vathi: at least here were found 12 bronze Geometric tripods (Odysseus had been given tripods by Alkinous on Corfu), later Greek sherds dedicated 'To the Nymphs', and a votive mask of the 1st C. AD bearing Odysseus' name — all suggesting that if this was not Odysseus' home at least people here 2000 years ago thought it was. Artefacts from the area, including the tripods, are in the museum at Pelikata.

Earthquakes Ithaka, Kefallinia and Zakinthos were all badly hit by earthquake in 1953; all have rebuilt, but on Kefallinia and moreso Zakinthos entire Venetian towns have been lost.
Kefallinia KEFALLINIA, once part of Odysseus' kingdom and lying spoon-in-spoon with Ithaka, is the largest and most mountainous island of the Ionian group. Forests of fir cover the slopes, giving them a sombre look, while peaks 5000 ft high burst incoming rain clouds, sudden thunderstorms watering the occasional meadowlands and valleys rich with flowers,

fruit and shrubs in a landscape otherwise lacking the luxuriance of Corfu or Zakinthos.

During the Residency here of Sir Charles Napier, roads were built and the water supply improved — "every hour not employed to do her good appears wasted"; he played host to his friend Byron who admired the island in those last months before crossing over to Messolongi.

Sami Visitors arriving by boat will probably put in at Sami, on the channel separating Kefallinia from Ithaka. Here Don John of Austria's fleet lay at anchor before its triumph over the Turks at Lepanto. The town is entirely modern; a busy transit point rather than a congenial place to stay, its vast pebbly beach too impersonal. On the hills above the town are the remains of ancient Sami, capital of the island in **Argostoli** Classical times. Preferable is the modern capital of Argostoli, beautifully situated along an inlet within the great Bay of Livadi to the west. The Archaeological Museum has an extensive collection of Mycenaean finds; indeed only at Mycenae itself have greater treasures been found. In the **Museums** Koryalenios Public Library and Folk Museum there are some fascinating photographs of 19th C. Argostoli and of the 1953 earthquake.

The British-built causeway and bridge across the inlet **Around the** have turned its inner reach into a lagoon, a walk of 5 kms **lagoon** all around; at the furthest point in the walk are the considerable walls of ancient Kranioi. Another walk is to the north where inlet and bay become one — here there is a reconstructed sea mill. In 1835 an Englishman discovered **The mysterious** that sea water was rushing into a rock tunnel and disappear- **sea mill** ing underground, to rise again no one knew where. He built a corn-mill on the spot, but the mystery of the water was not solved until the 1960s when Austrian scientists dumped dye down the tunnel and to their astonishment found it appearing again 16 kms away in the semi-underground lake at Melissani near Sami, having plunged beneath the central mountain range. The 1953 earthquake has retarded the flow and the present mill turns by electricity. By bus from **Beaches** Plateia Valianos you can reach two of the finest beaches in these islands, Platis Yialos and Makris Yialos, 3.5 kms south of town.

On a hill outside the village of Travliata, 8 kms southeast of Argostoli, soars the perfect phantom of the medieval **Castle of** past, the Venetian Castle of St George. Until the mid-18th **St George** C. the island capital stood beneath its massive battlements from which there are splendid views. During the second half of 1823 Byron lived between here and the sea at Metaxata: "Standing at the window of my apartment in this beautiful village, the calm though cool serenity of a beautiful and transparent Moonlight, showing the Islands, the Mountains, the Sea, with a distant outline of the Morea traced between the double Azure of the waves and the skies, has quieted me enough to be able to write".

Napier's cross-island road to the north is long and arduous, though to save making it a round-trip you can leave the island from Fiskardo, the Corfu-Patras ferry calling there. On the west coast, at the neck of a headland surmounted by a ruined Venetian castle, is the picturesque

Assos village of Assos, its colour-washed houses in gay relief to the stern grandeur of the sea and mountains around. A sand beach lies just to the north. Continuing to the extremity of the peninsula brings you to the only place on Kefallinia left undamaged by the 1953 earthquake: the 18th and 19th C.

Fiskardo houses at Fiskardo are typical of the island's pre-concrete architecture. A ruined church on the nearby headland could be 11th C. Norman — Fiskardo takes its name from the Norman conqueror of Sicily Robert Guiscard who died here in 1085. There is swimming from the rocks in the secluded coves to the north and south of the village.

Zakinthos ZAKINTHOS lies off the Peloponnese, the southernmost island of the Ionian crescent sheltering the entrance to the Gulf of Patras. It is reached by ferry from Killini. Topographically it is divided in two: spreading away from the port is a fertile plain described by Edward Lear as "one unbroken continuance of future current dumplings and plum puddings"; and beyond, rugged mountains, hilltop villages, stone-walled vineyards and, along the inhospitable west coast, cliffs dropping sheer into the sea. In springtime the plain is like a garden overrun with flowers; at the August harvest there is the remarkable sight of acres of currants spread out to dry in the shrivelling sun. To the Venetians the island was "Zante, fior di Levante"

Zakinthos town was the finest monument to Venetian architecture in Greece — 'the Venice of the Ionian Sea'. At

Zakinthos noon on 12 August 1953 it all came crashing down, a great
town fire ravaging even the broken remains. Only Agios Dionisios, church of the island's patron, and a bank and a school survived — and anyway they were all modern. A few lineaments of the Venetian town remain, in the street plan principally, the lemon-washed arcades nostalgically incorporated in new facades, the ikons in rebuilt churches.

The churches most worth visiting are Agios Nikolaos sto Molos in Plateia Solomou, the oldest in the town (1483),

Churches and Kiria ton Angelon (Our Lady of the Angels) north of the Xenia. Towards the south end of town, the Panagia Faneromeni was before 1953 the finest church; further on is Agios Dionisios.

Museums On Plateia Solomou is the Zakinthos Museum displaying examples of the island's church art from the 12th to 19th C. Further back in the town towards the Castle Hill is the Solomos Museum containing manuscripts and mementoes of three great Zantiot poets, Ugo Foscolo, Andreas Kalvos and Dionisios Solomos. Solomos (1798-1857), like Chaucer and Dante, chose to work in the vernacular, establishing demotic as the language of Greek literature. He and Kalvos **Castle Hill** lie in the mausoleum below. From the Venetian kastro atop the hill there is a sweeping view from Messolongi to Navarino.

A circular excursion round the island can be made by crossing the plain to Makerado (11 kms) where the church **Around the** has an exceptionally sumptuous interior, then up into the **island** hills and over a wild and rolling plateau to Maries (32 kms), and back down again along the length of the plain, perhaps turning towards the sea for a swim off the sand beach at Alikes (16 kms from town). The closest beach to town is at **Beaches** Tsilivi, 5 kms to the north. The best swimming is at the tip of the Vasiliko peninsula (15 kms) — a pleasant enough excursion for its own sake — at Porto Roma or Yerakes. The long crescent of sand at Lagana (8 kms) on Keri Bay is crowded at weekends.

THE ISLANDS OF THE WINE-DARK SEA

The Aegean

Greece is a country of two equal and intermingling parts, land and sea; and the Greek is as much at home when ploughing the blue Aegean as when growing vines among the high islands of his mountain villages. Obsidian from the island of Milos unearthed in a cave in the Argolid at a level corresponding to a date of 7000 BC is the earliest evidence of sea-borne trade anywhere in the world. By 2500 BC a fairly homogeneous culture extended over the length and breadth of the Aegean. Already the "wine-dark sea" was at the heart of the Greek world.

Sea routes

One of the greatest pleasures of a visit to Greece is to sail these waters from island to island. Piraeus is usually your starting-point and you follow the sea routes like the spokes of a wheel. Often you have to double back to Piraeus to reach another group of islands on another spoke unless you can cut across on a wave-scudding caique. Or from Syros, Mykonos, Naxos and Rhodes you can set out on a lesser spin of radiations.

There are 1425 islands in the Aegean but only 166 are inhabited. Many are all but barren and rise from the sea like carved and sculptured rock; the withering light "seems to melt, as if it were eating the islands; it lies heavy like the sheaves of a yellow harvest made of air, flattened into wide smooth circles like the sun" (Freya Stark). Where forests grew they have long since gone for triremes and caiques; the ubiquitous goat has reduced the land to desiccated steppe. That is not always true, but it is true often enough; and even where the inhabitants can stretch a living from their vineyards, their oil, their fishing, it may not be sufficient to dissuade them from their age-old recourse — emigration to the mainland cities or abroad. To counteract this, many

Traditional and tourist-developed islands

islands are being scheduled for tourist development. Airports, extra shipping services, modern hotels and discotheques lure tourists who spend money which improves the islanders' standard of living. Sometimes it is done well — and it is often the larger islands that are able to absorb visitors without losing their Greek character; occasionally the result is disasterous. There are still many islands where the boat rarely calls, where life is traditional, where knowing some Greek would help, and where too the visitor should expect little in the way of amenities and, importantly, immediate medical help. There are benefits either way according to your circumstances and desires.

THE CYCLADES

The Cyclades (Kyklades) in the central Aegean form a rough circle (kyklos) around sacred Delos upon which they were dependent in ancient times, though the islands more perfectly encircle Syros, capital of the modern nome. Neither uninhabited Delos nor Latin-flavoured Syros, however, offer examples of that sparkling white-cubed architecture for which the Cyclades are so well known. Houses are often linked together, forming blank fortress-like exterior walls, bastion after cubic bastion rising up the hillsides behind, a bewildering maze of narrow lanes within, defences in fact against the pirates who terrorised the Aegean until the early 19th C. Often the principal village or town of an island, Chora as it is locally called (though usually it officially takes the name of the island itself), was located well inland for this reason; only in the past century or so have the little island ports really come to life, leaving the old choras marooned on their heights.

Cycladic architecture

From Rafina on the east coast of Attika boats go to Andros and to Kea in the northern Cyclades; Kea may also be reached from Lavrion in Attika.

The northern Cyclades from Attika

ANDROS is an impressively mountainous and well-wooded extension of Euboea. Batsi, on the west coast, is the liveliest and most agreeable place to stay, while 7 kms south are the scant but superbly sited ruins of Paleopolis from where a road along the steep-walled valley of Messaria leads to the introspective chora on the far side of the island.

Andros

Despite its proximity to Attika, KEA was until recently one of the least visited of the Cyclades. Much of the land is idle, and the hillsides are carved with defunct terraces. You land in the northwest, in the attractive small port of Livadi (Classical Korissia). Round the bay to the east is the fishing village of Vourkari (beaches both here and by the port), opposite which on a promontory a Minoan-type palace is being excavated. About 5 kms above the port is the chora. This was ancient Ioulis and vestiges of an ancient temple are visible in the ruined Venetian kastro, but this charming little Cycladic town is a relic of a more recent age, of a time before the drift from the land. Ten minutes walk to the east, amongst mulberry trees, there is a large lion, carved out of the rock.

Kea

The chora

Paved mule tracks wind between the fields in the surprisingly rich interior, making for pleasant walks — to Poiessa on the west coast via the deserted monastery of Agia Marina, built into a fine Hellenic tower; or to Karthaia on

Walks across the island

the east coast where there is an ancient acropolis, with ruins of a Doric temple of Apollo beautifully situated on a platform overlooking the sandy shore.

The other northern Cyclades, Syros, Tinos and Mykonos, can be reached direct from Piraeus, while Delos is served by caiques from Mykonos.

Syros

Until the growth of Piraeus early this century, Ermoupolis on SYROS was the major port of the Aegean and is still the largest town in the Cyclades. Mills and tanneries around the bay, dry docks opened in the last decade or so, and the sight of several large freighters awaiting the welder's torch are all signs of a modest revival and pleasing for their unexpectedness and incongruity. The town is handsomely

Ermoupolis

19th C., with much Neo-Classical and Italianate architecture. The quayside is lined with lively cafes and tavernas, and with shops selling loukoumi (Turkish Delight), a speciality of the island. But going up Odos Ermou to the grandiose Plateia Maiouli with its public buildings, its arcaded cafes, its opera house where no opera has been performed since 1914 — these are the rouge on cheeks that have lost their bloom.

Centre of Catholicism

The double breasts of Ano-Syra (on the left) and Vrontado rise behind the lower town; the latter is the Orthodox quarter, the former the Roman Catholic — Syros and Tinos are the centres of Catholicism in Greece, a legacy of Venetian domination and, on Syros, later French protection as well.

Galisa, Finika and Delagratsia, all to the southwest, have good beaches; the last two are mentioned in the *Odyssey* as cities ruled by the father of Odysseus' swineherd Eumaeus.

Tinos

On 25 March and 15 August, lame and sick pilgrims from all over Greece come to the church of the Panagia Evangelistria on TINOS with its wonder-working ikon in hope of a cure. There is nothing lame or sick about the inhabitants who with miraculous alacrity accost their visitors with all manner of religious gee-gaws — causing other islanders to warn, "They will rob you of all you possess". The town has some traces of Venetian architecture and an ordered, relentless whiteness. The interior is more interesting, with its compact Cycladic hamlets picked out in white upon the green hillsides and — as on Andros — the intricate lace-like designs of the many Venetian dovecotes, the local expression of an imported Italian mania for building towers. The best swimming, protected from the meltemi, is in the quiet bay of Agios Nikolaos at the southwest corner of the island.

Mykonos

The impact of MYKONOS is only felt once you get within it. From the boat deck you see it built upon a barely sloping crescent projecting from the featureless hills behind: it lacks the drama of Hydra's climbing amphitheatre with its harbour as the stage. But Mykonos' defence against marauding pirates — and in 1822 the Turkish navy — was to construct a casbah closed to the sea, a confusing maze of narrow cobbled streets where sounds carry with crystal clarity, where whitewashed houses are almost painfully dazzling. Architecturally, the town is best appreciated during the sauna-heat of siesta, or well past midnight at full moon when its cubes and cupolas seem lit by an interior radiance — during those few hours, that is, of asbestos silence when Mykonos retires into its shell and is no longer playing the role of Cycladic Carnaby Street, filled with funfair noises and funfair people.

The Cycladic town par excellence

Only one of the famous windmills still flutters — flour is ground on the mainland and imported; Mykonos has found easier ways of making money. The international set comes in droves, the nightlife is wild and rock and roll rampages from the stereo speakers of alleyway discotheques. Uncountable boutiques sell souvenirs, jewellery and the strikingly coloured weaves for which Mykonos has always been noted. A quiet kafeneion is hard to find and the tavernas are scenes, even for Greece, of exceptional pandemonium. If it's a party you want, this is it.

Fleshpots

There's respite, however, at the unvisited Archaeological Museum at the north end of the harbour. The prize is a 7th C. BC pithos depicting the Trojan war in Archaic comic-strip form. Achaean warriors, faintly conscious of seeming ridiculous, peer from hatches in the flanks of their wooden horse-on-wheels.

The Archaeological Museum

Beaches on the exposed north coast are badly hit by the meltemi; better to head south. Crossing the island, bright white little churches, especially gay with their red-painted roofs, illuminate the parched fields and stony hillsides. A bus runs to Plati Yialos; from there you walk or take a boat (boats also from town) to the nude beaches beyond (Paradise, Super Paradise, Elia), all excellent, with good sand and superb crystal clear water. I came with my wife who frankly was the best looking woman on the beach, though there's a lot to be said for making comparisons.

Nude beaches

On mornings when the meltemi isn't blowing too strongly, several small boats set out on the 30-minute crossing to DELOS. You are usually given 3 hours to scoot through it all, which can just be enough, otherwise a second visit is necessary. (It would be nice to stay at the Xenia here but

Delos

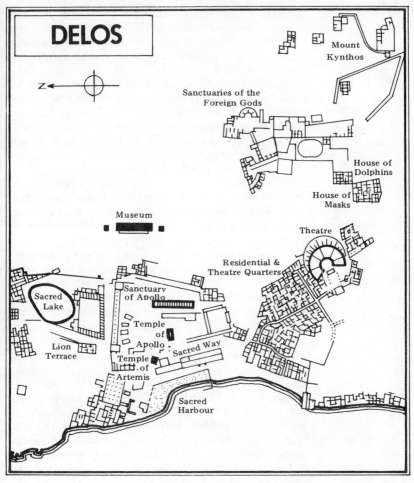

DELOS

Z ←

Mount
Kynthos

Sanctuaries of the
Foreign Gods

House of
Dolphins

House of
Masks

Museum

Theatre

Residential &
Theatre Quarters

Sacred
Lake

Sanctuary
of Apollo

Temple
of
Apollo

Lion
Terrace

Sacred Way

Temple
of
Artemis

Sacred
Harbour

its 4 rooms seem always to be taken by archaeologists.) The
problem is that everyone comes to the island at once and
you have little time to linger, little opportunity to feel the
place. Maybe that's why I thought Delos overrated: it was
August and its extensive tracts of foundations and sculp-
tureless pedestals — particularly in the area of the sacred
and public buildings — lay about like burnt sliced onions on
this small dry brown frying pan of an island. In springtime
it's different, I'm told, with bright red poppies and the
white and delicate blues of anemones bobbing about on the
green waves of long-stemmed grasses. Holy places impress
themselves upon you through all your senses and it might
be better not to rush about but to touch the stones — "The
The Sacred Isle   modest stones of Greeks,/ Who gravely interrupted death

by pleasure." (Durrell) — and catch the fragrance of the season, for here the radiant Apollo was born and "all Delos was immeasurably filled with ambrosial perfume; and the vast earth laughed, and the deeps of the grey sea did rejoice" (Theognis of Megara).

Birth of Apollo

Pregnant by Zeus and rejected by every spot of earth at jealous Hera's bidding, Leto finally found humble refuge where Poseidon had fixed floating Delos to the sea-bed. Here on Mt Kynthos according to one version of the myth, by the Sacred Lake according to another, Leto in her labour stood grasping a date palm while Artemis, born to her the day before, assisted at her brother's birth.

History of the island

Enrichment of the island began after the Persian wars when the treasury of Athens' maritime league was located here until removed to the imperial city in 454 BC. Following the plague that killed Pericles and thousands of others at Athens in the early years of her war with Sparta, the Athenians, at the command of an oracle, in 426 BC purified Delos, disinterring its dead and decreeing that no-one must ever die or be born here again. But in Hellenistic and Roman times the Delian Festival in honour of Artemis and Apollo became no more than an excuse for international trade fairs; Syrian, Egyptian and other merchants founded important trading houses at Delos; the population swelled to 20,000; and the island became the largest slave market in Greece, as many as 10,000 slaves sold here in a single day. In 88 BC, during the First Mithridatic War, the Parthian general Menophanes, by way of striking against Rome, seized the island, killed every man on it, and sold all its women and children into slavery in turn. The city was razed to the ground, never to recover; in the 2nd C. AD Pausanias observed that if the temple guard were withdrawn the island would be uninhabited. Turks and Venetians worked the marble ruins as a quarry; nearby islanders and Classically-minded English aristocrats embellished their homes with fragments of sculpture bought or looted; and the colossal Apollo cut base and figure from a single block of Naxian marble, still recognisably intact when sketched by the Dutch painter Segur de Vries in 1672, was soon after reduced to the near-formless torso that you see today, the rest having been hacked away and taken to the lime kilns. Since 1873 Delos has been excavated by the French School; the finest sculpture has been removed to Athens, the shattered remainder exhibited in the island's museum.

Depredations

Touring the site

A selection of guide books to the site can be obtained at the tourist pavilion. The highlights of the visit are the dis-membered Apollo, the Lions and the Sacred Lake, the residential and theatre quarter, and the climb up Mt Kynthos.

Except in rough weather, you land at a point between the *Sacred Harbour* on the left, the *maritime quarter* with its warehouses on the right, and ascend to the wide, paved *Sacred Way* leading off to your left. At its far end, to the right, is a vast precinct, the *Sanctuary of Apollo*, enclosing temples, altars and other vestiges of 1000 years of worship. The *Great Temple of Apollo* is here, and in front of it the *base* on which the colossos stood. Left of the Sacred Way, by the Temple of Artemis, you will find the *colossos Apollo* lying broken out in the sun where the Venetians left it — so cool to the touch, even where the sun strikes it directly. Its mass is impressive and burgeoning still with an inner power — it really ought to be reassembled on its base. Further on is the *Terrace of the Lions*, five lean beasts with eternity in their jaws; they survey the dried-up *Sacred Lake*, an evocative palm tree growing at its centre, planted by a French lady archaeologist in commemoration of Leto's labour.

The great statue of Apollo

The Lion Terrace and Sacred Lake

The museum

Circling round the lake you come to the *museum* and the *tourist pavilion*, a short distance in front of which is the small *Sanctuary of Dionysos*, sporting several choregic monuments in the shape of huge phalluses. Passing through the *Sanctuaries of Foreign Gods* you begin the stepped ascent of *Mt Kynthos* (only 368 ft) where Apollo and Artemis were worshipped in Archaic times and Cycladic dwellings of the late 3rd millenium have been found. But the reasson for the climb is the sweeping view of the Cyclades. "It is the most perfect imaginable island scenery, just as the mountain scenery of Apollo's other great shrine at Delphi is, as mountain scenery, the most perfect imaginable" (Robert Liddell) — it's a matter of luck: on the days of my visits the haze had reduced Paros and Naxos to shadows and Syros was entirely invisible.

The view from Mt Kynthos

Between the foot of Mt Kynthos and the maritime quarter, Delos is like Pompeii. There is a fine view of the excavated city from the upper tiers of the theatre, abutting which is a 3-storey 'hotel' where visitors to the festival may have stayed. Further uphill is the *House of the Masks*, named after its mosaic pavement, perhaps a hostel for actors. The paved street descending from the theatre is lined with Hellenistic and Roman workshops and expansive villas set around open courtyards such as the *House of Dionysos* and the *House of the Trident*, again named after their vividly coloured mosaics. There's a sense of bustle only temporarily absent, the long centuries of silence a passing siesta.

The ancient city

Barren landscapes and declining populations mark Kithnos and Kimolos, two islands sometimes served on the eastern Cyclades run. On SERIFOS, at least, the rocky and mountainous terrain achieves some character and from the hot landlocked harbour hard-worked terraces rise against a bony crag, the chora like a wave breaking on its edge. It's rewarding to make the steep walk up, and then back for a swim in the sand-rimmed bay. In summer at least one boat calls here daily enroute for Sifnos and Milos.

The landing at SIFNOS is made at the unattractive Bay of Kamares; this whole west coast is bare and unappealing and to the traveller merely sailing by conveys an erroneous impression of the island. You must take the bus the 5 kms up to the Cycladic villages of Apolloni or Artemona which undulate along the island's spine; individually, their houses are as fine as those on Mykonos, though the composition suffers from lack of compression. Artemona has several good tavernas and a lively nightlife. The eastern slopes of the island dropping down below are well-watered and green; Kastro, on the coast, turns out to be one of the loveliest villages in the Aegean with a delightfully medieval air with arches and projecting wooden balconies, its crumbling Venetian houses hugged against the hillside by 14th C. walls, built perhaps from the stones of the island's ancient capital here. The longest beach in the Cyclades is on the south coast, at Plati Yialos, now developing as a resort.

Volcanic MILOS, its mountains encircling a great gouging bay, was once a pirate haven where the pasha was paid to turn a blind eye while the inhabitants prospered through the disposal of booty. The port of Adamas is unremarkable, but there is the strange sight of purple-blossomed brine trees watered by the sea, and along the bay's encircling peaks the glittering sentinels of shrines and chapels. A winding road ascends to Plaka (4 kms), burning white against the volcanic soil. It spreads across the acropolis of the ancient city where near the walls the Venus de Milo was found in 1820 and spirited off to the Louvre. Nearby are extensive early Christian catacombs. Thucydides dramatically presents that moment of arrogance, with Nemesis standing in the wings, when the Athenian envoys argue that might has given them the right to dictate to the Melians. Only after months of siege did the Melians surrender, the men put to death, the women and children sold into slavery. Cruise ships often put in at the fishing village of Apollonia, opposite Kimolos, for its proximity to Phylokope where excavations have revealed a Minoan/Mycenaean city. There are good beaches along the coast here.

Daily boats from Piraeus, often calling at Syros enroute, serve the central and southern Cyclades — Paros, Naxos, Ios and Thera. Less frequently, boats calling at Naxos go on to Iraklia, Shinoussa, Koufonissi, Karos, Amorgos and Donoussa; boats calling at Ios or Thera go on to Anafi, Folegandros and Sikinos.

The symmetry of Profitas Elias (2530 ft) and the gentle contour of its slopes already from a distance establish the coherence and harmony that make PAROS the most endearing island of the Cyclades. The island is this single mountain, its skirts the flaring coastal plain, treeless but cultivated with wheat and barley and the vineyards that produce the island's dark red wine. The genial impression is confirmed as you enter its broad bay, sand beaches and a scattering of villas and farmsteads around it, the island's main village, Paroikia, running over a slight rise in the shoreline to the right — a rhythm of white houses and blue domes, a ruined 13th C. Venetian kastro (incorporating the remains of a temple of Demeter) and a few windmills — a visual iambic recalling Archilochos, the 8th C. BC lyric poet who was the first to write in that metre and was born on Paros. Paroikia has the architecture if not the size of Mykonos — nor has it been transformed by a surfeit of tourist-minded shops and tavernas. The main street soon establishes its own Greek tempo, past small fruit shops and grocers to whitewashed walls cascading with bougainvillia and houses large and small of modest grandeur, graceful arches decorating some, outside staircases on others leading to upper-storey balconies. A solitary bell suspended from its tower leads you round another corner in search of its hidden chapel. Though only three or four streets in depth, it's possible, as I did, to get lost altogether. Paroikia's cathedral, the Panagia Ekatontapiliani ('of the hundred doors', though more likely a corruption of *katapoliani*, 'on lower ground'), is the finest in the Aegean. Said to have been founded by St Helena, mother of Constantine, on the spot where she had her vision of the True Cross, the existing church was built two centuries later at the behest of Justinian by the same architects of the great Agia Sophia in Constantinople. Not that you should expect magnificence; interest lies in its peculiarities, for it is really three churches in one: the main cruciform structure with a patterned interior of green, purple and yellow stone; the basilica of Agios Nikolaos, its columns from a 6th C. BC Doric temple, to the left of the apse; and a baptistry off the south

transept with a font for total immersion. There is an archaeological museum nearby.

Paros assisted the Persians at Marathon, so that Miltiades
later led an expedition against the island and while failing
to take it broke his leg and died of gangrene. After the
defeat of Xerxes, Paros became subject to Athens and her
marble preferred for sculpture. The quarries lie about 8 kms
east of Paroikia — abandoned for centuries, marble was
again taken from them in 1844 for Napoleon's tomb.

Excursions
from Paroikia
Following a lovely green valley to the north coast you
come to the fishing village of Naoussa (10 kms) with its
tiny caique harbour, half-submerged kastro and good
beaches freshened by breakers rolling in past the headland. The Valley of the Butterflies is 10 kms in the other
direction — in fact an area of ivy-covered trees at the foot
of a slope, with many bright orange moths. There is another
such valley on Rhodes, where the tourists nearly out-
number the moths — at least that is not the case here. A
caique from Paroikia takes you to the islet of Antiparos
where in a vast cavern, seemingly supported by stalagmite
columns, the French Ambassador to the Porte celebrated
midnight mass on Christmas 1673, illuminating the cave
with hundreds of torches, and paying 500 bemused Parians
to attend.

Naxos

NAXOS is the largest of the Cyclades, the gauntness of its
interior relieved by fertile and well-watered valleys beyond
sight or salt of the sea where the air is sweet with an earthy
fragrance. Lemons and oranges, figs and pomegranates
provide the islanders with a healthy income, which along
with their traditional coolness towards visitors adds up to a
reluctance to compromise with modern tourism. Byron
liked it. The main road winds through a graceful valley,
dividing the northern from the southern ranges, to the
Villages of olive-covered plain of Tragaias where Chalki, a Cycladic
the interior village - interspersed with Venetian tower-houses and
interesting Byzantine churches, sits within medieval walls;
it then continues to Filoti, on the north flank of Mt Zia
(3290 ft — highest in the Cyclades), with its Frankish
kastro, and to Apiranthos, a decaying though well-built and
beautiful white village towards the far side of the island.
Unfinished From Chalki you can follow another road down to the
kouros coast at Apollona where a colossal unfinished kouros lies in
the quarry and the beach is covered with smooth-worn
marble stones.

From 1207 until 1566 when the Turks took the island,
Naxos town was the capital of the Venetian dukes whose
feudal sway extended over the entire Cyclades. Their

The Dukes of Naxos

memory is preserved by the occasional coat of arms over house-fronts along the steep claustrophobic alleyways of the upper town with its sections of medieval walls. On an islet connected to the town by a causeway is a great marble rectangle, the portal to a temple of Apollo (c530 BC), framing Delos in the distance — though some, recalling how "gently and sweetly, Dionysos, with his merry train of satyrs and maenads, came to Ariadne's rescue" (Robert Graves) after Theseus abandoned her here on his way home to Athens from Knossos, ascribe the temple to the god of wine. Naxian wine is good, but you should make a point of pausing along the quayside to enjoy a citron, the local liqueur, a distillation of the sweetness, bite and fragrance of the lemon's flesh and peel.

Ariadne and Dionysos

Beaches

There are excellent sandy beaches south of the town, but no road to them — you need good feet for the daily walk, or should take a tent and water for a longer stay. The fourth beach, past a headland, is frequented by nude bathers.

Amorgos

The most easterly of the Cyclades, primitive and unspoilt AMORGOS rises like a wall from the sea, three mountain peaks along its narrow spine, precipitous cliffs along its south coast. Sheer walls guard the entrance to the harbour at Katapola, too, at the centre of the island, a lively place considering its small size, and with good beaches. The ruins of ancient Minoa lie above, and an hour's steep climb beyond is the chora, wonderful mountain scenery all around; and finally, built into a cliffside across the island is possibly the most magnificently situated monastery in Greece, the Hozoviotissa, pendent over the blue.

Ios

IOS derives its name from the Ionians who with their unfailing sense for the graceful settled on this beautiful island. Homer is said to have died here, though the tomb claimed as his at Plakotos, at the north tip, is a much earlier prehistoric grave. Arrival is through a winding bay, the chora clinging to the first of three symmetrical hills, charming at a distance. You imagine it inviolate, belonging to another world. It has in fact been lately ruined by a plague of locusts who pack snack bars, boutiques and discotheques, appreciating nothing, giving nothing, taking everything. It is better to sail on.

'Homer's tomb'

Sikonos and Folegandros

Sikonos and Folegandros to the west are the two driest islands of the Cyclades and barely populated. Their choras, and what cultivation there is, are set well back from the coasts — remarkably precipitous in the case of Folegandros. Both islands, however, are being developed for tourism.

211

Thera

Battering hailstones and gale force winds drove us through the Naxos channel. Against the wet watercolour sky of mingling black and grey, Thera's odd abrupt outline, a smashed asteroid flung from the cosmos by some mightier-than-Olympian god, defied the furious waves. That night, pressed against the cathedral wall at clifftop Phira, listening to the shrieking wind which tore at corners and at rooftops, watching incandescent talons ripping through the black curtains of the horizon, it seemed the entire island might yet crack and tumble into the sea. I never so much doubted the ground on which I stood. It was a suitably atmospheric arrival, but any will do. THERA (also known as Santorini) is the most extraordinary island in the Aegean, extraordinary for its beauty, its history, its tragedy and the legends of a lost world which have struck a chord of wonder and yearning over thousands of years. Only 96 kms north of Crete, this was a highly sophisticated outpost of Minoan civilisation built, unwittingly, upon one of the greatest volcanoes on earth. Around 1450 BC the island was torn apart by an explosion unequalled by man or nature since, and as its greater part was hurled through the sky or sank beneath the sea, so also, some believe, a gigantic tsunami broke upon the shores of Minoan Crete, mortally wounding that most graceful of civilisations. The memory of the event may have entered the mythology of Mediterranean man, surviving in the legend of Atlantis. (For more on this, read *The End of Atlantis* by J.V. Luce.)

The caldera

Today you sail into the great caldera of the shattered volcano, its ribboned pumice walls rising hundreds of feet sheer above you. These are the cliffs of crescent Thera; the circular outline is continued to the west by Therasia, 9 kms distant. Floating islands of gathered pumice chunks roll within this inland sea, the black jagged lava dome of Kaimeni island, the new volcano which last seriously erupted in 1938-41, at its centre. The boat calls first below Oia at the northwest horn of Thera, and then either berths at Ormos Athinios (buses and taxis to Phira), weather permitting, or anchors off Skala Phira from where you make the 30-minute zig-zag climb (672 ft) on foot or mule to Phira running high along the cliff edge. From up here, Kaimeni sits like a gigantic black octopus within the lagoon, still active, sometimes smoking, and as a prelude to further eruptions or earthquakes usually discolouring the water around it. Kaimeni can be visited by motorboat from Skala Phira.

Phira

Half Phira was destroyed by earthquake in 1956. Some houses have been abandoned, others built further along, but all still hang upon the precipice, staring into the abyss which sooner or later will shrug or yawn and bring them down again. Why do these people do it? Every observation suggests that the land is used more extensively, more productively on Thera than anywhere else in Greece. Perhaps they don't want to build upon any of their usable soil. Despite its sterile appearance late in summer, the soil produces an abundance of tomatoes, wheat (there are numerous threshing-floors around the island) — and excellent grapes for wine. In this case tourism is complementary to the staple product, since it's the tourists who consume most of the wine. The 2½ hour walk to Oia, a

Oia and Skaros smaller, run-down version of Phira, takes you after a short distance through Skaros, the ruined medieval capital built by the Naxian dukes. In spring musk thistles grow from the castle walls, a delicate pink stock clings to the cliffs, and as you walk on there are beautiful views down the intricately-terraced slopes, bright red and yellow with corn poppies and Bermuda buttercups, with Anafi, Amorgos and Ios across the blue. Another walk, southeast, is to the monastery on Megalos Agios Ilias, the highest point on the island (1857 ft), from where you can see the mountains of Crete.

Pirgos At its base is Pirgos, with many fine old Cycladic houses and a blank-walled ruined Venetian kastro. The bus comes only this far; ancient Thera (signposted) is another hour's walk (or by taxi). The ruins are strikingly situated on the rocky spine of Mesa Vouno, the black sand beaches of Kamari (the ancient port) to the north, Perissa to the south

Ancient Thera (bus in summer from Phira). No one building is particularly well-preserved; the site is more important for its position and its extent. The ruins are mostly Ptolemaic — Kamari was an Egyptian naval station — but the site was inhabited from the 9th C. BC through Byzantine times.

On the southwest horn of the island, 1 km beyond the village of Akrotiri (12 kms), are the excavations of the Minoan settlement that have turned up the magnificent frescoes now in Athens. Reproductions, as at Knossos,

The Minoan would enhance the visitor's appreciation of the site, but
settlement still it is fascinating. Banks of ash have been pushed back
at Akrotiri around the buildings, some of them 2 and 3 storeys high. They were first damaged by earthquake and then 2-3 years later buried by the great eruption of c1450 BC. Prof Marinatos, who led the excavations from 1967, is buried within one of the buildings he uncovered, opposite where he was killed in 1974 by a collapsing wall.

The museum Back in Phira the museum contains mostly Geometric through Roman artefacts, though it's intended to build a new museum for the Akrotiri frescoes, etc. — and extraordinary intention considering the geological possibilities.

THE EASTERN SPORADES

The Eastern Sporades, more fertile than the Cyclades, are scattered down the coast of Asia Minor. Samothraki and Lemnos have been included in the chapter on northern Greece from where they are most easily reached. From Piraeus, the boat passes under the long, high island of
Samos Ikaria, and in the distance, at the western end of SAMOS, you can already see 4740-ft Mt Kerkis, mantelled in forests that have survived — so rare on Aegean islands — since ancient times. Eastwards there is a pass, but then the mountain backbone arches again, with great spurs falling away from Ambelos (3740ft), precipitous along the north coast, but enclosing a series of plains and good beaches along the south. On Samos the friendly sound of splashing streams reminds you of the island's richness, where even the birds gave milk, so Menander said. Today wines, tobacco and olives are exported all over the world, sustaining a large population in scattered mountain villages and in the island's three ports.

Karlovassi, along the north coast, is uninteresting, but now the boat thrums along the beautiful mountain coastline to Vathy (or Samos). From Ano Vathy, above, with its red tiled roofs and timbered houses reminiscent of northern Greece or Turkey, you look down upon the deep-cut bay
The ports and sense a Levantine mood. Across the island you can see Turkey, only 3kms of blue water marking the divide. On the south coast of the island, with a wonderful view down the Dodecanese and across the Strait of Mykale to Turkey is the lazy seafront village and port of Pithagorion, named for the great mathematician born in ancient Samos on which the present village in part stands. Pithagorion is for
Beaches many reasons the best place to stay. To the west there are several good beaches, some sandy, some pebbly, all protected from the northern meltemi. There are the Turkish mountains running down to Cape Kanapitza, indolently viewed from a cafe table. And around you are the formidable remains of the ancient city.

Ancient Samos Aesop and Epicurus, as well as Pythagoras, once lived in ancient Samos. So did Aristarchos, the first to state that the earth revolved around the sun, and also the explorer Kolaios who around 650 BC made his name and fortune by sailing to the Pillars of Hercules. The walls of the city climb steeply over the hill of Astypalaea, its towers and central
Wonders of the sectons in good condition at the crest. But it was under the
ancient world rule of Polykrates, says Herodotos, that three of the greatest building and engineering feats in the Greek world were carried out. The first was the harbour mole on whose

foundations its modern counterpart still projects far out from the coastline. The second was the kilometre-long Tunnel of Eupalinos cut through Astypalaea, a guarantee of water supply at times of siege, an escape route too if necessary. The tunnel took 15 years to dig and was completed in 524 BC; the centre has now collapsed but you can still explore deep inside using a flashlight. The **Temple of Hera** third — and this was ranked among the seven greatest wonders of the world — was the Temple of Hera, 8 kms along the coast and past the airport at a place called Kolonna for the single skew column rising now from the vast limestone foundations. According to legend, Hera, Queen of Olympos, was born along the torrent Imbrasos here, and since c1000 BC there has been a sanctuary on this spot dedicated to her. In the early 8th C. BC a megaron surrounded by a peristyle of columns was constructed here, the earliest example of a true Greek temple. A later temple, already the largest in Greece, was destroyed by fire in 525 BC; Polykrates at once ordered the construction of the yet larger one whose ruins you now see. Comparable in size to the Olympeion in Athens which was to take 700 years to complete, Polykrates' temple had progressed to its still astonishing dimensions within 3 years when, in 522 BC, he was tricked, captured and crucified on the mainland by the Persians, and construction ceased. What you might most regret, however, is the loss of Kolaios' little ship, which like some space capsule was long exhibited on the site.

Chios Like Samos, CHIOS enjoys fertility and a good climate. With Samos and several mainland cities including Ephesos and Miletos, it was a member of the Ionic Confederation that succumbed first to Croesus of Lydia, then to Cyrus of Persia. The confederation's unsuccessful revolt against Persian domination was assisted by Athens and decided Darius on his punitive expediton against the Greek main-landers in 490 BC. For 300 years until 1566, when the Turks captured the island, Chios prospered under the Genoese and, unusual for Greece, developed a native aris-tocracy whose country houses set within gardens surrounded by high mud-brick walls remain typical of Kambos, the long fertile plain abounding in citrus groves extending south of Chios town. The new aristocracy are the successful shipowning families who seem equally to abound on Chios. Unlike Samos, however, Chios has suffered hor-ribly from natural and man-wrought devastation. In 1822 the islanders rose against the Turks. It is said that the ladies of Constantinople were furious at losing their source of mastic (used for making a liqueur and a sweetmeat, as the basis for chewing gum and, most importantly for the ladies, as a breath sweetener). A Turkish force landed on Chios, murdering and abducting the largely unarmed population. These regulars were soon joined by every armed, greedy and vicious Turk who could cross over from the mainland. In the end, 25,000 Chiots were killed, 41,000 taken to Constantinople for sale as slaves — along with sacks of human heads, noses and ears that were strewn around the streets where the putrefying flesh was left to be trampled into the mire. The massacre shocked Europe and led Delacroix to paint his famous if insufficiently grisly 'Scenes from the Massacres of Scio', now hanging in the Louvre. The island's social structure was destroyed, and in 1881 a further 5000 Chiots were killed by earthquake.

The port

Facing Turkey's Karaburnu peninsula 8 kms distant, Chios has a nondescript commercial air relieved only occasionally by a projecting Turkish balcony and by the inevitable kastro, this time Genoese, with crumbling towers, gates and gun embrasures, some of them bearing the arms of the Giustianini, the old Turkish quarter huddled within. The modern town almost entirely obscures ancient Chios.

Nea Moni

8 kms west is the convent of Nea Moni, founded in the 11th C. to house a miraculous ikon and visited for its fine mosaics. Though there is no evidence for the claim, Kardamila, 27 kms to the north, is touted as Homer's birthplace. The upper town is picturesque and there's good swimming along the north coast. Volissos, 40 kms to the

Homer's home
town

northwest, was once the home of a clan claiming descent from Homer and is promoted as the place where he lived and worked.

Pirgi, 24 kms south of Chios town, is certainly the most unusual and attractive spot on the island. Round-roofed houses line narrow streets spanned by arches as a protection against earthquakes, and the houses

Mastic growing
country

are strangely decorated with geometric patterns cut into plaster and coloured — sgraffito it is called, an Italian fashion, but executed here during the Turkish occupation and strongly Islamic in character. This is a medieval fortress town in the heart of the mastic growing region, the fortifications necessary against the Turks who came, raiding for women. Though lacking any sgraffito, the best example of a fortified town is Mesta to the west, no streets, but alleyways, dark and tunnel-like with no windows on the ground floors. At Emborio, on a promontory along the southeast coast, a Bronze Age settlement, thought to be a rival to Troy, has been unearthed. There is good swimming off the black pebble beach here.

Sappho's island   LESVOS (Lesbos) is visited less for its antiquities than for its beauty and its literary associations. Aesop came from Lesvos, while the landscape between Mytilene and Methymna provided the setting for Longus' erotic pastoral *Daphnis and Chloe*; but most importantly this was Sappho's isle — "I love delicacy, and the bright and the beautiful belong for me to the desire of the sunlight": *the* poetess the ancients called her, in the same way that Homer was *the* poet. In Sappho's time (7th/6th C. BC), this third largest Aegean island after Crete and Euboea was a major trading and cultural centre renowned for its high standard of education and its comparative freedom for women — two attributes it retains today. Its capital, Mytilene, was an important ally of the Athenians during the Peloponnesian War until its oligarchs attempted to join with the Spartans. Outraged and embittered by the betrayal the Athenian assembly despatched a galley with orders to put every citizen to death. It is one of the more dramatic moments in Thucydides, for the following day brought a change of heart and a second galley was sent racing across the Aegean, its crew sleeping in turns, eating and drinking at their oars, sweeping into Mytilene just as the death sentence was being read out.

Mountainous and rugged, with strange forests of petrified conifers and sequoias in the largely barren west, green with olive, pine, oak and chestnut trees in the east, Lesvos contains some of the wildest and also the most romantic, idyllic scenery in Greece. The weather is mild, the beaches are good, and there is an agreeable lingering of Turkish influence — here at least they ruled with restraint.

Mitilini   Probably the finest thing about sailing into what was the ancient harbour of Mytilene (modern Mitilini) is imagining that moment of reprieve 2400 years ago; the waterfront is lively enough, and this is the place to enjoy some of the best ouzo and olives in Greece, but the town is without particular interest. There are good views, however, along the coast and across to Turkey from the Kastro, and all about the landscape is superb, especially across the peninsula along the shores of Yera Bay where also there is excellent swimming.

Molivos   Molivos (anciently Methymna), 62 kms distant on the beautiful northern coast, is built against a headland surmounted by a Genoese castle. Its towerhouses, fishing harbour and a long beach make it the most appealing place to spend some time, Skala Eressou, at the southwest end of Lesvos, is by a long beach beneath the rocky acropolis of the ancient city where Sappho was born.

THE DODECANESE

Like the Eastern Sporades, the Dodecanese closely follow the Turkish coastline, their extremities sometimes embraced by the headlands of Asia. The islands themselves are often indented, usually mountainous and, the moreso as you head south, blessed with a warm and sunny climate the year round. They are also undeniably Greek in character, though they were part of the Ottoman Empire until 1912, governed with increasing harshness by the Italians until the British occupation in the closing years of the Second World War, and only united with Greece in 1947. Nevertheless, part of the pleasure of the Dodecanese is the varying degree to which Classical, Byzantine, Crusader, Turkish and Italian influences make themselves felt on each island. They may be reached by sea from Piraeus (via the Cyclades or Crete) or from Thessaloniki, while there are air services from Athens to Kos and Rhodes. Going back to the time of Suleiman the Magnificent in the 16th C. the Dodecanese have enjoyed certain privileges — the Greek government allowing a lower rate of duty on many imported goods (including spirits). However, when passing between the Dodecanese and the rest of Greece, you must clear through customs.

If Delos is the holy island of Classical Greece then PATMOS is the holy island of Christianity where St John the Divine received his vision of the Apocalypse and wrote *Revelations*. Patmos is suitably an island of extremes, the most northern of its group, the most arid, one of the smallest and perhaps the most beautiful with a wildly undulating coastline of coves and headlands, hidden beaches which require a boat to reach, a lively port and, high above, the atmospheric medieval Chora helmeted by the fortified Monastery of St John.

The island of the Apocalypse

Skala

The boat ties up at Skala, deep within a lovely, almost entirely enclosed bay, a narrow beach extending north-wards along the waterfront. The houses are white, their doors and shutters painted ochre and in muted blues and greens. The impression is bright, pleasant and friendly, and there are some good kafeneions by the arcaded plateia — an Italian legacy — where breakfast or an evening drink is attended by the gentle rocking of sailboats and caiques at their moorings. After Rhodes and Kos, Patmos is the most visited of the Dodecanese, but mostly by cruise ships which come and go again within a few hours; otherwise, even at the height of summer, it is a peaceful and relaxing place.

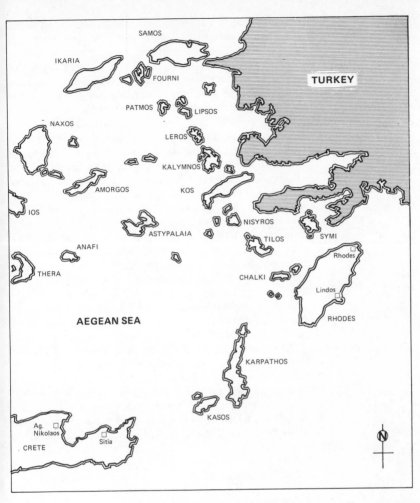

A donkey path climbs steeply up towards Chora, or you can follow the more gradual, winding road. There are buses and taxis. Halfway up is the Grotto of the Apocalypse (signposted), which you enter via the chapel of Agia Anna built over its yawning opening. Rock ledges are identified as the saint's desk and bed, and ikons vividly depict the moment of cosmic revelation which enroute from God to St John blasted a three-way fissure near the mouth of the cave — odd, that; as though the Word could not be bothered to go in by the very obvious front door.

Continuing upwards, the views are spectacular. You see that Skala is built on a narrow isthmus, the bay on one side, the open Aegean on the other. The arid island landscape is so deeply incised by coves and bays that from here to the sea

St John's grotto

Climbing towards Chora

sometimes seems a stunning blue lake amidst rolling slopes of brown and dun-green. Though often shuttered, and quiet except for the meltemi whistling across its narrow streets, Chora is beautiful — substantial 16th and 17th C. houses of several storeys with marvellous wooden doors and elaborately wrought knockers. And rising above them are the crenelated battlements of the Monastery of St John, founded in 1088 with the permission of the Byzantine emperor by the Blessed Christodoulos, a monastery with teeth, to fend off pirates and foreign powers and preserve the most important monastic collection in Greece outside of Mt Athos. Inside, all is white and angular, arcades, terraces and patios open to the sun. The view finally from the rooftops is of gleaming, burning whiteness; tiled Byzantine cupolas; glittering sea; Naxos, Paros, Kos in the far distance like basking whales. It is far more superb a view than that from stunted Delos. Below, the Library contains hundreds of parchments and hand-written books, many of them exquisitely illuminated, and 33 leaves from a 6th C. *Gospel of St Mark*. In the Treasury are jewellery, church furniture, embroidered stoles and numerous ikons, the most interesting being one of St Nicholas in mosaic, no piece greater than one twenty-fifth of an inch across.

Beaches Roads from both Chora and Skala (boats from Skala, too) take you to Grikou beach, 3.5 kms south of Skala, with a few tavernas, a couple of hotels, good swimming in a lagoon-like bay, and out at the tip of a spit of sand a great rock, its cave inhabited in prehistoric times. The alternative is Kambos, 8 kms to the north by road or boat, some rooms to let, better sand than Grikou, but not nearly as attractive a situation.

Leros LEROS is remarkably similar to Patmos in configuration, but with none of its interest and little of its charm. Porto Lakki, at the head of a vast, still bay on the west coast, was a major Italian naval base and will be your likely port of call. It is a dreary, crumbling place. Platanos, on the east coast, is livelier and there are some fine views from the Byzantine kastro. Nowhere on the island is the swimming especially good. A peculiarity of Leros is that property is inherited through the female line, nearly all land and houses belonging to women.

Kalymnos Only 2 kms of sea separate Leros and KALYMNOS, an imposingly mountainous island whose inhabitants rely on fishing and the declining rewards of sponge diving for their livelihood. The Aegean's depleted sponge beds oblige the divers to search along the North African coast; they are gone from Easter until summer's end and only when they return does the island really come to life. Kalymnos town, looking southeastwards towards Kos, presents to the arriving visitor an ascending flight of predominantly blue-and white-painted houses, a display of the Greek national colours calculated in decades past to annoy the Italians. There are several interesting neo-Byzantine churches, the finest being Agios Christos in the clock tower square by the waterfront.

Luxuriant valleys and sandy beaches

Kalymnos' once extensive tree-cover was stripped by the Turks, though between the bony mountain ranges running east to west are two beautiful valleys rich in fruit: the village of Vathy lies where one valley meets the east coast and oranges and tangerines grow succulent in the volcanic soil; the other valley runs westwards from Kalymnos town, the old chora with medieval castle lying 3 kms along the way, to Linaria Bay (5.5 kms). From here northwards to Myrties (7.5 kms) and Masouri (8.5 kms) there are many good sandy beaches backed by groves of cypress, pine, lemon, fig, tangerine and oleander. Small boats from Myrties cross in 10 minutes to the islet of Telendos rising 1300 ft from the sea, a small fishing village with a simple taverna on its shore. There are ruins of a monastery and castle to explore, solitude and beautiful views, especially by morning light, of the Kalymnian mountains to enjoy.

Kos

Second in size to Rhodes in the Dodecanese, the long low profile of KOS is interrupted only once by a mountain. Well-irrigated and green, this is a garden island of lemons and oranges, grapes, melons, almonds and honey inhabited by farming people, not fishermen. Half the population is Greek Orthodox, the other half Muslim. Kos is ringed by miles of lovely sand beaches, though those on

Beaches

the north coast (Tigaki, Marmari, Mastichari) are exposed to the meltemi; Kardamena on the south coast is more sheltered, and Agios Stefanos, near Kefalos towards the southern tip of the island, is the best of all (perhaps the best in the entire Dodecanese). Bicycles are a favourite form of transport over this gentle landscape.

Kos attracts far fewer visitors than Rhodes, though its appeal amongst the cognoscenti goes back at least as far as Ptolemaic Egypt when vacationing pharaohs spent the odd fortnight here.

Hippocrates and the Asklepieion

Hippocrates, 'father of medicine', taught and healed in a sacred grove on high ground 3 kms behind what is now the harbour of Kos town. The views of verdant hillsides, the Aegean and the shores of Asia Minor cannot be much less therapeutic now than they were then, in the late 5th, early

221

4th C. BC. Proximity to Asia, also to Egypt, was no accident, for there medicine of a sort had been practised for centuries before, though it had been inextricably bound up with magic and religious mumbo-jumbo. The Hippocratic method was rational and based on observation, with the course of illnesses recorded — an approach adopted and advanced by the Arabs following their conquest of Greek Alexandria and only accepted again in Europe 2000 years after Hippocrates' time. A Hellenistic sanctuary, the Asklepieion, was built upon the site after Hippocrates' death, now an uncertain assortment of picturesque ruins worth visiting mostly for the pleasantness of its situation.

Back in town, on Plateia Eleftherias, is a museum containing a 4th C. BC statue of Hippocrates himself, plus many other Greek and Roman marbles displayed in rooms surrounding an open courtyard decorated with a Roman mosaic floor. Hippocrates is said to have lectured under a spreading plane tree and the locals claim their Platonos Ippokratos is it. Certainly it is a venerable tree and Plateia Platanou is pleasingly cool, green and shaded, bordered by a Turkish wall with a refreshing fountain. The nearby excavations have revealed a layered jumble of medieval, Greek and Roman ruins, once the agora area, while further back in town, by the old acropolis, is a Hellenistic theatre, a Roman bath with mosaics, and a paved Roman way lined with houses à la Pompeii. Jutting out into the sea is the Castle of the Knights of St John, 15th C., its battlements crumbling, wildflowers waving across the stones and views of infidel Turkey through the embrasures.

Lesser islands

Astipalaia Astipalaia lies furthest west of the Dodecanese, too far back from the front line for the Knights of St John to bother with it; all Western influence on the island is Venetian. It is mountainous, though not dramatically so; the most attractive village is Livadi, southwest of Chora with its Venetian castle. The boat serving Astipalaia from Piraeus via the southern Cyclades also calls at Nisyros, Tilos **Nisyros** and Simi, lying between Kos and Rhodes. Nisyros is thought once to have been attached to Kos and separated by a volcanic explosion. It is itself a volcano, circular and rising towards a 4-km wide crater at its centre, a further and still warm volcanic cone within that. The best views are from Nikia, on the crater's rim, especially when the island's many almond trees blossom in February. As on Astipalaia, **Tilos** the women of Tilos still wear traditional costume. Nearly the entire population is engaged in agriculture. But on Simi **Simi** the soil seems allergic to cultivation, and turning from their earlier craft of boat-building, Simiots have taken to sponge

Hellenistic, Roman and Crusader monuments

diving. Nearly enclosed by two mountainous peninsulas of Turkey, Simi is itself as impressively mountainous as Kalymnos. The 18th C. monastery of St Michael Panormitis on the southwest coast attracts visitors from Kos and Rhodes for its festivals at Orthodox Whitsun and on 7-9 November. It contains a magnificent ikonostasis.

Rhodes

As you sail into RHODES the walled, medieval town rises honey-coloured from the sea, a romantic spectacle of turrets, towers and battlements built by the Knights of St John to defend the island against the Infidel, but conquered in 1523 by Suleiman the Magnificent and made still more exotic by the domes and minarets of Turkish mosques. (The siege, which held the attention of all Europe for 6 months, was only won when the Sultan's 100,000 troops persuaded the 180 surviving Knights — out of an original complement of 650, aided by 200 Genoese, 50 Venetians, 400 Cretans and 600 inhabitants — to accept honourable terms.) The island is green and wooded. A range of hills runs from north to suuth, Mt Ataviros down the west coast exceptionally rising to 3985 ft. In contrast to the starkness of many other Aegean landscapes both lush island and mellow town seem un-Greek. Surrounding the largely 14th C. Old Town of Rhodes, the New Town is brimming with modern hotels, chic restaurants and a smart set of travellers — many of them Scandinavians — who fill the rooms and cafe tables and send prices sky-high. Indeed, tourists come in such overwhelming numbers from spring to autumn that accommodation can be a problem.

The Old Town

For a brief 60 or 70 years the Colossus of Rhodes, a gigantic bronze statue reckoned to be one of the Seven Wonders of the Ancient World, stood astride the entrance to Mastraki Harbour. An earthquake toppled it (c250 BC) and some centuries later it was taken off piecemeal to Asia Minor and melted down as scrap. South of this old port and the Commercial Harbour is the Old Town.

When the Knights of St John retreated from Asia Minor and the Holy Land they based themselves in Rhodes. Their architecture borrowed heavily from the Gothic of their native lands — principally France and Spain — and com-

The Street of the Knights

bined both military and religious styles. The Steet of the Knights (Odos Ippoton), narrow and cobbled, is lined with the inns of the various nationalities making up the Order. Of these the Inn of the Tongue of France, on the right, about halfway up from the port, is architecturally the most distinguished. The street is silent, severe, broken only by the splashing of water from a Turkish fountain, the details of escutcheons on the solid walls and stone traceries around the doorways and windows. The street runs gently upwards towards the Palace of the Grand Masters, residence of the head of the Order and meeting place for senior knights. The Palace contains many splendid Roman and early Christian mosaics.

The Palace of the Masters

Nearby is the pink dome and minaret of the Mosque of Suleiman, built immediately after the Turks had driven the Knights from the island. The Knights were probably the most formidable opponents of Islam in the Eastern Mediterranean, conflict caused not only by religion but by trade. Rhodes was a flourishing commercial outpost of the West and a threat to Turkish shipping. So the Knights defended themselves with massive walls and gates which you can tour at close hand by gathering at the courtyard of the Palace at 5pm on Tuesdays and Saturdays (3pm in winter).

Mosque of Suleiman

The walls

On either side of the Street of the Knights are the Museums of Archaeology and of the Decorative Arts, the former once the Hospital of the Knights, the latter an arsenal. The Hospital is the most important medieval building in the Old Town, in excellent condition and witness to the original function of the Order: the care of the ill and needy. In this respect, the courtyard and, up the steps and to your left, the infirmary which could bed 100 patients, are of interest. Beyond the infirmary and passing the refectory are three rooms containing sculpture: in the third is the 3rd C. BC Aphrodite Thalassia — 'The seawater had sucked at her for centuries till she was like some white stone jujube, with hardly a feature sharp as the burin must originally have left it. Yet such was the grace of her composition — the slender neck and breasts on that richly modelled torso, the supple line of arm and thigh — that the absence of firm outline only lent her a soft and confusing grace. Instead of sharp Classical features she had been given something infinitely more adolescent, unformed. The ripeness of her body was offset by the face, not of a Greek matron, but of a young girl.' — made famous by Lawrence Durrell in his *Reflections on a Marine Venus.*

The Hospital of the Knights and Archaeological Museum

The Marine Venus

Around the island	At the beginning of the first millenium BC the Dorians replaced the early Minoan and Mycenaean colonists and built three cities: Ialisos, Kamiros and Lindos. Only later did they federate and build the town of Rhodes as their capital.
Ialisos	Ialisos lies nearest to Rhodes, about 8 kms down the west coast route, and has hardly been excavated. But the view from Mt Philerimos — its acropolis — is marvellous and there is a church and ruined castle of the Knights and a Byzantine monastery. 36 kms from Rhodes along the same
Kamiros	coastal route is Kamiros, the entire groundplan of the ancient city excavated. If you turn inland about halfway between Rhodes town and Kamiros you come to Petaloudes,
The Valley of the Butterflies	the wooded gorge where thousands of butterflies gather from June through September — though unlike the flocking tourists they are usually camouflaged against the trees, leaves and rocks.
Lindos	But the place most worth visiting is Lindos, 55 kms down the east coast, perhaps the Aegean's most perfect blend of nature, antiquity and the Middle Ages. There is a
The acropolis	majestic panorama from the clifftop acropolis hovering 380 ft above the sea, fortified by the Knights, earlier occupied by the Sanctuary of Athena Lindia, a surviving temple exquisitely sited at the edge of the cliff at the southernmost point of the acropolis. There is an excellent beach below and a lovely village with many 15th C. houses combining Gothic, Byzantine and Oriental features. Lindos is renowned for its pottery: reproductions of medieval ware bearing floral motifs.
Beaches	All along the coast to Lindos there is the enjoyment of green hillsides spilling into sea-scalloped sandy coves. If you want a more secluded beach than that at Lindos, go on to the long, shallow Bay of Lardos, fringed with sand dunes.
Other lesser islands	The sea approach to Rhodes from Piraeus via Crete takes you to Kasos, Karpathos and Chalki enroute. If you have read — and you should read — *Journey to a Greek Island* by the Greek-American Elias Kulukundis whose forebears
Kasos	came from Kasos, then that island will loom large in your imagination. In unravelling his ancestral past, Kulukundis tells of his visit to this small island inhabited by barely more than 1000 people, ravaged and depopulated by the Egyptians acting for the Turks during the War of Independence, later resettled by families who had the enterprise to take the lead in the switch from sail to steam. There are Kasiot shipping families living in London today. Many Kasiots emigrated to Egypt and were employed in cutting the Suez Canal; the pilots of the first ships through both the Suez and Panama canals were Kasiots. The island is

Karpathos

mountainous, little visited, traditional; its few villages are all within walking distance of Ophrys (or Phry), the port on the north coast. Travellers who like Crete for its wild mountain scenery and want more of the same, with still greater isolation, should come to Karpathos. In size, though not in population, it is comparable to Kos. 4000-ft Mt Kalolimno divides the island in half. The south is well-watered and fertile. The port, Pigalia, is here. But the most interesting village on Karpathos is Olimpos, a mountain village in the north and the oldest settlement on the island. Doric words are still traceable in the vocabulary, the houses are solidly built, with wooden locks and keys as in Homer, and the inhabitants habitually wear traditional costume. Bare

Chalki

and hilly Chalki is nearest Rhodes and numbers less than 400 inhabitants, the population steadily declining. A church and castle of the Knights, built of Hellenic remnants, stand in the all but abandoned chora 900 ft by mule path above the port.

Kastellorizzo

Kastellorizzo is the furthest east of the Dodecanese (only 2 kms from the south coast of Turkey) and the smallest. It is served by boat from Piraeus via Rhodes. Emigration is encouraged by poverty and the suspicion that Kastellorizzo will one day be ceded to Turkey. The little port with its wooden Turkish balconies is charming from a distance, but decay and a sense of departure are evident close to.

Each of the above islands may also be reached by local boat from Rhodes once weekly.

CRETE

Character of
the island

In size, diversity, beauty and history Crete (Kriti) is an island apart, a world of its own. It is the largest of the Greek islands and, after Sicily, Sardinia and Cyprus, the fourth largest island in the Mediterranean. Over its length of 257 kms and its width which varies from 12 to 61 kms is a compression of landscapes of continental variety: palm-lined beaches, 8000-ft mountains capped with snow, cliffs, caves, coves, lowland plains and alpine meadows and a magnificent gorge which is the deepest in Europe. Even the simplest bus ride from A to B is an absorbing adventure.

Crete sets the southern limit of the Aegean and lies on the same latitude as Sousse in Tunisia or Palmyra in Syria. Equidistant from Athens and the coasts of Turkey and Libya, it combines the blazing summer climate of North Africa with the cool breezes of the open Mediterranean, and its people and culture too, though fundamentally European, display the spontaneity yet mystery of African and Asian influences. The island has been in the hands of Rome, Byzantium, the Arabs, Venice and the Ottoman Empire. Only in 1898 were the Turks tossed out, and only in 1913 was Crete officially united with Greece. Centuries of struggle have shaped the Cretans into a rugged, rebellious and proud people, their character described in the novels of Nikos Kazantzakis. But like the early Cretan spring there is the gentler spirit of the brilliant Minoan civilisation which flourished here 4000 years ago with its luxurious palaces, joyful frescoes, the first and possibly finest civilisation in Europe.

Heraklion

Most people who come to Crete arrive in the early morning at HERAKLION. The ship ties up near the old orange harbour walls of the Venetians. This is the major commercial and tourist drop-off town on the island. It's not very pretty and has almost the dusty disorder of a Wild West town, though some of the side streets are charming, there's a Venetian fountain and loggia, a small park with a bust of El Greco (alias Dominikos Theotokopoulos, a native son) and the Archaeological Museum with its Minoan collection, which if nothing else would make the visit more than worth while.

Fountain Square

At the centre of the town is the Plateia Venizelou, more commonly known as Fountain Square for its 17th C. Venetian fountain around which are several cafes where you can enjoy a pastry and get your bearings. Facing north towards Odos 25 Avgoustou, lined with banks and travel offices and running north down to the old harbour, you can

227

The loggia	see on its right the reconstructed loggia and behind it the Venetian armoury, now the town hall. Wander into the narrow streets here for some delightful glimpses of old balconied houses softly pasteled. On your immediate right, on the corner of Odos Daidalou, is the 14th C. Venetian
Church of St Mark	Church of St Mark, now housing copies of frescoes from churches around the island — helpful in planning your tour.
The market	Behind you, across the traffic lights, is Odos 1866, an outdoor market and excellent place to see and meet people under the guise of buying a tomato. The older Cretans come down from the mountains wearing their knee-high leather boots which protect them from the thorny hillsides (in summer the slopes are grey and brittle with thorns, but in spring the spurge is still green and fresh and flowering).

East from the traffic lights is Plateia Eleftherias (Liberty Square) where you will find the Archaeological Museum. From here you can begin a circuit of the walls (4 kms). The strongest of their day anywhere in the Mediterranean, for

The land walls and grave of Kazantzakis 22 years (1648–69) they withstood the final Turkish siege. Embedded in the most southerly bastion is the grave of Nikos Kazantzakis, author of *Zorba the Greek, Christ Recrucified*, etc. He was buried here when the Orthodox Church refused him sacred ground. The inscription on his stone replies, "I hope for nothing. I fear nothing. I am free." A reconstruction of the study of Kazantzakis, with

The Historical Museum his furniture, belongings and books, is in the Historical Museum opposite the Xenia hotel on the seafront. The museum also contains a collection of art, handicrafts and historical mementoes dating from the early Christian era to the present.

The Archaeological Museum Before going to Knossos and the other sites, and again afterwards, you should visit the Archaeological Museum, for nearly everything removed from the sites and used to build up our picture of Minoan civilisation is here, including sealstones, Linear B tablets and all the original frescoes. Also there is a scale reconstruction of Knossos. The rooms are arranged chronologically and geographically, and many of the labels are in English, so that the visitor with a limited schedule may move through fairly quickly yet still grasp in outline the development of Minoan civilisation and appreciate the museum's highlights. For a more detailed study of the collection, a guide book in English by the museum's director, Dr Alexiou, with an introduction by Professor Platon, is available in the entrance hall.

Minoan myth and history In that way that legend has of collapsing centuries of hazily recalled events into one good story, King Minos (Minos was

228

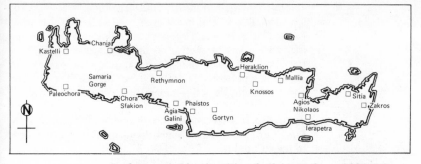

in fact probably the title of all kings from 2000 BC onwards) was born the son of Zeus by Europa, while his wife
Pasiphae, developing an uncontrollable lust for bulls, gave
birth to the Minotaur. It was this creature who dwelt in the
labyrinth designed by Dedaelus beneath Knossos, and to
whom Greek youths were sacrificed until Theseus, with the
help of Ariadne, put an end to it. (Mary Renault's novel
The King Must Die, tells the story.) Minoan defence and
power lay in controlling the sea. Their cities and palaces
were absolutely secure and so developed like grand terraced
villa complexes, stone foundations supporting wooden
pillars and floors upon floors of rooms decorated with
brilliantly coloured frescoes. Everything, their palaces,
their frescoes, their pottery showed an exuberance in life
expressed with a graceful insouciance prefiguring millenia
later the Provence of the Middle Ages and perhaps the Paris
of the Third Republic.

But the bull lurked sinisterly beneath the palace. Bulls'
horns, like crenellations, decorated the walls of Knossos.
Every Minoan palace had its bull arena, and frescoes depict
men and women leaping over bulls in a ritualised bull-dance
that makes modern bullfighting look like a sport for sissies.
The Minoans had an obsession with bulls, or rather with
what the image of the bull symbolised. It has been con-
jectured that the bull and its roar was linked to the roar of
the earthquakes which flattened Minoan cities every
century or so. The Minoans were supreme on the sea,
extending their influence over the whole of the Aegean and
even to Libya and Egypt, but they lived in terror of the
land and eventually, perhaps with the massive and unequalled explosion of volcanic Thera (c1450 BC) and the
consequent tidal wave, their civilisation was washed out.

**The destruction
of Minoan
civilisation** In fact the cause of Minoan civilisation's seemingly
sudden end is hotly debated. Some argue that invading
mainland Mycenaeans − or Dorians later on − burnt the
the palaces; others, while accepting some theory of natural
catastrophe, argue that Thera's tidal wave or its ejection of

229

volcanic ash were of insufficient magnitude to account for Minoan collapse; and it has even been suggested that what we see at Knossos, Phaestos and elsewhere around the island were not palaces at all but vast necropolises where the 'bathtubs' and plumbing features were part of an embalming process, the 'joyful' frescoes, like their counterparts in Egypt, depicting funeral ceremonies and a wished-for afterlife, and that these sombrely monumental and decorative appurtenances of a death-cult were rejected by the Minoans themselves when they turned, through drama, to the cult of life.

Knossos The PALACE OF KNOSSOS is 5 kms east of Heraklion, an easy pilgrimage on foot for some, otherwise quickly reached by local bus departing every 15 minutes from Plateia Kornarou by the harbour. Initial poking about was done by Schliemann, but the full work of excavation was undertaken from 1900 by the English archaeologist Sir Arthur Evans and paid for out of his own pocket. Evans' idea was to help the imagination of the amateur by partly reconstructing the palace, using the original materials where possible, but resorting to concrete as well. This has been welcomed by some people and criticised by others, but since the other palaces, like Phaestos, have not been reconstructed, you can learn about palace design at Knossos and then vividly imagine rooms and grand staircases rising up from the barer excavations elsewhere.

A tour of A tour of the palace is conveniently begun at the *West*
the palace *Court* (1) where there is a bronze bust of Sir Arthur Evans. The west facade of the palace would have been perhaps 40-45 ft high; from the direction of smoke stains here Evans deduced that it was springtime when the final fire consumed the palace; a south wind is common in spring. The *West Porch* (2) was the ceremonial entrance; visitors
Corridor of the would then have passed through the *Corridor of the*
Procession *Procession* (3) where the Procession fresco and the Cup Bearer were found. The southwest corner of the palace has fallen down the slope, so it is by cutting through intervening rooms that you come to the spot where the *Priest King*
The Prince of or *Prince of the Lilies* fresco (4) was discovered. (In fact the
the Lilies feathered crown was found separately from the human figure and it is more likely that it adorned a sphynx led by
The Central the man.) The *Central Court* (5), where bull-dancing might
Court have been performed lies before you, its original paving in place. On the left is the *Throne Room complex* (6), an *antechamber* leading to the Throne Room itself, at the left
The Throne of which down a flight of steps is a *lustral basin*. The
Room *Throne Room* when excavated was decorated with a river

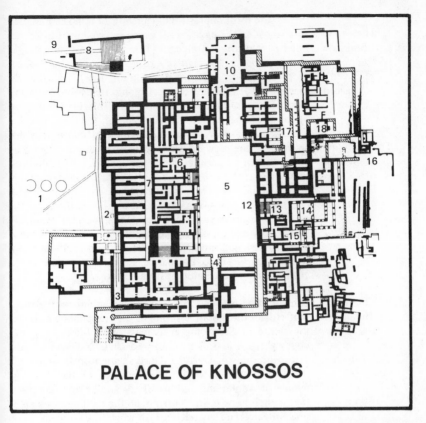

PALACE OF KNOSSOS

scene (not preserved); this has been replaced by two *griffins*, a complete fantasy of Evans' and painted for effect in AD 1930. The *'throne'* — for so it was called, being the fanciest piece of furniture discovered at Knossos — at least was found where you see it. (The Throne Room is railed off, so waiting till the coast was clear, I leapt over and sat upon it, joining that select list of throne-warmers which includes Minos himself, presumably Evans, certainly Henry Miller and one or two other Kilroys.)

Storerooms

Off the northwest corner of the Central Court a passage leads to the *Corridor of the Magazines* (7); the north magazines were apparently for storing textiles, those to the south, with their large pithoi, for storing liquids. Marks of burning are evident at the entrances of some of the magazines. Beyond the northwest corner of the palace is the *Theatral Area* (8) and the *Royal Road* (9). Returning via the *North Pillar Hall* (10) and the *north entrance passage* (11) with the relief of the Charging Bull, you cross to the *domestic quarters* to the east of the Central Court. Here is

'The oldest road in Europe'

one of the most impressive monuments of Minoan architecture, the *Grand Staircase* (12) which received light from the open *Hall of the Colonnades* (13). The magnificent *King's Room* or *Hall of the Double Axes* (14) could be partitioned by folding doors (note the pivots in the floor). The *Queen's Megaron* (15) is graced by the Dolphin fresco and there are evidences nearby of the Minoans' amazing plumbing systems: drainage or fresh water pipes in the floor and the famous *flush toilet*. Even the method of controlling the speed and direction of water which had to run from one storey down to another shows an appreciation of hydrodynamics; at the *east bastion* (16) you can observe how the water would have flowed through its courses, its speed checked by a series of parabolic curves. Below the *Corridor of the Draughtboard* (17) where Evans found a beautiful inlaid ivory and crystal gaming board you can see *terracotta pipes* so designed and fitted as to resist the pressure of fresh water introduced to the palace system. Near here (18), *giant pithoi* indicate another storage area.

The Grand Staircase

The Queen's Megaron

The plumbing system

South of Heraklion

Gortyna

Shortly after leaving Heraklion the bus grinds up the road that crosses the mountains running like a backbone through the centre of Crete, the great mass of Mt Ida looming on your right, and at 45 kms stops by a 7th C. basilica of Agios Titos, the ruins of Gortyna (Gortys), the Roman capital of the island, spread about on either side of the road. A temple of Apollo and another of Isis and Serapis lie across the road along with the museum; on the right-hand side is a small theatre and an odeion into which the Romans built the 2500-year old Law Code of Gortyna inscribed in 'ox-plough' writing — one line running from left to right, the next from right to left, and so on. But impatience calls: Phaestos lies only 16 kms further on.

Phaestos

From where the bus lets you off you climb a bluff to the pavilion, and there below on the level terrace are the ruins of PHAESTOS, the hillside rolling down behind them into the vast Messara Plain ringed by distant mountains. The panorama itself is magnificent and you think what fine and beautiful people these Minoans were, to build a palace and city here, their frescoes of birds and flowers matching opaque walls to open terrace views of fields beyond. The ruins are unreconstructed, mostly at foundation level, yet especially after a visit to Knossos, easy to trace and understand. What is far more impressive here than at Knossos is the situation of the palace, described by Henry Miller as "the last Paradise on earth". Several writers and travellers have compared the masculine, and sometimes forboding, sense of Knossos to the feminine and serene atmosphere of Phaestos. It is certainly equal to Knossos in design, but probably held a secondary political position allowing its populace, known for their wit, to lead more relaxed lives.

The famous 'Mister Alexandros' who enthusiastically guided so many people around the site retired to his nearby village a decade or more ago. I spoke to a cynical Zacharias who gripped his cigarette between his teeth, inhaled long and deeply, coughed and thumped his chest, and flung out his arm to a monastery beyond. "You see that monastery? The monks do no work. They take money from the people who work in the fields, people like my father who worked in the fields all his life. That is how it was here at Phaestos. Then it was the Minoans, now it is the church. Ha-ha! Now I am here" — drawing on his cigarette — "and it is better than working in the fields".

Agia Triada

The bus can drop you off a further 2 kms beyond Phaestos where there is a turning on the left and a ½ km walk to Agia Triada; alternatively you can follow the pleasant path west along the ridge from Phaestos, a 45-minute walk, to this Minoan villa like a pocket-sized palace which probably stood by the sea when the water level was higher.

Beaches at Matala and Agia Galini

After Phaestos the road divides, the left fork going off to Matala, that stretch of fine beach and cave-riddled cliffs made famous in the late 1960s by troglodytic hippies. Following the right fork, the road descends to the village of Agia Galini (75 kms from Heraklion), which looks uninspiring at first approach, never becomes especially lovely even when you get to know it well, but which once at least was a delightful place to spend some time. Then as now in spring the mountains rising up behind the beaches were still glistening with snow at their peaks and there was the pervading fragrance of thyme and lentisk. Fishing boats went out at night with lights shining from their sterns, and if you were up when they returned and they'd had a good catch, a taverna suddenly re-opened under the star-thick sky, bottles of wine were passed around, fish were fried up on the grills and you shared freely in the good fortune. Donkeys guffawed explosively in the midnight fields, reminding you how quiet the village could be and you could hear the waves lapping outside your window, the cocks crowing to the dawn. And on Saturday nights half the village carried chairs down to the harbour-front for the mobile picture show. The generator cranked up, someone threw a sheet over a balcony, and you sat stupefied watching John Wayne killing Indians who spoke only dubbed

Greek. But with the opening now of snack bar/discotheques like Bozo's and Zorba's the village is fast sacrificing its simplicity to its rapacity. Zorba's tries to create 'atmosphere' with photos on the wall of Agia Galini the way it was before Zorba's and Bozo's and their mindless clientele began to disfigure it.

The road from here to Rethymnon (52 kms) carries you through high mountains capped with snow into May, their lower slopes covered with flowers, valleys rolling with green wheat and lovely white mountain villages all along the way. The first stretch, where it climbs high above the cliff-coast, provides spectacular views. At Koxares you can instead return to the south coast and head west for Chora Sfakion.

West of Heraklion

The new National Highway runs west along the north coast from Heraklion to Rethymnon (79 kms) and Chania (137 kms), though by first following the old inland road you can detour to the attractive village of Tylissos (13 kms) with excavated Minoan villas and detour again for Fodele (26 kms), thought to be the birthplace of El Greco who never lost his feeling for Byzantine style and the Cretan landscape.

El Greco's birthplace

Rethymnon

On a narrow point of land surrounded by the sea, with slender minarets rising from narrow streets, RETHYMNON is the most Oriental of Cretan towns. Although severely damaged during the Second World War, it is still strongly marked by its Venetian and Turkish past.

The Venetian harbour

For colour go to the tiny Venetian harbour, a neglected area, houses crumbling, paint peeling off, but full of charm. Standing here with your back to the fishing boats looking up at the small semicircle of narrow houses with wrought-iron balconies (Turkish houses have wooden balconies, supported by angular stays), you could imagine this was all there was to a sleepy and forgotten village, no hint of Rethymnon crouching behind. In the fortress there's a mosque and solitary date-palm. On Odos Man. Bernardo, off Plateia Titou Petuchaki, is another mosque now used as a theatre; you can climb the spiral stone steps to the top of its minaret for a good view over the rooftops. Nearby is a Venetian fountain; and there's also a small Archaeological Museum, nicely laid out, with a collection of small bronzes from a Roman shipwreck off Agia Galini, and coins covering every period on Crete. In July the Cretan Wine Festival is held in the Public Garden. Kafeneions and tavernas liven both the Venetian and the long beach-lined new harbour (though there are better beaches to the east and west of the town).

Climbing a minaret

Wine festival, tavernas and beaches

It's a 22-km excursion to the Monastery of Arkadi, symbol of Crete's ageless dilemna, freedom or death. On

The Monastery of Arkadi	9 November 1866, hundreds of rebels, men, women and children, blew themselves up here rather than surrender to the besieging Turks. The ornate 17th C. Venetian church combining Classical, Renaissance and Baroque elements is defiantly at odds with the wild landscape.

The port for Chania

Souda Bay, a major Greek and NATO naval base, is the alternative port of arrival for visitors to Crete, and the best if you want to concentrate on the wilder western end of the island. CHANIA, 6.5 kms to the west, is the capital of Crete, a distinction it has retained from the 19th C. when the Pasha installed his seraglio here. There are two Chanias,

The modern and Venetian towns

the modern town on the plain where the bus stations, market (modelled on the one in Marseille) and cinemas are, and the old Venetian town of narrow streets clustered around the horseshoe harbour, the 17th C. Mosque of the Janissaries on the right, reconditioned to house the National Tourist Organisation. Tall Venetian houses of pink, ochre, green and much cream with brilliantly contrasting shutters line the promenade; all the roofs red tiled, balconies and outside staircases in elaborate ironwork. With the mosque as your view, people strolling by and in the late afternoon fishermen repairing their nets, this is the place to park yourself at a cafe or taverna. Then go for a walk through the narrow streets behind, one side in cool shadow, the other bleached in sunlight, with curiosities like the church at 51 Odos Zambeliou which is now a coal cellar where black-faced Beelzebubs load up the sacks. To the east on the

Church of Agios Nikolaos

delightful Plateia 1821 is the Church of Agios Nikolaos, its Venetian campanile and beautiful Turkish minaret witnesses to its conversions. The Archaeological Museum on Odos Halidon occupies the vaulted Venetian Church of San Francesco, a Turkish fountain in the adjoining garden. The collection includes several graceful Minoan sarcophagi.

West of Chania there's a fine sandy beach at Platanias (11 kms). Further on at Maleme is the airport where in 1941 the Germans staged their massive parachute invasion

Kastelli

of Crete. Subdued Kastelli (43 kms) is the port for twice-weekly arrivals from Piraeus via Monemvasia and Gytheion.

Palaiochora

From here you can go directly down to Palaiochora on the south coast, a small village with a 13th C. Venetian fort and a large sandy beach. At least twice a week in summer there's a caique service from Palaiochora to Agia Roumeli and Chora Sfakion.

The road to Omalos

The bus ride from Chania to Omalos is another intoxicating mountain adventure. In the high cool air the village people are cheerful and redfaced, the moon floats bright in the clear blue afternoon sky, and nobody takes any notice of the hairpin turns and precipitous drops. In fact, riding the bus is a social occasion during which everyone chatters and the driver divides his time between looking at the road and acting as master of ceremonies. Finally the road levels off and the round Omalos plain spreads before you, mysterious and beautiful, like a lost world.

The Gorge of Samaria

From a lodge on the far side you descend into the GORGE OF SAMARIA, the largest in Europe, with sheer walls rising nearly 2000 ft in some places, at the Iron Gates closing to only 5 metres across. From the lodge to Agia Roumeli on the coast the distance is about 19 kms and the walk can be comfortably done in 6-7 hours, though there's no reason not to spend the night somewhere enroute. The gorge has been gouged out by torrents of rain down from the White Mountains and during the rainy season and after the thaw a sizeable stream runs its length. In the summertime much of the bed is dry which makes passage easy, but April is the best time to make the walk — the stream is low enough to let you through and the vegetation is at its height of fullness and beauty. There was an oracle of Apollo here and various nymphs and nereids are said to have inhabited the region. Certainly the presence of the gods and goddesses of nature is powerfully with you as you walk along.

The gorge opens up into a valley, the afternoon sunlight refreshing after the recent shadows. High stone-walled lanes snake past occasional cottages, flowers and grass on the walls, chicks along the lane, goats in the gardens. Fresh, idyllic, absolutely quiet except for a goat bell or a child

Agia Roumeli

calling "kalispera". This is Agia Roumeli; the mountains quickly deflate to low hills and you can smell the salt breeze in your face. A gigantic fan of stones spreads out towards the sea; there's a taverna on the beach and caiques call here at least 3 times a day, the last around 4pm, for Loutro and Chora Sfakion, or west to Palaiochora.

At the taverna I meet Pavlos, a fisherman from Sougia to the west. He is missing his right hand and some fingers on his left. He says that's from fishing. He dynamites the fish at night and sometimes doesn't throw the stick soon enough. He's drinking ouzo and retsina and gives me some fried fish he's caught. Pavlos says when he was young, 25 years ago, he did the gorge in 3 hours and that was before they put in the path. Easy to imagine; he's singing and laughing and drunk, and now he goes off fishing again, blowing up fish with boisterous enthusiasm.

Sfakia

The Sfakia region is mountainous and largely inaccessible except on foot or by looping along the coast in a boat. Its centre is Chora Sfakion which can be reached by road from the north coast. The land is rugged, stark and magnificent; the people have become legendary as fighters and brigands. Their origins are unknown: some say they are pure Dorians, others that they are Saracens, but their fearlessness and independence is not doubted. This is the one part of Crete that the Venetians and Turks were never able to subdue, and from their mountain strongholds the Sfakians led the resistance against the German occupation during the Second World War. To this day, there are areas of Sfakia where the writ of Athens does not run.

Rebels and brigands

The land of Sfakia is covered with blood and tales of battles both with outsiders and amongst themselves. Family feelings are strong, vendettas are common, traditions are preserved. But the visitor gets only a hint of this now and again, perhaps a terrific fight or the sight of a gun or just a story told in a village. Treat the Sfakians with respect and respect will be returned.

Loutro

Instead of going direct from Agia Roumeli to Chora Sfakion, put in at Loutro. You sail into a beautiful cove of crystal green and turquoise water, some houses round the pebbly beach and palms. For all the world a South Pacific lagoon. Many of the houses stand empty. Some are derelict, others uninhabited for the moment as families move up into the mountains with their goats and sheep. Mountains climb behind the village and following a steep path you can reach Anapolis (also bus from Chora Sfakion), a village now but once a town of 70,000 which flourished in Roman and Byzantine times. The ruins of its giant walls remain. Another path, a bit dangerous, clutches its way along the coast to Chora Sfakion. Loutro is entirely without electricity and there is only one telephone. Chickens and turkeys run in and out of doorways; at night, apart from the dim oil lamps, there is only the light of the moon which casts a pale glow over the harbour water and the whitewashed houses.

Anapolis

Just at the jetty where the boat ties up is a cafe run by friendly, toothless, stubble-chinned old Andreas. He makes you a coffee on his single burner inside, and now you ask him about Daskalogiannis. Andreas speaks no English and then I knew maybe a dozen words in Greek, but like all Greeks Andreas can convey anything vividly with his gestures, expression and tone. So this old man sits over the coffee he has made for me and tells me about his great-great-grandfather, Daskalogiannis, national hero and leader of the Cretan uprising against the Turks at the end of the 18th C. The Pasha invites Daskalogiannis to Heraklion to talk. The Turks can't subdue Sfakia and ask only that the Sfakians pay a tax. Daskalogiannis says no and the Pasha

The Cretan hero, Daskalogiannis

237

has him skinned alive and thrown into the sea. Andreas is cutting the flesh off his face. He doesn't flinch, to let me know Daskalogiannis did not flinch. Only the women, before Daskalogiannis goes to Heraklion, cry no, don't go, but Daskalogiannis says it is his duty and he is not afraid. Dear old Andreas with his kafeneion and that picture on his wall inside of bearded Daskalogiannis and his wife.

Chora Sfakion

The phantoms of Frangokastello

The heyday of Chora Sfakion has passed and now it's small and dull, merely a transit point in your travels. But the situation is excellent, with mountains dropping into the sea to the west, and to the east a littoral between the mountainsides and the coast and 9 kms along Frangokastello, a Venetian fortress emblazoned with the Lion of St Mark. Cretans claim that on 18 May, at dawn, you can see the ghosts of warrior Sfakians dancing round the castle. The road out of Chora Sfakion loops and winds against the bare rising hills as though, when viewed from high up, it had been laid solely for some grand aesthetic purpose, a tentacle unwound from a Minoan vase to decorate the land.

Eastern Crete

You should not miss a visit to eastern Crete. If it cannot boast the largest Minoan palaces, it does possess three major Minoan sites at Mallia, Gournia and Zakros, as well as several lesser ones. There is also the most beautiful of the upland plains on Crete, Lasithi; the best known of the frescoed churches, at Kritsa; and the only town of any size on the south coast, Ierapetra. Unfortunately, the beaches on the north coast have attracted a number of large hotels, but the Cretan landscape, although less severe at this end of the island, is sufficiently spectacular to withstand almost the worst excesses.

Karteros Beach

Amnisos

Limin Chersonisou

If you take the old road (not the highway) from Heraklion towards Agios Nikolaos (67 kms) you pass, about 1 km east of the airport, probably the best bathing place close to the city, Karteros Beach. Before the road starts to climb again over Kakon Oros (Bad Mountain) there is a turning on the left to the Minoan site of Amnisos, suggested as one of the ports of Knossos. The House of the Lilies (from its fresco) has been excavated to the east of a prominent rock; to the west are some remains of what might be harbour installations. Limin Chersonisou (27 kms) is an old village grown into a small, relaxed town with several new hotels. The swimming attracts lots of visitors, including a good number from the local American air base. Pine-shaded tavernas look over the water, beneath which — when it isn't too windy, often a problem on Crete — you can see shapes indicating the line of the ancient harbour for Lyttos, an all but vanished Classical city to the south.

Mallia

About 9 kms eastwards is the Minoan PALACE OF MALLIA. The modern village is strung along the road; a little way north are several large hotels by a very good beach. Finally there is the site, about 3 kms further to the east of the village (buses to Mallia terminate at the site). At this point the narrow coastal strip has opened out and in a particularly satisfying position between the mountains and the sea is the palace, ranking in size after Knossos and Phaestos. Dating from the Neo-Palatial period as do the principal remains at the other two sites, it has the same general layout, but inevitably more of the feel of Phaestos, little restored and the pithoi as tall as most of the remains.

The Lasithi Plain

About 2 kms west of Limin Chersonisou a turning to the right leads up through olive groves and several pretty villages: in Potamies the monastic church of the Panagia has some good 14th C. frescoes (key from the village priest), as does the Church of Agios Antonios in Avdou. Finally you go through a pass, guarded by derelict stone windmills, into the LASITHI PLAIN, which lies in a bowl of mountains, the highest of which is Mt Dikti to the south (7050 ft). The plain spreads before you like a garden, almost completely flat, with countless windmills to irrigate the rich land; dotted around its edges are several small villages. The area produces a lot of grain (also fruit and potatoes) and, although machinery now does much of the harvesting, in August you can still see cattle pulling laden sleighs around the earth threshing floors, and the villagers winnowing the wheat with large olive wood prongs. You should try to see the first operation: I watched a woman who was perched uncomfortably on top of a large stone on a wooden sled driving two yoked cows in front of her around one of these circular floors, separating the wheat from the straw. The air was full of swallows diving after the countless insects, but the best moments came when she produced a large plate and had to juggle with an avalanche of dung from one of the animals, to prevent the grain being fouled, before depositing it in a neat pile to one side. Earlier she had stopped and offered me a handful of plums and a large apple, apologising that she had only the one apple to give.

The 'Diktaion Cave'

On the far side of the plain is the pleasant village of Psychro, a good base for walks around Lasithi and up to the 'Diktaion Cave', the alleged birthplace of Zeus, about half an hour to the west. This cave is worth a visit, although it may not be the one which the ancients associated with Zeus (according to Robert Graves it definitely is not). It descends steeply, with numerous stalagmites and stalactites at the bottom, the daylight above distressingly remote. Hereabouts the guide will point to the exact spot where Zeus was born, whereas the ancient legend only speaks of the infant being hidden in the 'Diktaion Cave' by Mother Earth after his birth in Arkadia, to prevent him being eaten by his father, Kronos. As the poet Kallimachos said of the Cretan claim that Zeus was also buried on the island, "the Cretans are always liars" — or perhaps they are just developing the myth. In any event, there is no doubt that the Earth Goddess was worshipped here from the Minoan through to the Archaic period, since many votive offerings have been found, and in the upper part of the cave there was a sacred enclosure.

Worship of the Earth Goddess

Outside again, the plain seen in the evening light is like an enormous tapestry, or a Brueghel painting, with ant-like humans coming home from the fields after the day's harvesting.

Agios Nikolaos

Barely more than a decade ago, AGIOS NIKOLAOS was just an attractive small port, and the only development was the Minos Beach complex in the bay on the west. Now it could be a resort on the Costa Brava: if that's what you like, it's ideal — large hotels, discos, bars, boutiques — but it hasn't got much to do with Crete. I have to admit the swimming is good, off rocks into clear turquoise water, and that owing to the nearby mountains the town enjoys a superb position. Other features are the 'bottomless pool', an inner harbour where quite often in summer there is outdoor music, and a small museum in the west of town with finds from Lasithi nome of which Agios Nikolaos is the capital.

Kritsa

Kritsa, 12 kms to the southwest, is an attractive village with probably the finest frescoed church on Crete — the Panagia Kera, situated amongst olive groves on the right of the road 2 kms before the village. The whitewashed church has 3 aisles with powerful frescoes of the 14th and 15th C. The south aisle shows scenes from the life of the Virgin Mary and her mother, St Anne. The middle aisle shows the life of Christ — the Last Supper is particularly fine. The north aisle depicts aspects of Paradise. There are also panels of saints and martyrs and in the north aisle you can see the founders of the church. The Cretan church "was an imitation, in symbol, of the Cosmos", "a microcosm of the whole universe, create and uncreate" (Michael Llewellyn Smith) — from Christ in his cupola representing heaven, down to the church founders on the lowest, earthly level.

From Agios Nikolaos to Sitia (73 kms) the scenery is very beautiful. Initially, there are several villages in fertile pockets of land on the Gulf of Mirabello, and the Sitia mountains can be seen ahead. At 19 kms you pass the site of Gournia, which lies on a hillock on the right hand side of the road, indicated by a small sign. GOURNIA is the best preserved Minoan town yet excavated. It was in an important position at the northern end of the shortest and easiest north-south trade route across the island, and possessed a harbour in the cove below. You can walk around the narrow, stepped streets between the small houses of this Minoan township as you might do in a Greek hill village like Arachova or the chora of a Cycladic island such as Kea or Ios. There is a knowledgeable but garrulous guide who can quickly point out the obvious features.

Gournia

Sitia

My memories of Sitia are slightly affected by once being moored on the end of the town sewage pipe, but travel writers are perhaps a little too kind to this unremarkable, small port. The Venetians who made Sitia one of the four capitals of the island were disappointed enough by the outcome to remove the cannons from the fortress to go elsewhere. Below the decayed Venetian kastro, the houses straggle down the hill to the harbour, which is now largely concerned with the export of raisins. Little to enthuse over, but it is a quiet place and has several good tavernas along the quay.

East of Sitia the road passes over one of the most satisfying stretches of country in eastern Crete — villages of one-storey houses with outside ovens and amphoras for chimneys, and (in August at least) hills covered with purple thyme. After about 15 kms there's a left turn to the isolated monastery of Toplou, which is worth a detour of 4 kms. It looks like a castle, and has long had a reputation as a centre of resistance (Toplou means 'cannon' in Turkish) and for hospitality to refugees and travellers alike. After an earthquake in the early 17th C. had destroyed the original 14th C. foundation, the monastery was rebuilt in a style showing Venetian influence. Its most famous possession is an ikon called 'O Lord Thou Art Great', painted in 1770 by Ioannis Kornaros, a great masterpiece of Cretan art. The main road continues to Palaikastro (overgrown excavations of a Minoan town nearby); 3.5 kms to the north is the long sand beach and tall palms of Vai, so often praised for its seclusion that now it's become an open air dormitory in summer.

Monastery of Toplou

Palaikastro

Vai

Ano Zakros

Ano Zakros (37 kms from Sitia) is a large village, like a modern Gournia, clinging to the hillside above a green valley, and nurtured by a gushing spring. It's pleasant to walk up to the spring, through the narrow streets, past plots of vines, and flowers and jolly women, and along the open, concrete ducts full of freshwater crabs. About 1 km out of Ano Zakros, on either side of the road to Kato Zakros, the remains of a Minoan villa of the Neo-Palatial period have been found: there was a wine-press in the building, although olive oil must have been at least as important a product to the Minoans of the region. You continue through the olive groves, then along the ridge above a huge gorge known as the 'Valley of the Dead' (from the number of caves which were there used for Minoan burials) until the road descends to the beautiful bay of Zakros. Two head-lands enclose the bay which has a good beach lined with a dozen or so buildings and a banana grove behind. In the north corner of the bay, near the mouth of the gorge, is the **The palace at** PALACE OF ZAKROS, perhaps the most romantically **Kato Zakros** situated of all the Cretan palaces.

Zakros seems to have been an important centre for the import into Crete of rich materials from the East; though similar to the other Neo-Palatial palaces and, like them, destroyed c1450 BC, it was never reoccupied or plundered so that excavations since 1962 under Professor Platon have **Its treasures** turned up some superb treasures: over 50 stone vessels of diverse style and decoration, many bronze saws and swords, chalices, a rock crystal rhyton, countless vases, bronze ingots from Cyprus and tusks of ivory from Syria — the best of these can be seen in Room VIII of the Archae-ological Museum in Heraklion. Possibly the most famous find from Zakros is the Mountain Shrine Rhyton, which has reliefs of goats romping around the hillside and was origin-ally covered with gold leaf.

Ierapetra From Pakia Ammos back at the Gulf of Mirabello you can turn south for IERAPETRA (18 kms) through a plain which stretches from coast to coast, full of olive trees. No substantial Minoan remains have been found at Ierapetra, which is surprising in view of the apparent trade link across the island to Gournia. Hellenistic and Roman ruins lie just outside of town, but there is little to see. The Venetians or Genoese left a fine fort by the sea and the Turks a minaret and a charming fountain in the bazaar area in the west of town, but Ierapetra's attraction does not lie chiefly in these relics. The town faces across the Libyan Sea to Africa (you know it too, when the hot sirocco blows) and an easy-going atmosphere pervades the idle seafront: there, men sleep in the afternoon shade as if nothing other than the arrival of a long forgotten vessel from Africa or the East could stir them. But that trade has long gone, and Ierapetra's prosperity depends now largely on the olives, tomatoes and other vegetables grown in the region. There are also plenty of tavernas, pastry shops, and even discotheques to accept the money of the travellers and idlers who've come in increasing numbers recently to this lazy coast, but the Ierapetrans take the invasion easily as if they've seen it all before.

I couldn't test the reputedly good wine, because it had run out wherever I went. (This was in September; it's often difficult in the later summer months to find local wines in Greece, as it's the slack time before the next harvest comes in.) I confess too I missed the museum in the town hall, said to possess the finest Minoan clay larnax (bathtub-shaped sarcophagus or vice-versa) in Crete. It just didn't seem to matter.

PRACTICAL INFORMATION

The background section at the front of this Guide has already introduced you to many aspects of Greece. It should be referred to in conjunction with this practical information section which goes into detail on travel, accommodation, tavernas, etc. Information applying to Greece as a whole appears first, and is followed by place by place listings.

TRAVEL

Air. Olympic Airways are the sole operators within Greece. Their head office in Athens is at 96 Syngrou Avenue (Tel: 92.921). The following is a partial list of destinations served by Olympic from Athens, with current one-way fares in drachmas.

Corfu	1000
Heraklion	785
Ioannina	680
Kalamata	495
Kos	855
Mykonos	555
Mitilini	775
Rhodes	1080
Thera	665
Thessaloniki	795
Zakinthos	640

Aircraft charter. For a group of 5 or more, chartering a light aircraft can be cheaper than flying by scheduled airline. Contact Olympic Aviation Airtaxi at Athens airport (Tel: 9813.565) for details.

Rail. The country's railway network is operated by the Hellenic Railways Organisation (OSE). Their head office is at 1-3 Karolou Street, Athens (Tel: 5222.491). A selection of destinations with one-way fares in drachmas, both first and second class, from Athens follows.

Corinth	120	80
Kalamata	380	253
Kalambaka	111	74
Mycenae	168	112
Olympia	432	288
Patras	311	207
Thebes	104	69
Thessaloniki	587	391

There is a 20% discount on round-trip fares. Special season and touring tickets (for second class only) are also available and offer substantial discounts.

Bus. OSE also operates buses throughout the country. Information and tickets can be obtained at their head office. Additionally, a number of private companies cover particular routes. A partial list of destinations with one-way fares in drachmas from Athens follows.

Corinth	88
Delphi	176
Epidavros	140
Igoumenitsa	385
Kalamata	254
Ioannina	364
Megalopolis	242
Monemvasia	361
Mycenae	125
Nafplion	145
Olympia	303
Osios Lukas	162
Patras	245
Sparta	243
Thebes	96
Thessaloniki	400

Round trip fares are usually less than double the one-way fare.

Sea. Boat tickets are available from the profusion of agents at any port. A partial list of ports served from Piraeus, with first, second, tourist and third (deck) class fares in drachmas follows. Port taxes are extra.

Aegina	94	—	—	71
Heraklion	759	596	438	325
Hydra	154	—	—	113
Kos	860	636	476	362
Lesvos	781	551	403	325
Monemvasia	520	335	268	222
Mykonos	540	333	269	222
Paros	550	309	240	201
Poros	134	—	—	102
Patmos	896	511	381	299
Rhodes	960	696	528	403
Spetsai	194	—	—	148
Thera	750	435	345	285

Most ports are served by car ferries.

There is also a fast (and more costly) hydrofoil service from Zea Marina (near Piraeus) to Aegina, Poros, Hydra, Spetsai, Monemvasia and other ports enroute.

Boat hire and yacht chartering. Depending on size, a speedboat will cost from $50 to $300 a day, while a sailing boat will cost from $100 to $300 a day. Rates include crew if desired. Caiques 30 to 70 ft long, carrying from 4 to 15 passengers, fully crewed, will cost from $150 to $300 a day, while a luxury class yacht can cost anything from $1000 to $3000 a day.

Information is obtainable from many travel agents in Greece, or by writing to the Association of Charterers and Yacht Experts, PO Box 341, Piraeus.

Car hire. Hertz and Avis, as well as many Greek companies, are to be found in Greece. Rates fall between 260 and 1650 Drs per day plus from 3.90 to 15.50 Drs per kiiometre. An international driving licence is essential.

Tours and cruises. Bus tours operate from Athens, Thessaloniki, Chalcidici, Heraklion, Chania, Rethymnon, Agios Nikolaos, Corfu, and Rhodes. The leading tour operator is CHAT (in Athens: 4 Stadiou Street, Tel: 323.4444), but there are many others, usually less expensive. A half-day tour of Athens, including a guided tour of the Acropolis, will cost around 365 Drs. A full-day tour of Athens, Corinth, Mycenae and Epidavros will cost around 775 Drs. There are also longer tours taking in as much of the country as you like.

There are also air tours of Crete, Rhodes and Corfu from Athens. A 30-day tour of Crete, taking in Heraklion, Knossos and Phaestos, will cost around 7230 Drs. Enquire at a travel agency, or try, for example, Sophios Tours, 5 Metropleos Street, Athens. Tel: 323.8727.

Organised cruises operate from Piraeus, Rhodes and Corfu. From Piraeus, a 1-day cruise of the Argo-Saronic will cost around $24, a 3-day cruise of the Aegean, calling at Mykonos, Delos, Thera Heraklion and Rhodes, from $150. Travel agents. will carry brochures and have full details.

Maps of nomes (1:200,000) for walking, from the National Ministry of Statistics, 14 Likourgou, Athens. Passport required.

ACCOMMODATION

Hotel rates below show the minimum/maximum rates authorised by the National Tourist Organisation (NTOG) and include a 15% service charge. Only minimum rates are shown for the luxury class hotels. All prices are in drachmas.

Luxury: single rooms without bath, 310; with bath, 520. Twin bedded rooms without bath, 535; with bath, 730.

A Class: single rooms without bath, 215-350; with bath, 370-600. Twin bedded rooms without bath, 360-615; with bath, 535-840.

B Class: single rooms without bath, 185-265; with bath, 265-457. Twin bedded rooms without bath, 275-440; with bath, 330-645.

C Class: single rooms without bath, 150-220; with bath, 190-320. Twin bedded rooms without bath, 200-325; with bath, 275-390. Three bedded rooms without bath, 240-390; with bath, 330-470.

D Class: single rooms without bath, 130-175; with bath, 175-220. Twin bedded rooms without bath, 195-230; with bath, 230-320. Three bedded rooms without bath, 235-275; with bath, 275-385. Two bedded rooms per bed, 95-115. Three bedded rooms per bed, 80-95.

E Class: single rooms without bath, 105-150; with bath, 135-200. Twin bedded rooms without bath, 150-215; with bath, 185-260. Three bedded rooms without bath, 180-260; none with bath. Two bedded rooms per bed, 75-108. Three bedded rooms per bed, 60-85.

Inns: single rooms without bath, 65-100. Two or three bedded room per bed, 60-80.

Reservations at any hotel in Greece may be made in advance by contacting the Hellenic Chamber of Hotels, 6 Aristidou Street, Athens. From abroad, telephone 323.6962 (8am-1pm Greek time). In Greece, telephone 323.7193 (8am-8pm). Or, in person, go to 2 Karageorgi Servias Street, Athens (near Syntagma Square), Tel: 323.7193; or reserve on arrival at Athens airport, East Terminal, Tel: 900.9437.

And don't forget, wherever you are in Greece the local Tourist Police will always help you find accommodation in their area.

Furnished rooms in private houses are categorised first, second and third class. Authorised room rates should be pinned up in every room. A single room without bath will cost from 105 to 220 Drs depending on class. A double room without bath will cost from 150 to 325. A room with bath will cost more.

Campgrounds are run by the NTOG, the Hellenic Touring Club and by private individuals. At NTOG sites, rates are 60 Drs per person from 16 June to 16

September, less off-season, and half-price for children aged 2 to 7. Caravans cost 60 Drs, cars with tents cost 50 Drs, less off-season. Huts are also available. Hellenic Touring Club campgrounds are cheaper.

PLACE LISTINGS

ATHENS

Accommodation
Amalia (L), 10 Leoforos Amalias. Tel: 323.7301. Overlooking the National Gardens.

Athenee Palace (L), 1 Kolokotroni. Tel: 323.0791. Central; discreetly elegant.

Athens Hilton (L), 46 Vassilissis Sophias. Tel: 72.0301. More than pleasant walking distance from the centre of town.

Grande Bretagne (L), Syntagma Square. Tel: 323.0251. What Claridges is to London, the Ritz to Paris.

Saint George Lycabettus (L), 2 Kleomenous, Plateia Dexamenis. Tel: 79.0711. New, tasteful, high up in Kolonaki with wonderful views.

Other luxury hotels: Acropole Palace, Caravel, King George, Kings Palace, Park, Royal Olympic.

Electra (A), 5 Ermou. Tel: 322.3222. Near Plaka.

Electra Palace (A), 18 Nikodimou. Tel: 324.1401. In Plaka.

King Minos (A), 1 Pireos. Tel: 523.1111. Near Omonia; approaching luxury standards.

Olympic Palace (A), 16 Filellinon. Tel: 323.7611. Between Syntagma and Plaka.

Aretoussa (B), 6-8 Metropoleos. Tel: 322.9431. Off Syntagma.

Athens Gate (B), 10 Leoforos Syngrou. Tel: 923.8302. Overlooking the Temple of Zeus and Hadrian's Arch.

Lycabette (B), 6 Valaoritou. Tel: 363.3514. In Kolonaki.

Omiros (B), 15 Apollonos. Tel: 323.5486. In Plaka.

Plaka (B), 7 Kapnikareas and Metropoleos. Tel: 322.2096.

Titania (B), 52-54 Panepistimiou. Tel: 360-9611. Near Omonia.

Achilleus (C), 21 Lekka. Tel: 322.5826. Off Syntagma.

Carolina (C), 55 Kolokotroni. Tel: 322.8148. Between Syntagma and Omonia.

Hermes (C), 19 Apollonos. Tel: 323.5514. Plaka.

Imperial (C), 46 Metropoleos. Tel: 322.7617. Near Plaka.

Phoebus (C), 12 Peta. Tel: 322.0142. Plaka. Best of its class.

Royal (C), 44 Metropoleos. Tel: 323.4220. Near Plaka.

Cecrops (D), 13 Spyrou Tsagari. Tel: 323.2138. Plaka.

Cleo's (D), 3 Patrou. Tel: 322.9053. Plaka.

Kimon (D), 27 Apollonos. Tel: 323.5223. Plaka.

Phaedra (D), 16 Cheraephondos and Adrianou. Tel: 323.8461. Pleasantly situated in Plaka; difficult to get a room.

Clare's House (Inn), 17 Phrynichou. Tel: 322.9284. Plaka, near Hadrian's Arch.

The Funny Trumpet (Inn), 30 Metropoleos. Off Syntagma.

Joseph House (Inn), 13 Markou Moussouri. Near Ardettos and the Stadium.

Pericles Student Hotel (Inn), 39 Kapnikreas and Adrianou. Plaka.

There are many other dorm-style places, but they come and go. Ask at a student travel office.

YMCA (XAN), 28 Omirou. Tel: 3626.970.

YWCA (XEN), 11 Amerikis. Tel: 3624.294.

For Youth Hostels in Athens and throughout Greece, contact the Greek Youth Hostels Association (Organosis Xenonon Neotitos Ellados), 4 Dragatsaniou, Plateia Klafthmonos, Athens. Tel: 3234.107.

Camping: Athens Camping Grounds, 198 Leoforos Athinon, Peristeri (on the road to Daphni). Tel: 571.5326.

Restaurants
All the luxury hotels have (expensive) restaurants serving international cuisine.

Others (less expensive) include:

Al Convento, 4-6 Anapiron Polemou. Tel: 739.163. Cheerful Italian.

Balthazar, 27 Tsocha and Vournazou. Tel: 6441.215. Inside a mansion; garden dining in summer.

Bouillabaisse, 28 Zissimopoulou, Amphithea (near Paleo Phaleron). Tel: 9333.459. Excellent seafood.

Delphi, 13 Nikis. Tel: 3234.869.

Zorbas, 28 Koumoundourou, Turkolimano. Tel: 425.501. One of several restaurants along the waterfront at this little yacht harbour at Piraeus.

Tavernas
Askimopapo (Ugly Duckling), 61 Ionon. Tel: 363.282. Charmingly rustic, with barrel organ music. Hidden away in Petralona, on the far side of Philopappou.

O Platanos, 4 Diogenous. Tel: 322.066.
One of the oldest tavernas in Plaka.
Psarra, on the steps at the intersection of
Erechtheos and Erotokritou in the heart
of Plaka. Enjoyable for watching the
world go by.
Rouga, 7 Kapsali. Tel: 729.934. Small,
spartan, but good atmosphere and food.
In Kolonaki.
Theophilou's, off Vyronos at 1 Vakchou
in Plaka. Tel: 322.3901. A tiny, quiet
courtyard in Plaka.
Vassilenas, 72 Etolikou, Piraeus. Tel:
4612.457. Renovated grocery store, roof-
top dining in summer. No menu, instead
an extraordinary succession of 18 courses.
Fixed price.
Zafiris, 4 Thespidos. Tel: 322.5460. A
Plaka landmark, frequented by con-
noisseurs of Greek cuisine. The speciality
is game. Booking essential.

Kafeneions and bars
Syntagma Square and Kolonaki Square,
packed with cafe tables, are popular places
for sitting out at night, the first inter-
national, the second stylishly upper class
Greek. Floca's and Zonar's, both at 9
Panepistimiou, near Syntagma, are famous
pavement cafes though exhaust fumes
from passing traffic overwhelm the
ambience.
   Some recommended bars:
Dewar's Club, 7 Glykonos, Dexameni
Square, Kolonaki. Tel: 415.412. From
9pm.
Larry's Bar, 20 Lykavitos, Kolonaki. Tel:
3600-100. From 8.30pm.
Red Lion, 16 Niridon, behind the Hilton.
From noon to 2am.

Entertainment
For up to date entertainment listings
visitors should buy a copy of 'The Athenian'
or 'Athenscope', both monthly magazines on sale at most kiosks and full of
much other useful information as well.
   There are tavernas with Greek music
and dancing, laid on mostly for the benefit
of tourists, and clubs and discos. The Jazz
Club, Ragava Square (Tel: 324.8056), in a
quiet part of Plaka, has live sessions some
nights, recorded jazz, blues and rock on
others. Not in Plaka is the Nine Muses,
43 Akademias (Tel: 604.260), one of
Athens' most fashionable discos.
   Boites are more discreet: intimate
places where one or a few performers sing
traditional or partisan or modern Greek

songs. Drinks start at 200 Drs. Skorpios,
Zygos and Zoom, all on Kydathinaion in
Plaka, are examples. Programmes start
around 10pm.
   Bouzoukia are places where Greeks
go to blow all their money, by buying
whisky at 2500 Drs a bottle and smash-
ing plates at similarly astronomical prices
— to the accompaniment of ear-splitting
amplified bouzouki music. These are
usually outside central Athens, often near
the sea, like Fantasia, Agios Kosmas
(opposite the West Airport), Tel: 981.0503.
The best bouzouki place, however, and
more traditional, is Harama at the
Kessariani Shooting Range (Skopeftirio),
at the 12th km out of Athens on the
National Road. Vassilis Tsitsanis, Greece's
best-loved bouzouki composer, and Sotiria
Bellou, last of the great rembetika singers,
perform here from 11.30pm nightly in
summer. A bottle of whisky costs 1900
Drs. Tel: 766.4869.
   More conventional nightclubs, with
striptease and international shows, are the
Las Vegas, 8 Othonos, Syntagma (Tel:
323.4831) and the Coronet, 6 Panepi-
stimiou (Tel: 361.7397).
   Check 'The Athens News' for cinema
programmes.
   Cultural events, including plays, films,
also concerts, are put on by the British
Council, Kolonaki Square (Tel: 363.3211),
the Hellenic American Union, 22 Massalias
(Tel: 362.2886), and also their French,
Italian and German equivalents.
   For the Athens Festival, Dora Stratou
Theatre, Son et Lumiere, etc., see the
background section.

Travel
Buses (blue) and trolleys (yellow) are the
chief means of getting around Athens and
environs. For Piraeus, take the 70 bus
from Omonia or the 165 bus (green) from
Filellinon at Syntagma. For the beaches,
take one of the buses departing from
Leoforos Olgas, at the Zappeion. Buses to
Sounion and other points in eastern Attica
depart from Mavromateon Street, near
Pedio Tou Areos Park.
Provincial bus stations: for the Peloponnese,
Macedonia, Epiros and the Ionian Islands,
100 Kifissou; for Euboea, Central Greece
and Thessaly, 260 Liossion. OSE buses
(Hellenic Railways) depart Larissis Railway
Station for Northern Greece, Peloponissou
Railway Station for the Peloponnese.
The electric train runs underground

through Athens with stops at Omonia and Monastiraki. Its chief use is for getting to Piraeus.

Trains to the provinces depart from Larissis (Northern Greece) and Peloponissou (Peloponnese) stations, northwest of Omonia. Get there on trolley 1 or 5.

Taxis, recognised by their grey colour and sonic boom, charge 8.50 Drs on hiring, 7.50 Drs per km within the Athens/Piraeus area. They're a fairly cheap and certainly practical way of getting around town. Car hire: Hertz, 12 Syngrou (Tel: 922.0102); Avis, 48 Leoforos Amalias (Tel: 322.4951); their Greek equivalent Hellascars, 7 Stadiou (Tel: 323.3487); and cheaper, Autorent, 118 Syngrou, near the Olympic terminal (Tel: 923.2514); plus many others, mostly along Syngrou and Amalias.

The Automobile and Touring Club of Greece (ELPA), 2-4 Messogion, Athens Tower (Tel: 779.1615), provides motorists with assistance and information, including gas coupons, hotel reservations, free legal advice, international driving licence, car hire, insurance, road assistance, camping information and information on road conditions.

Airline offices concentrate around Syntagma Square.

An airport bus departs from Leoforos Amalias by the Japan Airlines office near Syntagma. The fare is 24 Drs, the ride takes about 20 minutes, and the bus departs every 20 minutes from 6am to midnight.

Travel agents are also found mostly around Syntagma Square: Stadiou, Filellinon and Nikis Streets. American Express overlooks the square, entrance at 2 Ermou (Tel: 322.4075).

For student travel, call in at the Athens Student Travel Service, 1 Filellinon, or Host, 3 Filellinon.

Information

For brochures, maps and general travel information, go to the National Tourist Organisation of Greece (NTOG), 2 Karageorgis Servias, Syntagma Square (Tel: 3222.545), inside the National Bank of Greece. Their map of Athens is quite detailed, is keyed to squares, banks, post offices, museums, archaeological sites, etc., and lists bus and trolley routes.

To really put yourself in the picture, buy a copy of 'The Athenian' or 'Athenascope' at any kiosk. Between them they tell you just about everything you want to know about Athens, listing hotels, tavernas, nightspots, cultural and sports events, shops and markets, services and travel information.

Permit for Mt Athos from the Foreign Ministry, 2 Zalocosta. Tel: 361.0581.

Some embassies (a complete list can be found in either 'The Athenian' or 'Athenscope'):

Australia, 15 Messogion. Tel: 360.4611.
Canada, 4 Ioannou Gennadiou. Tel: 739.511.
New Zealand, 29 Vas. Sofias. Tel: 727.514.
United Kingdom, 1 Ploutarchou. Tel: 736.211.
USA, 91 Vas. Sofias. 712.951.

You may assume that there is an inn, also rooms in private houses, at any of the places listed below. Only NTOG and Hellenic Touring Club campsites are listed; private campsites may also be available. Restaurants and tavernas are mentioned only where they stand out from the generality.

ATTICA

Kaisariani
Travel: 39/52 bus from the University.

Daphni
Accommodation: Daphni Camping. Travel: 100 bus from Koumoundourou Sq, Athens.

Elefsis
Travel: 68 bus from Koumoudourou Sq.

Glyfada
Accommodation: Astir(L); Palace, Palmyra Beach (A); Delfini, Florida (B); Beau Rivage, Themis (C); Evriali (D). Taverna: Kyra Antigoni, 54 Pandoras. Travel: 30 bus from Zappeion.

Voula
Accommodation: Voula Beach (A); Aktaeon, Galini (B); Kabera, Palma (C); Miramare (D). Voula Camping.

Vouliagmeni
Accommodation: Astir Palace (L); Greek Coast (A); Hera (B); nothing cheaper. Taverna: To Limanaki, Avras. Travel: 89 bus from Zappeion.

Sounion
Accommodation: Aegeon (A); Sun (B);

Saron (C).
Taverna: To Sirtaki, Leof. Sounion.
Travel: buses from Mavromateon St.

Marathon
Accommodation: Golden Coast (B);
Marathon (C). Nea Makri Camping, to the
south.
Travel: buses from Mavromateon St.

ARGO-SARONIC
Travel: boats from Piraeus, hydrofoils
from Zea Marina. Poros can also be
reached from Galatas in the Argolid.

Aegina
Accommodation: Nausica (B); Brown (C);
Aktaeon (D) — all Aegina town, and many
more at Agia Marina. Moni Island Camping.
Tavernas: Maridaki, along the harbour;
Evangelos, at Agioi Asomatoi.

Poros
Accommodation: Saron (B); Aktaeon,
Manessi (C).

Hydra
Accommodation: Miramare (A); Delfini
(B); Hydra (C); Sophia (D).
Taverna: Kokkini, 1 Pinotsi St.

Spetsai
Accommodation: Spetses (A); Roumanis
(B); Faros (C); Acropole (D).

ARGOLID
Travel: bus to all places; train to Loutraki,
Corinth, Mycenae and Argos.

Loutraki
Accommodation: numerous hotels A-E.
Taverna: Horiatiki, 70 El. Venizelou.

Perachora
Accommodation: Anessis (D). Limni Ireou
Camping.

Corinth
Accommodation: Kypselos (B); Belle-Vue
(C); Byron (D); Emborikon (E). At
ancient Corinth: Xenia (A). Blue Dolphin
Camping, Lechaion.
Tavernas: Ippopotamos, at the harbour;
Fotis, 2kms along Patras road.

Mycenae
Accommodation: Agamemnon (C); Orea
Helene tou Menelaou (E). Mycenae
Camping.

Argos
Accommodation: Mycenae (C); Hermes
(D).

Nafplion
Accommodation: Xenia Palace (L); Xenia
(A); Agamemnon (B); Dioskouri (C); King
Othon (D); Hera (E). Nafplion Camping.
Tavernas: Kanaris, 1 Bouboulinas;
Savouras, 5 Bouboulinas.

Tolon
Accommodation: Solon (B); Aktaeon (C);
Assini Beach (D). Lido Camping.
Taverna: Kali Kardia, 54 Aktis.

Epidavros
Accommodation: Xenia II (B). Nikolas
Camping, Palaea Epidavros.

CENTRAL PELOPONNESE
Travel: bus to all places (except Vassai:
taxi from Megalopolis); train to Tripolis,
Megalopolis, Olympia, Patras and
Xilokastro.

Tripolis
Accommodation: Menalon (A); Semiramis
(B); Galaxy (C); Crystal (D); Averof (E).
Milia Camping.
Taverna: Kipos tou Sosoli, 40 John
Kennedy.

Megalopolis
Accommodation: Achillion (D).

Andritsaina
Accommodation: Theoxenia (B); Pan (D);
Vassai (E).

Olympia
Accommodation: SPAP (A); Apollon,
Neon Olympia (B); Ilis (C); Pelops (D).
Olympia Camping.
Taverna: Thraka, on the Pirgos road.

Patras
Accommodation: Acropole, Moreas (A);
Majestic, Galaxy (B); Esperia, Mediterranee
(C); Hellas, Splendid (D); Agios Georgios,
Megali Vretannia (E). Patron Camping,
Agia Patron.
Restaurant: Evangelatos, 9 Agia Nikolaou.
Tavernas in the upper town.

Kalavrita
Accommodation: Chelmos (B); Litsa
Kakanas (C); Paradissos (D).

Xilokastro
Accommodation: Apollo (A); Miramare (B); Periandros (C); Philoxenia (D); Kentrikon (E).

SOUTHERN PELOPONNESE
Travel: bus to all places except Kithera; train to Kalamata; air to Kalamata and Kithera; boat to Gytheion, Kithera and Monemvasia.

Sparta
Accommodation: Xenia (A); Menelaion (B); Dioscouri (C); Cecil (D); Sparti (E).

Mistra
Accommodation: Vyzantion (B).
Restaurant: Xenia, at the site.

Kalamata
Accommodation: Rex (B); Achillion (C); Grande Bretagne (D); Megas Alexandros (E). Patista Camping.
Taverna: Taygetos, 42 Athinon.

Pylos
Accommodation: Castle, Nestor (B); Navarinon (D).

Gytheion
Accommodation: Lakonis (A); Belle Helene (B); Pantheon (C); Aktaeon (D).

Monemvasia
Accommodation: B and E hotels at Gethira; private houses on the rock.

ROAD TO DELPHI
Travel: bus to all places except Osios Loukas (taxi); train to Thebes and Levadia. Frequent Andirrion-Rion ferries, passengers 7 Drs, cars 90 Drs.

Thebes
Accommodation: Dionyssion Melathron (B); Niobe (C); Averof (E).

Levadia
Accommodation: Levadia (B); Midia (C); Boiotia (D).
Restaurant and taverna: Xenia, Trofoniou Springs; Stilias, Magiakou Square.

Orchomenos
Accommodation: Elli (D).

Davlia
Accommodation: Pantheon (E).

Osios Loukas
Accommodation: Xenia (B).

Arachova
Accommodation: Anemolia (B); Apollon (D).
Taverna: Karathanassis, Papaioannou Sq.

Delphi
Accommodation: Amalia (A); Hermes, Pythia (C); Phoebos (D). Delphi Camping.
Restaurant and taverna: Xenia; Pan, Isaiah St.

Itea
Accommodation: Galini (B); Akti (C); Parnassos (D).
Taverna: Apolafsis.

Kirrha
Accommodation: Agiannis Camping.

Galaxidi
Accommodation: Ganymede (C); Possidon (D).
Taverna: Manolis, on the harbour.

Navpaktos
Accommodation: Amaryllis (B); Akti (C); Niki (D).

EUBOEA AND THE NORTHERN SPORADES
Travel: bus or train to Chalcis and bus throughout Euboea. Boats to Euboea from various mainland ports. Boat to Skyros from Kimi, Euboea; to Skiathos, Skopelos and Alonissos from Volos and Agios Konstantinos. Air to Skiathos.

Chalcis
Accommodation: Lucy (A); John's (B); Hara (C); Morfeus (D); Iris (E).
Tavernas: Karkadalidis, Voudouri Ave., on the seafront; Mouhritsa, 14 Ermou.

Limni
Accommodation: Avra (C); Ilion (E).

Loutra Aidipsou
Accommodation: numerous hotels A-E.
Restaurant: Egli Hotel, on the beach.

Eretria
Accommodation: Perigiali Eretrias (B); Delfis (C).
Restaurant: Tsolias (no name displayed), on the harbour just before the beach.

Karystos
Accommodation: Apollon Resort (B); Louloudi (C).
Restaurant: Miami, on the shore.

Skyros
Accommodation: Xenia (B); Aegeon (E).

Skiathos
Accommodation: Skiathos Palace (L); Esperides (A); Xenia (B); Koukounaries (C); Sporades (D).

Skopelos
Accommodation: Xenia (B); Avra (C); America (D).

Alonissos
Accommodation: Galaxy (C); Alonissos (D).

CENTRAL GREECE

Travel: bus throughout; train to Lamia, Volos, Larissa, Trikala and Kalambaka. Air to Volos and Larissa.

Thermopylae
Accommodation: Aegli (C); Asklepios (D).

Lamia
Accommodation: Leonideon, Samaras (C); Neon Astron, Anessis (D).
Taverna: Tripio Katostari, 25 Karaiskaki.

Ipati
Accommodation: numerous hotels A-D.

Volos
Accommodation: Pallas (A); Alexandros (B); Kypseli, Galaxy (C); Iasson (D); Europa, Pelion (E).
Restaurant: Kentrikon, Volos pier; good ouzeri, Halkias, on Koutarelia St.

Makrinitsa
Accommodation: Archontikon Mousli (A).

Larissa
Accommodation: Divani Palace (A); Astoria (B); Acropole, Olympion (C); Cecil, Pantheon (D).
Taverna: Zachariadis, 109 Eperou.

Trikala
Accommodation: Divani (B); Dina (C); Lithaeon (D); Olympia (E).
Restaurant: Frourio, on hilltop.

Pili
Accommodation: Aspropotamos (E).
Taverna: Anavrissoula.

Kalambaka
Accommodation: Motel Divani (A); Aeolikos Astir, Olympia (C); Rex (D); Epirotikon (E). Kalambaka Camping.
Taverna: Zogas.

NORTHERN GREECE

Travel: bus throughout except to Athos and, of course, to the islands; train to Edessa and Thessaloniki. Air to Kastoria, Thessaloniki, Kavala and Lemnos. Boat to Samothraki from Alexandroupolis; to Thasos from Kavala; to Lemnos from Kavala and from Piraeus via Lesvos. See Athos for travel there.

Kastoria
Accommodation: Xenia du Lac (A); Kastoria, Orestion, Kalithea (C).
Tavernas: Mavrotissa, by the lake; Omonia, Omonia Sq.

Edessa
Accommodation: Xenia (B), unpleasant; Alfa, Olympion (D); Olympia (E).
Taverna: Mitsos, 5 Karaoli.

Thessaloniki
Accommodation: Makedonia Palace (L); Mediterranean Palace, Electra Palace (A); City, Egnatia, Victoria (B); Amalia, Emborikon, Pella (C); Aegli, Ilios, Kastoria (D); Atlantis, Nea Ameriki (E). Evropi Camping, Asprovalta.
Restaurants: Krikelas, 32 Gramou Vitsi; Olimpos Naoussa, 5 Vas. Konstantinou.
Taverna: Nikos, 2 Agion Anargiron Sq.
Ouzeri: Kapetan Vaggelis, 21 Kalapothaki
Information: permit for Mt Athos from the Ministry of Northern Greece (Directorate of Civic Affairs), 48 El. Venizelou. Tel: 260.427. NTOG, 8 Aristotelous Sq. Tel: 27.18.88. Tourist Police, 10 Egnatia. Tel: 522.587.

Kallithea
Accommodation: Athos Palace, Pallini Beach (A); Ammon Zeus (B); Kallithea (C).

Ouranopolis
Accommodation: Eagles Palace (A); Xenia (B); Galini (D); Ouranopolis (E).
Taverna: Paralia, on the beach.

Athos

You must be male and you must get permission to visit either from the Ministry of Northern Greece (see Thessaloniki) or the Foreign Ministry (see Athens).

There is a limit on the days allowed for a visit (usually 5); also in summer there's a queue to get in, so you will be given a date a week or more later. You must then present yourself, with the necessary papers and your passport, at Karies, the administrative centre of Athos, where you will be given a 'diamonitirion' which enables you to stay in any one of the 20 monasteries, though usually only for one night at a time.

Karies is a long day's walk from the frontier. The most practical way is to go by sea. A caique runs, depending on the weather, from Ierisos to the monasteries of Vatopedi (2 hrs walk to Karies) and Iviron (occasional bus to Karies or one hour's walk). More dependable is the motor boat from Ouranopolis to Daphni (the last one leaves mid-morning), from where there is a connecting bus to Karies.

The boat from Ierisos stops at most of the monasteries on the east coast, continuing to Lavra; the boat on the west coast does likewise, continuing to those monasteries beyond Daphni. With the bus from Daphni to Karies and Iviron and back, and a very occasional boat round the end of Athos, the options of assisted travel are exhausted, and otherwise you must walk between the monasteries.

Travelling on Athos is unusual, with its own rhythm and rules, and much of the most useful information will come from other travellers. The evening meal is eaten quite early, about 6pm in summer, and the conducted visits to the churches, treasuries, etc., are usually in the late afternoon or early evening, so don't arrive too late at a monastery. Also the monastery gates close at sunset.

Kavala

Accommodation: Tosca Beach (A); Oceanis, Philippi (B); Panorama (C); Astoria (D); Pagaeon (E). Bati Kavala Beach Camping.
Restaurant and taverna: Zafira-Panos, on the harbour; Mihalis, 17 Erithrou Stavrou.

Thasos

Accommodation: Timoleon (B); Angelika, Lido (C); Astir (D).

Samothraki

Accommodation: Xenia (B); Akroyali (C); Ilios (E).

Lemnos

Accommodation: (in Marina) Akti Mirina (L); Lemnos (C); Aktaeon (D).

NORTHWEST GREECE

Travel: bus throughout; by air to Ioannina. Frequent Preveza-Aktion ferries, passengers 7 Drs, cars 52 Drs.

Igoumenitsa

Accommodation: Xenia (B); Tourist (C); Aktaeon (D); Rhodes (E).

Metsova

Accommodation: Flokas (B); Olympic (C); Egnatia (D); Athinae (E).
Taverna: Krifi Folia, in the plateia.

Ioannina

Accommodation: Palladion, Xenia (B); Galaxy, Olympic (C); Ilion, Paris (D).
Taverna: To Nissaki, ferry to port of Nissaki, island in the lake.

Dodona

Accommodation: Andromachi (B).

Parga

Accommodation: Lichnos Beach (B); Avra (C); Agios Nektarios (D); Acropole (E).
Taverna: To Kantouni.

Preveza

Accommodation: Almini, Minos (C); Averoff, Athinae (E).

Arta

Accommodation: Xenia (B); Amvrakia (C); Hellas (D); Rex (E).
Restaurant: Xenia, within the frourion.

Messolongi

Accommodation: Liberty (B); Avra (D); Diethnes (E).
Taverna: Haravgi, 1km on Agrilia road.

IONIAN ISLANDS

Travel: boat from Patras to Fiskardo and Sami (Kefallinia), Ithaka, Paxos and Corfu; from Igoumenitsa to Corfu; from Parga to Paxos; from Kilini to Zakinthos. Bus to Lefkas. Air to Corfu and Kefallinia.

Corfu

Accommodation: Corfu Palace (L);

Cavalieri (A); Astron, King Alkonoos, Olympiakon (B); Arcadion, Bretagne (C); Anessis, Constantinoupolis (D); Elpis (E). All of these are in town; there are numerous hotels from L to D round the island. Campsites north of town.
Restaurant: Rex, 66 Capodistriou.

Paxos
Accommodation: Paxos Beach (B); Agios Georgios (E).

Lefkas
Accommodation: Santa Mavra (C); Vyzantion, Patrae (E).

Ithaka
Accommodation: Mentor, Odysseus (B); Aktaeon (E).

Kefallinia
Accommodation: Ionion (C); Kyma (D); Krinos (E) (in Sami). Xenia (B); Armonia (C); Allegro (D) (in Argostoli). Myrto (B) (in Assos). Panormos (B) (in Fiskardo).

Zakinthos
Accommodation: Strada Marina, Xenia (B); Diana, Phoenix (C); Ionian (D); Emborikon (E), and many more in the town; also round the island.

CYCLADES
Travel: sea routes are mentioned in the text. You may also fly to Mykonos, Milos and Thera.

Andros
Accommodation: Lykion (B); Chryssi Akti (C); Avra (D) (in Batsi). B and C in Chora.

Kea
Accommodation: Itzia Mas (B); Karthea (C) (in Livadi).

Syros
Accommodation: Hermes (B); Europe (C); Kykladikon (D); Aktaeon (E) (in Ermoupolis). B and C hotels round the island.

Tinos
Accommodation: Tinos Beach (A); Tinion (B); Avra, Flisvos (C); Eleana (D).

Mykonos
Accommodation: Leto (A); Theoxenia (B); Manto (C); Apollon (D). Paradise Camping.

Delos
Accommodation: Xenia (B).

Serifos
Accommodation: Perseus (B); Maistrali (C).

Sifnos
Accommodation: Apollonia (B); Sifnos (C) (in Apollonia). Artemon (C) (in Artemona). Plati Yialos (B) (in Plati Yialos).

Milos
Accommodation: Adamas (B); Delfini (D) (in Adamas).

Paros
Accommodation: Xenia (B); Paros (C); Kontes (D); Pandrossos (E) (in Paroikia). Naoussa (B); Ambelas (C); Drossia (D) (in Naoussa).

Naxos
Accommodation: Ariadne (B); Apollon, Hermes (C); Oceanis (D).

Ios
Accommodation: Chryssi Akti (B); Armadoros (C); Aktaeon (D); Avra (E).

Thera
Accommodation: Atlantis (B); Panorama (C); Tataki (D); Lucas (E) (in Phira).

EASTERN SPORADES
Travel: by sea from Piraeus to Samos and, separately, to Chios and Lesvos; also, to all three on the Thessaloniki to Rhodes route. By air from Athens to Samos, Chios and Lesvos.

Samos
Accommodation: Xenia (B); Samos (C); Hera (D); Parthenon (E) (in Vathy). Delfini (C); Alexandra (D) (in Pithagorion).

Chios
Accommodation: Xenia (B); Aktaeon (C); Palladion (D); Apollon (E) (in Chios town).

Lesvos
Accommodation: Blue Sea, Lesvion (B); Rex (C); Lycabettus (D); Kentron (E) (in Mitilini). Delfinia (B) (in Molivos).

DODECANESE
Travel: there are three routes from Piraeus through the Dodecanese to Rhodes: the northern, via Patmos or Leros; the central,

via Astipalaia; the southern, via Crete, Kasos and Karpathos. Also by sea from Thessaloniki to Rhodes via the Eastern Sporades and Dodecanese; and sailings within the group from Rhodes. By air from Athens to Kos and Rhodes; from Heraklion to Rhodes; from Rhodes to Kos and Karpathos.

Patmos
Accommodation: Patmion (B); Astoria (C); Rex (D); Neon (E) (in Skala). Vamvakos (D) (at Grikou).

Leros
Accommodation: Xenon Angelou (B); Leros (C) (in Lakki). Alinda (B) (in Platanos).

Kalymnos
Accommodation: Thermae (C); Alma (D); Vazanellis (E) (in Kalymnos town). Drossos (C) (in Panormos). Delfini (C); Myrties (D) (in Myrties).

Kos
Accommodation: Continental Palace (A); Theoxenia, Kos (B); Elli (C); Dodecannessus (D).

Simi
Accommodation: Nireus (B).

Rhodes
Accommodation (over 100 hotels in the New Town): Grand Hotel Astir Palace (L); Chevaliers Palace, Mediterranean (A); Cactus, Plaza, Spartalis (B); Astoria (C); D'Or, Zeus (D); Stassa (E).
Restaurant: Casa Castellana, 33 Aristotelous, Old Town.
Tavernas: Fotis, 8 Menekleous, Old Town. Triton, by the beach, Lindos.
Information: NTOG, 5 Archbishop Makarios (Tel: 23.655). Tourist Police, 31 Alex. Papagou (Tel: 27.423).

Karpathos
Accommodation: Porfyris (C); Karpathos (D).

CRETE
Travel: by sea from Piraeus to Chania and Heraklion; via Thera to Agios Nikolaos and Sitia, and sometimes Heraklion; Kastelli via Monemvasia and Gytheion. Also from Rhodes to Sitia and Agios Nikolaos. By air from Athens to Chania and Heraklion; from Rhodes to Heraklion. Bus throughout Crete.

Heraklion
Accommodation: Astir, Astoria (A); Esperia, Kastro (B); Daedalos, El Greco, Selena (C); Arkadi, Florida (D); Kritikon, Moderno (E).
Restaurant: Maxim, 3 Koroneou.
Taverna: Klimataria, 8 Daidalou.
Information: NTOG, 1 Xanthoudidou (Tel: 282096). Tourist Police: Vas Konstantinou (Tel: 283.190).

Phaestos
Accommodation: Xenia (D).

Agia Galini
Accommodation: Acropolis (C); Livii (D); Aktaeon (E).

Rethymnon
Accommodation: Idaeon (B); Park (C); Acropole (D); Paradissos (E). Arcadia, also Elisabeth Camping near town.
Taverna: Chelona, at the Venetian harbour.

Chania
Accommodation: Kydon (A); Lissos (B); Chania (C); Piraeus (E).
Restaurant: Faros, by the old lighthouse.
Taverna: Kontosouvli, at the old harbour.

Palaiochora
Accommodation: Livykon (D).

Omalos
Accommodation: Xenia (B).

Chora Sfakion
Accommodation: Xenia (B).

Limin Chersonisou
Accommodation: Belvedere (A); Nora (B); Helena (C).

Mallia
Accommodation: Sirens Beach (A); Grammatikaki (B); Chryssi Mellissa (D).

Psychro
Accommodation: Zeus (D); Diktaeon Andron (E).

Agios Nikolaos
Accommodation: Minos Beach (L); Mirabello (A); Coral (B); Creta (C); Aegeon (E).

Sitia Accommodation: Sitia (C); Flisvos (D).	**Zakros** Accommodation: Zakros (C).
	Ierapetra Accommodation: Creta (C); Alkyon (D);
Palaikastro Accommodation: Itanos (E).	Venizelos (E). Ierapetra Camping.

SELECTED BIBLIOGRAPHY

A vast selection of books on Greece, in English, is available in Greece itself and it might be best to visit a good bookshop there (eg Eleftheroudakis, 4 Nikis Street, Athens — near Syntagma Square) for a first-hand browse. We include a list of titles the reader might like to acquaint himself with before or during his travels. If the book is available in paperback its title is followed by (P). In most cases we do not specify particular editions, translations, etc., but for books difficult to obtain, first date and place of publication are mentioned.

Anderson, Patrick *The Smile of Apollo, a Literary Companion to Greek Travel*
Aylen, Leo *Greece for Everyone* (4000 year historical survey)
Bradford, Ernle *Companion Guide to the Greek Islands*
Bury, J.B. *History of Greece* (ancient history)
Byron *Letters*, ed Lesley Marchand
Campbell, Patrick and Sherrård, Philip *Modern Greece*
Carpenter, Rhys *The Architects of the Parthenon* (P)
Durrell, Lawrence *Reflections on a Marine Venus* (P) (Rhodes)
Durrell, Lawrence *Prospero's Cell* (P) (Corfu)
Fermor, Patrick Leigh *Mani*
Fermor, Patrick Leigh *Roumeli*
Gell, William *Itinerary of Greece*, London 1819
Graves, Robert *The Greek Myths* (P)
Herodotos *The Histories* (P) (the Persian wars)
Holst, Gail *Road to Rembetika* (P), Athens 1977 (music of a Greek sub-culture)
Homer *The Iliad* (P)
Homer *The Odyssey* (P)
Kazantzakis, Nikos *Travels in Greece*
Kulukundis, Elias *Journey to a Greek Island* (Kasos)
Lancaster, Osbert *Classical Landscape* (P)
Leake, W.M. *Travels in Northern Greece*, London 1835
Lear, Edward *Journal of a Landscape Painter in Greece and Albania*, London 1851
Lear, Edward *Views in the Seven Ionian Islands*, London 1863
Liddell, Robert *Mainland Greece*
Llewellyn-Smith, Michael *The Great Island* (Crete)
Loch, S. *Athos: Holy Mountain*
Luce, J.V. *The End of Atlantis* (P) (Thera)
Miller, Henry *The Colossos of Maroussi* (P)
Papandreou, Andreas *Democracy at Gunpoint* (P) (early years of the junta by populist-socialist politician
Pausanias *Guide to Greece* (2nd C. AD) trans Peter Levi (P)
Pausanias *Description of Greece* ed J.G. Frazer, London 1898
Pindar *Odes* (P)
Plutarch *Lives of the Noble Greeks* (P)
Powell, Dilys *An Affair of the Heart* (Perachora)
Powell, Dilys *The Villa Ariadne* (Crete)
Renault, Mary *The Bull from the Sea* (P) (Hippolytos)
Renault, Mary *Fire from Heaven* (P) (Alexander)
Renault, Mary *The King Must Die* (P) (Theseus)
Sherrard, Philip *Athos: the Mountain of Silence*
St Clair, William *That Greece Might Still be Free* (War of Independence)
Thucydides *The Peloponnesian War* (P)
Wunderlich, H.G. *The Secret of Crete* (P) (interesting but sloppy theory that the Minoan palaces were really necropolises)

INDEX